THE DIY HOME APOTHECARY

Inspired by Dr. Nicole Apelian's Approach - 250+ forgotten powerful remedies for longevity

TOMMY B. ATTIA

Copyright

© TOMMY B. ATTIA, 2026

All rights reserved.

No part of this publication may be reproduced, distributed, or transmitted in any form or by any means, including photocopying, recording, or other electronic or mechanical methods, without the prior written permission of the publisher, except in the case of brief quotations embodied in critical reviews and certain other noncommercial uses permitted by UNITED STATES copyright law.

This publication is designed to provide helpful information for exam preparation purposes only. It is not intended to serve as professional nursing, medical, legal, or academic advice. Readers should always consult official sources and qualified professionals for guidance specific to their situation.

The information contained in this book is intended to provide helpful and informative material on the subjects addressed. It is not intended to serve as a replacement for professional medical advice. Any use of the information in this book is at the reader's discretion.

MEDICAL DISCLAIMER

IMPORTANT: PLEASE READ CAREFULLY

The information in *The DIY Home Apothecary* is for educational purposes only. This book does not diagnose, treat, cure, or prevent disease, nor replace professional medical advice.

Always Seek Professional Medical Care:

- Consult a qualified healthcare provider before starting any herbal remedy, especially if pregnant, nursing, taking medications, or have chronic health conditions.
- Never discontinue prescribed medications without consulting your physician.
- Seek immediate emergency care for serious injuries, severe symptoms, or life-threatening conditions.
- This book does not replace licensed medical professionals.

Individual Results May Vary:

- Herbs affect people differently based on biochemistry, genetics, and health status.
- Allergic reactions and adverse effects are possible with any substance.
- Always start with small doses and monitor your response.

Critical Safety Information:

- Proper plant identification is essential—misidentification can be fatal.
- Some herbs interact with medications or medical conditions.
- Pregnancy, nursing, children, elderly, and immunocompromised require special precautions.
- Quality and potency of herbs vary significantly between sources.

Wildcrafting Warnings:

- Only harvest plants you can identify with 100% certainty.
- Many plants have toxic look-alikes.
- Ensure legal permission to harvest.
- Avoid contaminated areas (roadsides, sprayed fields, polluted sites).

Emergency Medicine:

- Survival remedies are for situations where professional care is genuinely unavailable.
- When professional care is accessible, seek it immediately.
- Wilderness first aid training strongly recommended.

No Guarantees:

The author and publisher make no guarantees regarding effectiveness, safety, outcomes, or healing of any condition. Herbal supplements are not FDA-regulated like pharmaceutical drugs. Claims have not been evaluated by the FDA.

Use at Your Own Risk:

By using this information, you acknowledge that you assume full responsibility for your health decisions and that the author and publisher are not liable for any consequences.

Recommended Professional Consultation:

Consider working with licensed herbalists (AHG, RH), naturopathic doctors (ND), integrative physicians, or other qualified practitioners.

Your health is your responsibility. Use this information wisely and in consultation with qualified healthcare providers when appropriate.

By continuing to read this book, you acknowledge that you have read, understood, and agree to this medical disclaimer.

DEDICATION

To my grandmother,

Who taught me that the best medicine grows in the backyard, that healing begins in the kitchen, and that plant wisdom is older than any pharmacy.

Your hands—weathered from soil, stained from herbs, gentle in healing—showed me true self-reliance.

This book carries your legacy forward.

To the indigenous healers, traditional herbalists, and medicine keepers across all cultures and time,

Who preserved plant knowledge through persecution, who understood nature provides everything we need, and who never forgot what modern society lost.

Your wisdom runs through every page.

To Dr. Nicole Apelian,

Whose journey from debilitating autoimmune disease to vibrant health through plant medicine proves these remedies are powerful, legitimate, life-saving tools.

Thank you for showing us what's possible.

To every person told:

"There's nothing more we can do,"
"You'll have to live with this,"
"There's no cure,"

You are not powerless. You are not broken. The plants have been waiting to help you heal.

To my children, and all children,

May you grow up knowing that medicine grows from the earth, that your body knows how to heal, and that true health comes from connection—to plants, to soil, to ancestral wisdom.

May you never lose what I had to rediscover.

To the plants themselves,

Calendula, who heals our wounds.
Yarrow, who stops the bleeding.
Chamomile, who soothes us.
Ashwagandha, who strengthens us.
Elderberry, who protects us.

Thank you for waiting in fields and forests and gardens, ready to help the moment we remember.

And to you, the reader,

For having the courage to question, the wisdom to seek alternatives, and the strength to take your health into your own hands.

By reading this book, you join an ancient lineage of healers.

You are now a keeper of knowledge that must not be lost.

Use it. Share it. Pass it on.

The world needs healers.

You are one of them.

With gratitude and hope for a healthier, more self-reliant humanity,

---

Plant medicine is our birthright.
Healing is our natural state.
Self-reliance is our power.

May you reclaim all three.

THE DIY HOME APOTHECARY

FOREWORD

I wasn't supposed to be here.

Twenty years ago, doctors told me I had multiple sclerosis—incurable, degenerative, progressive. The prognosis: eventual wheelchair dependence and lifetime pharmaceutical management.

I was a scientist. I believed in evidence-based medicine. I took the medications.

And I got worse.

Then I started asking different questions: *What if my body isn't broken? What if it's responding to something—and I need to remove triggers and provide what it needs to heal?*

I turned to plants.

Not because I rejected science—I have a PhD in Natural Resources. I turned to plants *because of* science. Because humans evolved with these medicines for hundreds of thousands of years. Because our ancestors survived and thrived without pharmacies.

I studied herbalism intensively. I learned from indigenous healers and traditional practitioners. I experimented carefully, tracking everything.

My body responded.

The inflammation decreased. Brain fog lifted. Energy returned. Symptoms doctors called irreversible began disappearing.

Today, two decades later, I'm symptom-free. I survived 57 days alone in the Arctic on *Alone*—thriving in extreme conditions. I hike, work, teach, and live fully.

I healed myself with plants.

Why This Book Matters

The medical system excels at acute emergencies—trauma surgery, antibiotics when needed, diagnostics. But for chronic disease? It often fails us.

It manages symptoms without addressing root causes. It's built around pharmaceuticals that generate profit, not healing. It's increasingly inaccessible.

Meanwhile, the knowledge that sustained humanity for millennia—that plants heal, food is medicine, and the body self-repairs when given what it needs—has nearly been lost.

This book reclaims that knowledge.

The DIY Home Apothecary is the guide I needed when I was sick and desperate. Written with scientific rigor and traditional wisdom, it respects both modern research and ancestral knowledge.

What You Hold

This isn't folklore. Every remedy is grounded in:

- **Traditional use** (tested across generations)
- **Phytochemical understanding** (we know *why* they work)
- **Modern research** (many clinically proven)
- **Practical application** (real instructions you can follow)

Over 250 remedies for every health need—immune support, heart disease, anxiety, emergency care. You'll understand not just *what* to do, but *why* it works and *how* to do it safely.

More importantly, you'll reclaim **agency over your own health**.

The Path Forward

This requires effort. Learning plants takes time. Making remedies requires patience. Growing a garden demands consistency.

But you get in return:

Independence. No longer completely dependent on failing systems or unaffordable pharmacies.

Empowerment. Tools to respond when illness strikes.

Connection. To plants, your body's wisdom, the earth, your ancestors.

Health. Real, lasting health—not just managed disease.

Is herbal medicine a replacement for all modern medicine? No. Emergency surgery saved my life. Antibiotics saved my son's.

But for most health issues—chronic disease, prevention, immune support, stress, hormones—plants offer powerful, safe, accessible solutions.

Solutions you can make yourself.

My Hope for You

I hope this book becomes worn from use. I hope you write in margins, add observations, pass it to your children with notes about what worked.

I hope you plant calendula and watch it heal wounds. I hope you make elderberry syrup and stop colds. I hope you brew valerian and finally sleep.

I hope you experience what I did: the profound moment when you realize **your body knows how to heal— it just needed support, not suppression.**

Most of all, I hope you become your own healer. Not because doctors aren't valuable—they are. But because **you** live in your body 24/7. You notice changes, understand your constitution, and can respond immediately.

You have more power than you've been told.

This book shows you how to use it.

A Final Word

This knowledge isn't new—it's ancient. But desperately needed now.

We face chronic disease epidemics modern medicine can't solve. Healthcare systems strain and fail. We're dependent on complex supply chains while losing skills our great-grandparents knew.

Learning herbal medicine isn't regression—it's reclamation.

It's taking back wisdom that served humanity for 99.9% of our existence. Remembering we evolved with plants. Coming home.

The author has created something remarkable: a comprehensive, practical, scientifically-grounded guide honoring both traditional wisdom and modern understanding.

Trust the process. Start small. Be patient. Track results.

Prepare to be amazed by what's possible when you work **with** your body's healing capacity.

Your journey begins now.

The plants are waiting.

Table of Contents

MEDICAL DISCLAIMER iii
DEDICATION v
FOREWORD vii
CHAPTER 1: YOU WERE DESIGNED TO HEAL 1
    The Immune System, Inflammation, and Self-Repair 1
    Why Chronic Illness Is Not Genetic Fate 2
    How Herbs Communicate with Cells 3
CHAPTER 2: LONGEVITY THROUGH ANCESTRAL MEDICINE 6
    What Centenarians and Tribal Cultures Knew 6
    How Herbal Medicine Preserves Cellular Youth 8
    Why Inflammation Is the Real Aging Disease 11
CHAPTER 3: IMMUNE DEFENSE REMEDIES 13
    Focus: Staying Illness-Proof 13
CHAPTER 4: ANTI-INFLAMMATORY HEALING 48
    Focus: Arthritis, Autoimmune, Chronic Pain 48
CHAPTER 5: GUT & DIGESTIVE RESTORATION 81
    Focus: IBS, Bloating, Nutrient Absorption 81
CHAPTER 6: LIVER & DETOX REMEDIES 112
    Focus: Cellular Cleansing and Energy 112
CHAPTER 7: HORMONES & WOMEN'S LONGEVITY 147
    Focus: Cycle Balance, Fertility, Menopause 147
CHAPTER 8: BRAIN, MEMORY & MOOD 171
    Focus: Cognitive Function, Mental Clarity, Emotional Balance 171
CHAPTER 10: HEART, BLOOD & CIRCULATION 192
    Focus: Cardiovascular Health, Blood Pressure, Circulation 192
CHAPTER 11: SKIN, WOUNDS & FIRST AID 200
    Focus: Wound Healing, Burns, Infections, Emergency Medicine 200
CHAPTER 12: SLEEP, STRESS & NERVOUS SYSTEM 211
    Focus: Restorative Sleep, Stress Resilience, Nervous System Repair 211
CHAPTER 13: SURVIVAL & EMERGENCY MEDICINE 221
    Focus: Wilderness First Aid, Emergency Remedies, Self-Reliance 221
CHAPTER 14: A LIFETIME OF SELF-HEALING 233

Focus: Long-Term Vitality, Self-Reliance, Legacy 233

Section 1: Aging With Strength - The Longevity Protocol 233

Section 2: Travel Kits - Medicine Wherever You Go 238

Section 3: Growing Your Own Herbs - True Self-Reliance 241

Section 4: Teaching Your Family - Legacy Of Healing 247

Section 5: Integration - Making This Sustainable 252

CHAPTER 1: YOU WERE DESIGNED TO HEAL

Your body is not fragile. It is not broken. And it is not waiting for a pharmaceutical miracle to save it.

You were born with the most sophisticated healing system on Earth—a self-regulating, self-repairing biological masterpiece that has kept humans alive for hundreds of thousands of years. Long before hospitals, before antibiotics, before prescriptions, your ancestors survived plagues, infections, injuries, and environmental threats **because their bodies knew how to heal**.

That same intelligence lives in you.

The problem is not that your body has forgotten how to heal. The problem is that **modern life has overwhelmed its capacity to do so**. We are exposed to more toxins, stress, inflammatory foods, and immune triggers than any generation in history. Your body is still fighting—still trying to restore balance—but it's doing so while under constant siege.

This is why chronic illness has exploded. Not because humans suddenly became genetically defective, but because **we stopped supporting the systems that keep us healthy**.

In this chapter, you'll learn how your immune system actually works, why inflammation is both protector and destroyer, and how plants act as the missing bridge between your body's brilliance and the healing it's trying to accomplish.

The Immune System, Inflammation, and Self-Repair

Let's start with the truth: **your immune system is not just about fighting off colds**. It is your body's entire defense, repair, and regeneration network. It patrols for invaders—bacteria, viruses, fungi, parasites. It identifies damaged cells and removes them. It orchestrates wound healing, tissue repair, and even memory formation.

When it's working well, you don't even notice it. Cuts heal. Infections clear. You wake up energized.

But when it's **dysregulated**—either overactive or suppressed—everything falls apart.

The Two Faces of Inflammation

Inflammation gets a bad reputation, but it's not inherently evil. In fact, **acute inflammation is how you heal**.

When you cut your finger, your immune system immediately sends white blood cells to the site. Blood vessels dilate. The area swells, reddens, and warms. This is inflammation—and it's *exactly* what should happen. It's your body isolating the injury, clearing debris, killing pathogens, and rebuilding tissue.

This type of inflammation is **short-lived and life-saving**.

The problem arises when inflammation becomes **chronic**—when it never turns off. This happens when your immune system is constantly triggered by:

- **Poor diet** (processed foods, sugar, seed oils)

- **Gut dysfunction** (leaky gut, dysbiosis, food sensitivities)
- **Toxins** (heavy metals, pesticides, plastics, chemicals)
- **Chronic stress** (cortisol overload, sleep deprivation)
- **Infections** (hidden viruses, bacteria, parasites, mold)

When your body is stuck in a state of perpetual defense, inflammation stops being helpful and starts destroying you from the inside. It damages blood vessels, breaks down joint cartilage, disrupts hormone production, impairs brain function, and accelerates aging.

This is the root of nearly every chronic disease:

- Autoimmune conditions (rheumatoid arthritis, lupus, MS, Hashimoto's)
- Heart disease and stroke
- Diabetes and metabolic syndrome
- Alzheimer's and dementia
- Cancer
- Chronic pain and fibromyalgia

Here's the key insight: Your body *wants* to turn off inflammation. It has built-in mechanisms to do so—anti-inflammatory cytokines, regulatory T-cells, repair pathways. But when those systems are nutrient-depleted, toxin-burdened, and constantly re-triggered, they can't keep up.

This is where plants come in.

Herbs don't just "boost" your immune system blindly. The best ones are **immunomodulators**—they help regulate immune response, calming overactivity (autoimmunity) and strengthening underactivity (chronic infections). They reduce inflammatory signaling molecules. They protect cells from oxidative damage. They support the body's natural repair processes.

They remind your body what balance feels like.

Why Chronic Illness Is Not Genetic Fate

You've probably heard it before: "It runs in my family."

Maybe it's diabetes. Maybe it's heart disease, cancer, or autoimmune disorders. You've been told that because your mother had it, or your grandmother, you're destined for the same fate.

This is one of the most damaging myths in modern medicine.

Yes, genetics matter. But **genes are not destiny**. They are more like blueprints that can be expressed or silenced depending on your environment, lifestyle, and choices. The science of **epigenetics** has proven that your daily habits—what you eat, how you move, how you sleep, what toxins you're exposed to, and yes, *what plants you use*—can turn genes on or off.

Let me give you an example:

Two identical twins share the exact same DNA. One develops type 2 diabetes at 45. The other never does. Why? Because their *environments* were different. One ate inflammatory foods, lived a sedentary lifestyle, and accumulated visceral fat. The other ate whole foods, stayed active, and maintained metabolic health.

Same genes. Different outcomes.

This applies to autoimmune disease, cancer risk, heart disease, and virtually every other "genetic" condition. You are not a passive victim of your DNA. You are an **active participant** in how those genes are expressed.

And one of the most powerful ways to influence gene expression is through **phytochemicals**—the bioactive compounds in medicinal plants.

Studies show that compounds like:

- **Curcumin (from turmeric)** can turn off inflammatory genes linked to arthritis and cancer
- **Resveratrol (from Japanese knotweed)** activates longevity genes that protect against aging
- **Sulforaphane (from broccoli sprouts)** triggers detoxification genes that eliminate carcinogens
- **EGCG (from green tea)** inhibits genes that promote tumor growth

These aren't fringe claims. These are published, peer-reviewed findings showing that **plants talk to your DNA**—and when they do, they often tell your cells to heal, repair, and resist disease.

So no, you are not doomed by your family history. You are **empowered by your choices**.

How Herbs Communicate with Cells

Here's where it gets fascinating.

When you consume a medicinal plant—whether as a tea, tincture, or food—you're not just swallowing inert matter. You're ingesting **information**.

Every plant contains hundreds to thousands of bioactive molecules. These molecules interact with **receptors on your cells**—the same receptors that respond to hormones, neurotransmitters, and immune signals. In essence, plants "speak" the language your body already understands.

Let's break down how this works:

1. Plants Bind to Cell Receptors

Your cells have receptors on their surface—tiny docking stations that receive chemical messages. When the right molecule binds to a receptor, it triggers a cascade of activity inside the cell.

For example:

- **Cannabinoids in cannabis** bind to endocannabinoid receptors, reducing pain and inflammation
- **Ginsenosides in ginseng** bind to steroid hormone receptors, modulating stress response

- **Berberine in goldenseal** activates AMPK, a master metabolic switch that improves insulin sensitivity

This isn't random. **Plants evolved alongside animals for millions of years.** Many of the chemical pathways in plants mirror the pathways in our own bodies. This is why they work so well—and why they're often safer than synthetic drugs, which force receptors into unnatural states.

2. Plants Regulate Gene Expression

As we discussed, herbs don't just mask symptoms—they influence **which genes get turned on or off**.

When you drink a cup of **holy basil (tulsi) tea**, compounds called eugenol and ursolic acid enter your bloodstream and travel to your cells. There, they interact with transcription factors—proteins that control gene activity. They can:

- Suppress genes that promote inflammation
- Activate genes that produce antioxidant enzymes
- Enhance genes involved in stress resilience

This is why people who use adaptogenic herbs like **ashwagandha, rhodiola, and holy basil** report not just feeling calmer, but actually *becoming* more resilient over time. The plants are literally reprogramming how their cells respond to stress.

3. Plants Modulate Biochemical Pathways

Your body runs on interconnected systems—digestion, detoxification, hormone production, immune surveillance. When one system falters, others compensate (or collapse).

Medicinal plants are uniquely suited to **multi-system support** because they contain diverse compounds that work synergistically.

Take **milk thistle**, for example. Its active compound, silymarin, doesn't just protect liver cells—it:

- Blocks toxins from entering hepatocytes (liver cells)
- Stimulates regeneration of damaged liver tissue
- Increases production of glutathione, the body's master antioxidant
- Reduces liver inflammation and fibrosis

One plant. Multiple mechanisms. Whole-body impact.

This is the brilliance of **whole-plant medicine**. Unlike isolated pharmaceutical compounds that target one pathway and often create side effects, herbs work across multiple pathways simultaneously—supporting, balancing, protecting.

Your Body Is Waiting to Heal

Here's what I need you to understand: **healing is not a miracle**. It's biology.

Your immune system knows how to fight infection. Your liver knows how to detoxify. Your gut knows how to absorb nutrients. Your cells know how to repair damage.

But they can't do it without the right support.

Modern life has created a perfect storm of deficiency and toxicity. We're nutrient-starved and poison-saturated. We're stressed, sleep-deprived, and disconnected from the natural rhythms that regulate our biology.

Plants are the antidote.

They provide the phytochemicals, vitamins, minerals, and anti-inflammatory compounds your body is desperately lacking. They help restore the balance that modern life has stolen.

You were designed to heal.

Now it's time to give your body what it needs to do so.

CHAPTER 2: LONGEVITY THROUGH ANCESTRAL MEDICINE

There's a question that haunts modern medicine, one that researchers spend billions trying to answer:

Why do some people live to 100—sharp, mobile, and vibrant—while others are chronically ill by 50?

The answer isn't hidden in a pharmaceutical lab or a genetic testing facility. It's been sitting in plain sight for thousands of years, practiced by cultures that never had access to hospitals, yet somehow produced generation after generation of healthy elders.

They knew the plants.

From the Okinawan centenarians who drink turmeric tea daily, to the Hunza people of the Himalayas who use apricot kernels and wild herbs, to the Indigenous tribes of the Amazon who treat every ailment with forest medicine—**long-lived cultures have always been plant-medicine cultures**.

This isn't coincidence. It's biology.

In this chapter, you'll discover what centenarians and tribal healers understood instinctively: that **aging is not inevitable decline**, that inflammation—not time—is the true destroyer of youth, and that the right plants, used consistently, can preserve not just lifespan, but **healthspan**—the years you live with strength, clarity, and vitality.

What Centenarians and Tribal Cultures Knew

Let's travel the world and learn from the people who got it right.

The Blue Zones: Where People Forget to Die

Researchers have identified five regions on Earth where people live significantly longer than the global average—places called **Blue Zones**:

1. **Okinawa, Japan**
2. **Sardinia, Italy**
3. **Ikaria, Greece**
4. **Nicoya Peninsula, Costa Rica**
5. **Loma Linda, California** (a community of Seventh-day Adventists)

What do these populations have in common?

- They eat **whole, plant-based foods** (minimal processed food)
- They move naturally throughout the day (no gyms, just life)
- They live in tight-knit communities (low chronic stress)
- They have a sense of purpose (ikigai in Okinawa)
- And critically: **they use medicinal plants daily**

Let's look at just one example: **Okinawa**.

Okinawans consume **turmeric** almost daily—in teas, soups, and as a spice. Turmeric contains curcumin, one of the most powerful anti-inflammatory compounds on Earth. Studies show that Okinawans have some of the lowest rates of Alzheimer's disease, heart disease, and cancer in the world.

Coincidence? Not even close.

They also eat **bitter melon** (a blood-sugar regulator), **mugwort** (a digestive and immune tonic), and **Okinawan sweet potatoes** (rich in anthocyanins that protect the brain and cardiovascular system).

Their food **is** their medicine. And their medicine **is** their food.

The Hunza: The People Who Never Got Sick

High in the Karakoram Mountains of Pakistan lives a population called the **Hunza**. For decades, explorers and researchers were stunned by their longevity and absence of chronic disease.

Hunza elders routinely lived into their 90s and beyond—still working, still climbing mountains, still mentally sharp. Cancer, heart disease, and diabetes were virtually unknown.

What was their secret?

- **Apricot kernels** (rich in amygdalin, which some researchers believe has anti-cancer properties—though this remains debated)
- **Mineral-rich glacier water**
- **Wild herbs and greens** gathered from the mountains
- **Fermented foods** that supported gut health
- A diet based on **whole grains, vegetables, and minimal animal protein**

But perhaps most importantly: **they lived without chronic stress, in harmony with nature, and with deep respect for plant medicine passed down for generations**.

Indigenous Amazonian Healers: The Original Pharmacologists

The Amazon rainforest is home to an estimated **80,000 plant species**. Indigenous tribes like the Shipibo, Asháninka, and Yawanawa have been using these plants medicinally for millennia.

Western scientists are only beginning to understand what these healers have always known:

- **Cat's claw (Uncaria tomentosa)** – A powerful immune modulator and anti-inflammatory used for arthritis, autoimmune disease, and cancer support
- **Sangre de drago (dragon's blood)** – A tree sap that heals wounds, stops infections, and treats gastrointestinal ulcers

- **Ayahuasca** – A potent entheogenic brew used for deep psychological healing (now being studied for PTSD and depression)
- **Chuchuhuasi** – A bark used for pain relief, immune support, and vitality

These are not folk remedies. These are **sophisticated healing systems** developed through thousands of years of observation, experimentation, and spiritual practice.

When a shaman prepares medicine, they're not guessing. They're drawing on a vast, intergenerational knowledge base—**ethnobotany encoded in ritual, song, and story**.

Native American Medicine: Healing Through Relationship

Before colonization, Indigenous peoples of North America had thriving, plant-based healing traditions. Every tribe had its medicine people—those who knew which plants stopped bleeding, which reduced fever, which eased childbirth, which cleared infection.

Some of their most powerful remedies:

- **Echinacea** – Used by the Plains tribes for infections, snake bites, and immune support
- **Goldenseal** – A potent antimicrobial for wounds, digestive infections, and respiratory illness
- **White sage** – Burned for purification and used internally for sore throats and digestive issues
- **Willow bark** – The original aspirin, used for pain and fever
- **Slippery elm** – A demulcent that soothes the gut lining and heals digestive inflammation

What made Native American medicine so effective was not just the plants themselves, but the **relationship** with them. Plants were not seen as commodities to be harvested. They were seen as **relatives, teachers, allies**.

Healing was holistic—body, mind, spirit, and community.

This is a lesson we've forgotten in modern medicine, where healing has been reduced to symptom suppression and profit.

How Herbal Medicine Preserves Cellular Youth

Aging, at its core, is a process of **cellular breakdown**. Over time, your cells accumulate damage from:

- **Oxidative stress** (free radicals damaging DNA, proteins, and lipids)
- **Chronic inflammation** (the immune system attacking your own tissues)
- **Telomere shortening** (the protective caps on chromosomes wearing down)
- **Mitochondrial dysfunction** (your cellular power plants failing)

- **Glycation** (sugar molecules binding to proteins and causing tissue stiffness)

If you can **slow or reverse these processes**, you can slow or reverse aging.

And guess what? **Plants do exactly that.**

1. Antioxidants: Neutralizing Free Radicals

Every second, your cells produce energy—and as a byproduct, they generate **free radicals** (unstable molecules that steal electrons from healthy cells, causing damage).

Left unchecked, free radicals lead to:

- Wrinkled, sagging skin
- Cognitive decline
- Vision loss
- Cardiovascular disease
- Cancer

Your body produces its own antioxidants (like glutathione and SOD), but **plants provide additional, powerful reinforcements**.

The most potent antioxidant-rich plants:

- **Blueberries, elderberries, acai** (anthocyanins)
- **Green tea** (EGCG)
- **Turmeric** (curcumin)
- **Cacao** (flavanols)
- **Goji berries** (carotenoids)
- **Astragalus** (saponins and polysaccharides)

Studies show that people who consume high amounts of dietary antioxidants have:

- Slower rates of brain aging
- Lower risk of heart disease
- Better skin elasticity
- Reduced cancer incidence

---

2. Anti-Inflammatory Herbs: Silencing the Fire Within

We've said it before, but it bears repeating: **chronic inflammation is the single greatest driver of aging and disease**.

It's what turns a healthy 50-year-old into a stiff, foggy, tired 60-year-old. It's what causes joints to swell, arteries to harden, and neurons to die.

The good news? **Plants are master anti-inflammatory agents.**

Top anti-inflammatory herbs for longevity:

- **Turmeric** – Inhibits NF-kB (a protein complex that drives inflammation)
- **Ginger** – Reduces inflammatory cytokines; supports joint health
- **Boswellia (frankincense)** – Blocks inflammatory enzymes; used for arthritis and autoimmune disease
- **Devil's claw** – A potent pain reliever and anti-inflammatory for joint conditions
- **Licorice root** – Modulates immune response; soothes inflamed tissues

When you reduce inflammation consistently over time, you:

- Preserve joint function
- Protect cardiovascular health
- Maintain cognitive sharpness
- Support hormone balance
- Enhance energy and vitality

---

3. Adaptogens: Protecting Cells from Stress

Chronic stress accelerates aging by:

- Elevating cortisol (which breaks down tissue and suppresses immunity)
- Increasing oxidative stress
- Disrupting sleep and repair cycles
- Promoting insulin resistance and weight gain

Adaptogens are herbs that help your body resist the damaging effects of stress. They don't just calm you down—they **build resilience at the cellular level**.

Key adaptogenic herbs for longevity:

- **Ashwagandha** – Lowers cortisol, supports mitochondria, improves sleep
- **Rhodiola** – Increases energy, protects neurons, enhances endurance
- **Holy basil (tulsi)** – Reduces oxidative stress, balances blood sugar
- **Reishi mushroom** – Immune-modulating, anti-cancer, promotes longevity

- **Schisandra** – Protects the liver, enhances mental clarity, supports skin health

People who use adaptogens regularly report:

- Better stress tolerance
- Improved sleep quality
- Sustained energy without crashes
- Sharper mental focus
- Healthier aging overall

---

4. Telomere Protection: Guarding Your Genetic Clock

Telomeres are protective caps at the ends of your chromosomes. Every time your cells divide, telomeres shorten. When they get too short, cells stop dividing and enter senescence (a kind of "retirement" state)—or they die.

Short telomeres = accelerated aging.

But here's the exciting part: **certain plant compounds can slow telomere shortening or even activate telomerase** (the enzyme that rebuilds telomeres).

Plants that support telomere health:

- **Astragalus** – Contains cycloastragenol, which activates telomerase
- **Turmeric** – Protects telomeres from oxidative damage
- **Green tea (EGCG)** – Preserves telomere length
- **Ginkgo biloba** – Protects against DNA damage

Research shows that people with longer telomeres tend to:

- Live longer
- Have better cognitive function
- Experience fewer age-related diseases

Why Inflammation Is the Real Aging Disease

Let's bring it all together.

Aging is not about the passage of time. It's about the accumulation of damage.

And the primary source of that damage? **Chronic, low-grade inflammation.**

This type of inflammation—often called **"inflammaging"**—quietly destroys your body from the inside:

- It damages blood vessel walls → leading to atherosclerosis and heart disease

- It breaks down cartilage → leading to osteoarthritis
- It disrupts insulin signaling → leading to diabetes
- It kills neurons → leading to Alzheimer's and dementia
- It triggers abnormal cell growth → leading to cancer
- It weakens the immune system → leading to infections and autoimmune disease

The centenarians we've discussed—the Okinawans, the Hunza, the Indigenous elders—**they all kept inflammation low** through lifestyle and plant medicine.

They didn't need anti-aging creams or pharmaceutical interventions. They had:

- Anti-inflammatory diets (rich in polyphenols, omega-3s, fiber)
- Movement and purpose (which reduce stress)
- Strong social connections (which lower cortisol)
- And most importantly: **daily use of medicinal plants**

The Path Forward: Becoming Your Own Elder

You don't need exotic superfoods shipped from remote islands. You don't need expensive supplements or anti-aging clinics.

You need **the wisdom that's been here all along**—the plants, the practices, the ancestral knowledge that kept humans healthy for millennia.

In the chapters ahead, you'll learn exactly which plants to use, how to prepare them, and how to integrate them into your life so that aging becomes not a decline, but a **graceful unfolding of vitality**.

Your ancestors knew how to do this. Now it's your turn.

CHAPTER 3: IMMUNE DEFENSE REMEDIES

Focus: Staying Illness-Proof

Your immune system is not a static shield. It's a **living, intelligent network** of cells, tissues, and chemical messengers that adapt, learn, and respond to every threat you encounter.

When it's strong, you don't just "fight off" illness—you **prevent it from taking hold in the first place**. You move through cold and flu season untouched. You recover quickly when everyone around you is bedridden. You feel resilient, energized, protected.

When it's weak, you're vulnerable. Every virus finds you. Every infection lingers. You're tired, run-down, and constantly playing catch-up.

The remedies in this chapter are designed to **fortify your immune defenses year-round**—and to intervene powerfully at the first sign of infection.

These are not "boosters" in the trendy supplement sense. These are **deep immune tonics, antiviral warriors, infection fighters, and resilience builders** that have protected humans for thousands of years.

You'll learn to make:

- **Elderberry syrup** – The ultimate antiviral remedy
- **Astragalus tonics** – Long-term immune strength
- **Antiviral teas** – Blends that stop infections in their tracks
- **Infection-fighting tinctures** – Fast-acting liquid medicine for acute illness
- **Immune-boosting broths** – Nourishing food as medicine
- **Fire cider** – The legendary immune tonic
- **Respiratory steams and chest rubs** – For when infection hits the lungs
- **Throat sprays and gargles** – First defense against sore throats

Each remedy includes:

- ☑ **What it heals**
- ☑ **Why it works**
- ☑ **How to make it**
- ☑ **How to use it**
- ☑ **Safety notes**

Let's begin building your immune fortress.

REMEDY 1: Elderberry Syrup

What It Heals

Elderberry syrup is the **most powerful antiviral remedy in the home apothecary**. It:

- Shortens the duration of colds and flu by up to 4 days
- Reduces severity of symptoms (fever, body aches, congestion)
- Prevents viral replication
- Supports immune cell activity
- Acts as a potent antioxidant

Why It Works

Elderberries (*Sambucus nigra*) contain **anthocyanins**—deep purple pigments that inhibit the neuraminidase enzyme on the surface of flu viruses. This prevents the virus from entering your cells and replicating.

Studies show elderberry extract:

- Reduces flu symptoms faster than Tamiflu in some trials
- Increases cytokine production (immune signaling molecules)
- Protects cells from oxidative damage during illness

How to Make It

Ingredients:

- 1 cup dried elderberries (or 2 cups fresh)
- 4 cups water
- 1 cinnamon stick
- 1 tablespoon fresh grated ginger (or 1 teaspoon dried)
- 5–10 whole cloves
- 1 cup raw honey (added at the end)

Instructions:

1. Combine elderberries, water, cinnamon, ginger, and cloves in a pot.
2. Bring to a boil, then reduce to a simmer.
3. Simmer uncovered for 45 minutes, or until liquid is reduced by half.
4. Mash berries with a potato masher or fork to release remaining juice.
5. Strain through cheesecloth or a fine-mesh strainer into a clean bowl. Squeeze out every drop.
6. Let the liquid cool to room temperature (below 110°F to preserve honey's enzymes).
7. Stir in honey until fully dissolved.
8. Pour into sterilized glass bottles (amber or swing-top bottles work best).
9. Label with date.

Yield: About 2 cups of syrup

How to Use It

During illness:

- Adults: 1 tablespoon every 2–3 hours
- Children (2–12 years): 1 teaspoon every 2–3 hours
- Infants under 1 year: Do not use (honey is not safe for infants)

For prevention (during cold/flu season):

- Adults: 1 tablespoon daily
- Children: 1 teaspoon daily

Storage: Refrigerate. Lasts 3–6 months.

Safety Notes

- **Never consume raw elderberries**—they contain cyanogenic glycosides that cause nausea and vomiting. Cooking destroys these compounds.
- Safe for children over 1 year (due to honey content).
- If diabetic, reduce honey or use a glycerin-based version.

REMEDY 2: Fire Cider

What It Heals

Fire cider is a **legendary immune tonic and circulatory stimulant**. It:

- Warms the body and improves circulation
- Clears sinuses and respiratory congestion
- Fights bacterial and viral infections
- Stimulates digestion and metabolism
- Supports detoxification

Why It Works

Fire cider combines **antimicrobial, antiviral, and circulatory-stimulating herbs** in an apple cider vinegar base. Each ingredient plays a role:

- **Garlic:** Broad-spectrum antimicrobial
- **Ginger:** Anti-inflammatory, warming, circulation-boosting
- **Horseradish:** Clears sinuses, antimicrobial
- **Cayenne:** Increases circulation, stops infections
- **Onion:** Antimicrobial, expectorant
- **Citrus:** High in vitamin C
- **Apple cider vinegar:** Extracts minerals, antimicrobial

How to Make It

Ingredients:

- 1 large onion, chopped
- 10 cloves garlic, chopped or crushed
- 2 jalapeño peppers, chopped (seeds optional for extra heat)
- 1 cup grated fresh ginger
- 1 cup grated fresh horseradish root
- 1 tablespoon turmeric powder (or 2 tablespoons fresh grated turmeric)
- 1 teaspoon cayenne powder (or to taste)
- Zest and juice of 2 lemons
- Zest and juice of 1 orange
- Raw apple cider vinegar (with "the mother")
- Raw honey (to taste, added at the end)

Instructions:

1. Place all chopped/grated ingredients into a large glass jar (quart or half-gallon).
2. Fill the jar with apple cider vinegar, covering all ingredients by 1–2 inches.
3. Use a piece of parchment paper or plastic wrap under the metal lid (vinegar corrodes metal).
4. Seal jar and shake well.
5. Let sit in a cool, dark place for **4–6 weeks**. Shake daily.
6. After 4–6 weeks, strain through cheesecloth, squeezing out all liquid.
7. Add honey to taste (start with ¼ cup, adjust to preference).
8. Bottle in glass jars or bottles. Label with date.

Yield: About 3–4 cups

How to Use It

During illness:

- Take 1–2 tablespoons every few hours
- Can be taken straight (brace yourself—it's spicy!) or diluted in water or tea

For prevention:

- Take 1 tablespoon daily, especially in fall and winter

Other uses:

- Salad dressing base (mix with olive oil)
- Marinade for meats
- Added to soups and stews

Storage: Shelf-stable for 1–2 years in a cool, dark place.

Safety Notes

- Very spicy—start with small amounts
- May irritate sensitive stomachs (take with food if needed)
- Not suitable for infants or very young children due to honey and spice level
- Pregnant women: Consult herbalist (cayenne and horseradish can be stimulating)

REMEDY 3: Echinacea Tincture

What It Heals

Echinacea is a **powerful immune activator** best used at the **first sign of infection**. It:

- Activates white blood cells
- Increases interferon production (antiviral compound)
- Reduces severity and duration of colds and respiratory infections
- Speeds wound healing (topically or internally)
- Fights bacterial, viral, and fungal infections

Why It Works

Echinacea contains **alkamides, polysaccharides, and caffeic acid derivatives** that stimulate macrophages (immune cells that "eat" pathogens) and increase production of immune signaling molecules.

It works best when taken **at the onset of symptoms**—not as a long-term preventive (it can overstimulate the immune system if used continuously).

How to Make It

Ingredients:

- 1 part dried echinacea root (or 2 parts fresh root, chopped)
- 5 parts vodka (80 proof) or Everclear diluted to 60% alcohol

Instructions:

1. Place dried echinacea root in a clean glass jar (pint or quart).
2. Cover with alcohol, ensuring all plant material is submerged by 1–2 inches.
3. Seal jar tightly.
4. Label with herb name, date, and alcohol percentage.
5. Let sit in a cool, dark place for **4–6 weeks**. Shake jar daily.
6. After 4–6 weeks, strain through cheesecloth into a clean bowl, squeezing out all liquid.
7. Pour into amber dropper bottles.
8. Label with name, date, dosage.

Yield: Varies based on jar size (1 cup root yields about 1–1.5 cups tincture)

How to Use It

At first sign of illness (scratchy throat, fatigue, body aches):

- Adults: 4–5 mL (about 1 teaspoon) every 2–3 hours
- Children (2–12 years): 1–2 mL (20–40 drops) every 3–4 hours

Continue for 7–10 days maximum.

Do NOT use:

- Long-term (more than 2 weeks at a time)
- As a daily preventive (it's for acute infections only)

Pro tip: Echinacea tincture should cause a tingling sensation on the tongue—this confirms potency.

Safety Notes

- Safe for most people
- Avoid if allergic to plants in the Asteraceae family (ragweed, daisies, sunflowers)
- Not recommended for autoimmune conditions (stimulates immune response)
- Not for long-term use

REMEDY 4: Astragalus Immune Broth

What It Heals

Astragalus is a **deep immune tonic** used in Traditional Chinese Medicine for thousands of years. It:

- Builds long-term immune resilience
- Increases white blood cell production
- Protects against viral infections
- Supports recovery from chronic illness
- Enhances energy and vitality

Why It Works

Astragalus contains **polysaccharides and saponins** that modulate immune function, enhance T-cell activity, and support the body's "Wei Qi" (protective energy).

Unlike echinacea (acute use), astragalus is used **long-term** to build foundational immune strength.

How to Make It

Ingredients:

- 6–8 slices dried astragalus root
- 8 cups water (or chicken/vegetable broth)
- 4 cloves garlic, smashed
- 2-inch piece fresh ginger, sliced
- 2 carrots, chopped
- 2 celery stalks, chopped
- 1 onion, chopped
- Fresh or dried thyme, rosemary, or sage (optional)
- Sea salt and black pepper to taste

Instructions:

1. Place astragalus slices in a large pot with water or broth.
2. Bring to a boil, then reduce to a low simmer.
3. Add garlic, ginger, carrots, celery, onion, and herbs.
4. Cover and simmer for **2–3 hours** (the longer, the better—astragalus needs time to release its compounds).
5. Strain out astragalus slices (they're woody and not edible, but can be composted).
6. Season with salt and pepper.
7. Drink 1–2 cups daily.

Storage: Refrigerate for up to 5 days, or freeze in portions.

How to Use It

- Drink 1–2 cups daily during cold/flu season
- Use as a base for soups and stews
- Especially beneficial for those recovering from illness or with chronic fatigue

Safety Notes

- Safe for long-term use
- Avoid during acute infections with high fever (use cooling herbs instead)
- Generally safe for children and elderly

REMEDY 5: Antiviral Herbal Tea Blend

What It Heals

This tea is a **multi-herb antiviral formula** that:

- Fights viral replication
- Reduces respiratory symptoms

- Soothes sore throats
- Supports immune function
- Calms inflammation

Why It Works

Each herb contributes unique antiviral and immune-supportive properties:

- **Elderflower:** Diaphoretic (induces sweating to break fevers), antiviral
- **Peppermint:** Clears sinuses, relieves headaches, antimicrobial
- **Yarrow:** Reduces fever, antiviral, anti-inflammatory
- **Lemon balm:** Antiviral (especially against herpes family viruses), calming
- **Thyme:** Antimicrobial, expectorant (clears mucus)

How to Make It

Ingredients (dried herbs):

- 2 parts elderflower
- 2 parts peppermint leaf
- 1 part yarrow flower
- 1 part lemon balm leaf
- 1 part thyme leaf

Instructions:

1. Mix all dried herbs together in a bowl.
2. Store in an airtight glass jar, labeled with name and date.
3. To brew: Use 1–2 teaspoons of tea blend per cup of hot water.
4. Steep covered for 10–15 minutes.
5. Strain and drink hot.
6. Add honey and lemon if desired.

How to Use It

During active infection:

- Drink 3–5 cups daily, as hot as you can tolerate
- Best taken at first sign of symptoms

For prevention:

- Drink 1–2 cups daily during cold/flu season

Safety Notes

- Safe for adults and children over 2 years
- Peppermint may reduce milk supply in nursing mothers (use sparingly)
- Generally very safe and gentle

REMEDY 6: Garlic Honey

What It Heals

Garlic honey is a **potent antimicrobial and immune booster**. It:

- Fights bacterial, viral, and fungal infections
- Clears respiratory congestion
- Supports cardiovascular health
- Boosts immune cell activity

Why It Works

Garlic contains allicin—a sulfur compound with proven antimicrobial properties. **Raw honey** is antimicrobial, soothing, and preserves the garlic's potency.

Together, they create a **synergistic infection-fighting remedy** that's also delicious.

How to Make It

Ingredients:

- 1 cup fresh garlic cloves, peeled

- Raw honey (enough to cover garlic)

Instructions:

1. Place peeled garlic cloves in a clean glass jar (pint size works well).
2. Cover completely with raw honey.
3. Use a clean spoon to stir and release air bubbles.
4. Seal jar loosely (fermentation gases need to escape).
5. Let sit at room temperature for **1–2 weeks**, turning jar upside down daily to coat all garlic.
6. After 2 weeks, store in pantry or refrigerator.

The garlic will ferment slightly, creating a sweet-savory, mellow flavor.

How to Use It

During illness:

- Eat 1–2 cloves of garlic honey every few hours
- Take 1 teaspoon of the honey alone (it absorbs garlic's medicinal compounds)

For prevention:

- Eat 1 clove daily during cold/flu season

Other uses:

- Drizzle over toast, cheese, or roasted vegetables
- Add to salad dressings
- Stir into tea

Storage: Shelf-stable for 1+ year. Improves with age.

Safety Notes

- Not for infants under 1 year (due to honey)
- May cause heartburn in sensitive individuals
- Garlic is a blood thinner—consult doctor if on anticoagulant medications

REMEDY 7: Thyme and Sage Throat Spray

What It Heals

This spray is a **first-line defense for sore throats**. It:

- Kills bacteria and viruses on contact
- Reduces throat pain and inflammation
- Prevents infections from settling deeper
- Supports immune response in throat tissues

Why It Works

Thyme contains thymol—a powerful antimicrobial volatile oil. **Sage** is astringent, antimicrobial, and anti-inflammatory. Together, they coat and protect throat tissues while killing pathogens.

How to Make It

Ingredients:

- 2 tablespoons dried thyme
- 2 tablespoons dried sage
- ½ cup vodka (80 proof) or apple cider vinegar
- 1 tablespoon raw honey (optional, for soothing)
- 5 drops peppermint essential oil (optional, for flavor)

Instructions:

1. Place thyme and sage in a small glass jar.
2. Cover with vodka or vinegar.
3. Seal and let sit for 2–4 weeks, shaking daily.
4. Strain through cheesecloth into a bowl.
5. Add honey (if using) and peppermint oil.
6. Pour into 2 oz amber glass spray bottles.
7. Label with name and date.

How to Use It

At first sign of sore throat:

- Spray directly into throat 4–6 times per day
- Hold spray in throat for a few seconds before swallowing

Safe for children over 5 years (alcohol evaporates quickly).

Safety Notes

- Safe for most people
- If using vinegar-based version, it's milder and safe for children over 2 years
- Avoid if allergic to mint family plants

REMEDY 8: Oregano Oil (Antibiotic Alternative)

What It Heals

Oregano oil is one of the **strongest natural antibiotics**. It:

- Kills antibiotic-resistant bacteria
- Fights fungal infections (Candida)
- Clears respiratory infections
- Supports gut health (eliminates pathogens without harming beneficial bacteria)

Why It Works

Oregano contains **carvacrol and thymol**—compounds with proven antimicrobial activity against E. coli, Staph, Strep, and other pathogens.

Studies show it's as effective as some pharmaceutical antibiotics—without promoting resistance.

How to Make It (Infused Oil Method)

Note: True medicinal-strength oregano oil requires steam distillation (essential oil), which isn't practical at home. However, you can make a potent infused oil for topical and mild internal use.

Ingredients:

- Fresh oregano leaves (preferably *Origanum vulgare*)
- Olive oil or fractionated coconut oil

Instructions:

1. Bruise or chop fresh oregano leaves to release oils.
2. Fill a jar ¾ full with oregano.
3. Cover completely with oil.
4. Seal jar and place in a warm, sunny spot for 2–4 weeks.
5. Strain through cheesecloth.
6. Store in amber glass bottles.

For stronger medicinal use, purchase high-quality oregano essential oil (look for at least 70% carvacrol content).

How to Use It

For infections (using essential oil):

- Dilute 2–3 drops essential oil in 1 tablespoon carrier oil (olive, coconut)
- Place under tongue or swallow in a capsule
- Take 2–3 times daily for up to 10 days

Topically (infused oil or diluted essential oil):

- Apply to fungal infections (athlete's foot, nail fungus)
- Use in chest rubs for respiratory infections

Safety Notes

- **Very potent**—always dilute essential oil before use
- Can irritate mucous membranes if too concentrated
- Avoid during pregnancy
- Not for children under 2 years

REMEDY 9: Respiratory Steam with Eucalyptus and Thyme

What It Heals

This steam opens airways and fights respiratory infections. It:

- Clears sinus congestion
- Loosens mucus
- Kills airborne pathogens
- Soothes inflamed respiratory tissues

Why It Works

Eucalyptus contains eucalyptol (cineole)—a decongestant and antimicrobial. **Thyme** contains thymol—antimicrobial and expectorant.

Inhaling steam carries these volatile oils directly to respiratory tissues.

How to Make It

Ingredients:

- 2 tablespoons dried eucalyptus leaves (or 5 drops eucalyptus essential oil)
- 2 tablespoons dried thyme (or 3 drops thyme essential oil)
- 4 cups boiling water

Instructions:

1. Boil water in a large pot.
2. Remove from heat.
3. Add eucalyptus and thyme (or essential oils).
4. Place a towel over your head and lean over the pot (keep face 12 inches away to avoid burns).
5. Breathe deeply through nose and mouth for 10–15 minutes.
6. Repeat 2–3 times daily during respiratory illness.

Safety Notes

- Keep face far enough from steam to avoid burns
- Not for children under 5 years (they can't safely lean over hot water)
- Supervise older children closely

REMEDY 10: Immune-Boosting Herbal Electuary (Honey Paste)

What It Heals

An electuary is a **medicinal paste made with honey and powdered herbs**. This immune-boosting version:

- Strengthens immunity
- Fights infections
- Reduces inflammation
- Tastes delicious (making it easy to take daily)

Why It Works

Combines multiple immune-supporting herbs in a form that's easy to consume and preserves potency.

How to Make It

Ingredients:

- ½ cup raw honey
- 2 tablespoons astragalus root powder
- 1 tablespoon reishi mushroom powder
- 1 tablespoon turmeric powder
- 1 teaspoon cinnamon powder
- ½ teaspoon ginger powder
- ¼ teaspoon black pepper (enhances turmeric absorption)

Instructions:

1. Place honey in a bowl.
2. Add all powdered herbs.
3. Stir thoroughly until a thick paste forms (add more honey if too thick).
4. Store in a small glass jar with tight-fitting lid.
5. Label with name and date.

How to Use It

- Take 1 teaspoon daily (straight or stirred into warm water or tea)
- Increase to 1 tablespoon 2–3 times daily during illness

Storage: Shelf-stable for 6–12 months.

Safety Notes

- Not for infants under 1 year
- Safe for children and adults
- Turmeric may stain clothing

REMEDY 11: Vitamin C Rosehip Syrup

What It Heals

Rosehip syrup is a **vitamin C powerhouse** that:

- Boosts immune function
- Reduces duration of colds
- Supports collagen production and wound healing
- Acts as a powerful antioxidant
- Strengthens capillaries and reduces bruising

Why It Works

Rosehips contain **more vitamin C than oranges**—up to 20 times more by weight. They also contain bioflavonoids that enhance vitamin C absorption and provide additional immune support.

Unlike synthetic vitamin C, rosehips provide the **full vitamin C complex** with cofactors that improve bioavailability.

How to Make It

Ingredients:

- 1 cup dried rosehips (or 2 cups fresh, chopped)
- 4 cups water
- 1 cup raw honey
- Juice of 1 lemon (optional, adds more vitamin C)

Instructions:

1. Place rosehips in a pot with water.
2. Bring to a boil, then reduce to simmer.
3. Simmer uncovered for 45–60 minutes, until liquid reduces by half.
4. Mash rosehips with a potato masher.
5. Strain through cheesecloth or fine-mesh strainer (rosehips have tiny hairs that can irritate—strain thoroughly).

6. Let cool to below 110°F.
7. Stir in honey and lemon juice.
8. Pour into sterilized glass bottles.
9. Label with date.

Yield: About 2 cups

How to Use It

For prevention:

- Adults: 1 tablespoon daily
- Children: 1 teaspoon daily

During illness:

- Adults: 1 tablespoon 3–4 times daily
- Children: 1 teaspoon 3–4 times daily

Other uses:

- Drizzle over pancakes or yogurt
- Mix into sparkling water
- Add to smoothies

Storage: Refrigerate for up to 3 months.

Safety Notes

- Very safe for all ages (except infants under 1 due to honey)
- High vitamin C content may cause loose stools in very large doses
- Generally well-tolerated

REMEDY 12: Colloidal Silver Spray (Immune Support)

What It Heals

Colloidal silver is **antimicrobial silver particles suspended in water**. It:

- Kills bacteria, viruses, and fungi on contact
- Prevents wound infections
- Treats sinus infections (as nasal spray)
- Supports immune function during acute illness

Why It Works

Silver ions disrupt bacterial cell walls and interfere with viral replication. It's been used as an antimicrobial for centuries—before antibiotics existed, silver was medicine's primary infection fighter.

How to Make It

Note: Making true colloidal silver requires a colloidal silver generator (available online, $50–$200). However, you can purchase high-quality colloidal silver (10–20 ppm) from health stores.

DIY method (if you have a generator):

1. Follow your generator's instructions (typically involves suspending silver electrodes in distilled water)
2. Run for prescribed time (usually 20–30 minutes for 10 ppm solution)
3. Store in amber glass bottles away from light
4. Label with concentration and date

How to Use It

For immune support:

- 1 teaspoon held under tongue for 30 seconds, then swallowed
- 1–3 times daily during illness

As nasal spray:

- Spray 2–3 times per nostril for sinus infections

Topically:

- Apply to cuts, burns, or skin infections

- Use as wound wash

Throat spray:

- Spray into throat for sore throat or oral infections

Safety Notes

- Use only high-quality colloidal silver (avoid ionic silver or silver protein)
- Short-term use only (1–2 weeks during acute illness)
- Long-term excessive use can cause argyria (blue-gray skin discoloration—extremely rare with proper dosing)
- Not for long-term daily use
- Controversial in mainstream medicine—research both sides

REMEDY 13: Ginger Lemon Immune Shots

What It Heals

These concentrated shots provide **rapid immune activation**. They:

- Stimulate circulation
- Warm the body (useful at onset of chills)
- Provide concentrated vitamin C
- Have antimicrobial and anti-inflammatory properties
- Boost energy during illness

Why It Works

Ginger: Contains gingerols and shogaols—anti-inflammatory compounds that stimulate circulation and support immune response.

Lemon: High in vitamin C and citric acid, which supports immune function and creates an alkaline environment hostile to pathogens.

Cayenne: Increases circulation, bringing immune cells to infected areas faster.

How to Make It

Ingredients (per shot):

- 1-inch piece fresh ginger, peeled
- ½ fresh lemon
- 1 pinch cayenne pepper
- 1 teaspoon raw honey
- Splash of warm water (optional, to dilute intensity)

Instructions:

1. Juice or finely grate ginger (use cheesecloth to squeeze out juice).
2. Juice lemon.
3. Combine ginger juice, lemon juice, cayenne, and honey in a small glass.
4. Stir well.
5. Take as a shot (drink quickly).

Or make a larger batch:

1. Juice 10 lemons and 1 cup fresh ginger.
2. Mix in ¼ teaspoon cayenne and ½ cup honey.
3. Store in glass bottle in refrigerator.
4. Shake before each use.
5. Take 2 tablespoons as needed.

How to Use It

At first sign of illness:

- Take 1 shot every 2–3 hours

For prevention during exposure:

- Take 1 shot daily

Pro tip: Follow with a glass of water—it's intense!

Safety Notes

- Very spicy—not suitable for young children
- May irritate sensitive stomachs (take with food if needed)
- Cayenne is a mild blood thinner—consult doctor if on anticoagulants

---

REMEDY 14: Propolis Tincture

What It Heals

Propolis is **bee resin**—a sticky substance bees collect from tree buds and use to seal their hives. It's one of nature's most powerful antimicrobials. It:

- Kills bacteria, viruses, and fungi
- Speeds wound healing
- Reduces inflammation
- Supports oral health (treats gum disease, canker sores)
- Boosts immune function

Why It Works

Propolis contains over **300 bioactive compounds**, including:

- Flavonoids (antioxidant, anti-inflammatory)
- Phenolic acids (antimicrobial)
- Essential oils (antiseptic)
- Vitamins and minerals

It's been called "nature's antibiotic" and has proven activity against antibiotic-resistant bacteria.

How to Make It

Ingredients:

- Raw propolis (available from beekeepers or online)
- High-proof alcohol (Everclear or 95% grain alcohol works best—propolis is resinous and needs strong alcohol)

Instructions:

1. Freeze propolis for a few hours (makes it easier to break apart).
2. Grate or chop frozen propolis into small pieces.
3. Place in a glass jar.
4. Cover with alcohol (use a 1:5 ratio—1 part propolis to 5 parts alcohol).
5. Seal jar tightly.
6. Let sit for 2–4 weeks, shaking daily.
7. Strain through cheesecloth (it will be very sticky—propolis stains, so use old cloth).
8. Pour into amber dropper bottles.
9. Label with date.

Yield: Varies by batch size

How to Use It

For sore throat:

- Add 10–20 drops to warm water and gargle
- Or drop directly on back of throat

For immune support:

- Take 20–30 drops in water, 2–3 times daily during illness

For wounds:

- Apply diluted tincture topically (or use propolis salve)

For oral health:

- Add 5–10 drops to toothpaste or use as mouthwash (diluted in water)

Safety Notes

- Generally very safe
- Rare allergic reactions in people allergic to bee products
- Stains clothing and surfaces (be careful)
- Safe for children in small doses (5–10 drops)

REMEDY 15: Medicinal Mushroom Immune Tea

What It Heals

This tea combines **multiple medicinal mushrooms** for deep immune support. It:

- Modulates immune function (strengthens weak immunity, calms overactive immunity)
- Protects against viral infections
- Supports cancer recovery
- Reduces inflammation
- Enhances energy and stamina

Why It Works

Medicinal mushrooms contain **beta-glucans**—complex polysaccharides that train and activate immune cells (macrophages, natural killer cells, T-cells).

Each mushroom brings unique properties:

- **Reishi:** Calming, immune-modulating, anti-cancer
- **Chaga:** Highest antioxidant content, immune-boosting
- **Turkey tail:** Cancer-fighting, gut-healing
- **Cordyceps:** Energy-enhancing, respiratory support

How to Make It

Ingredients:

- 2 tablespoons dried reishi pieces
- 2 tablespoons dried chaga chunks
- 1 tablespoon dried turkey tail pieces
- 1 tablespoon dried cordyceps
- 8 cups water
- Optional: cinnamon stick, ginger, or honey for flavor

Instructions:

1. Place all mushrooms in a large pot with water.
2. Bring to a boil.
3. Reduce to lowest simmer and cover.
4. Simmer for **2–4 hours** (mushrooms need long extraction).
5. Strain out mushroom pieces (save them—they can be re-simmered 1–2 more times).
6. Add cinnamon, ginger, or honey if desired.
7. Store in glass jars in refrigerator.

Yield: About 6 cups

How to Use It

- Drink 1–2 cups daily as a long-term immune tonic
- Especially beneficial during cancer treatment, chronic illness, or immune deficiency
- Can be reheated or enjoyed cold

Storage: Refrigerate for up to 5 days, or freeze in portions.

Safety Notes

- Very safe for long-term use
- Generally well-tolerated by all ages
- May have mild blood-thinning effects (consult doctor if on anticoagulants)

REMEDY 16: Olive Leaf Extract Tincture

What It Heals

Olive leaf is a **potent antiviral and immune modulator**. It:

- Fights viral infections (especially herpes, Epstein-Barr, flu)
- Lowers blood pressure
- Reduces inflammation
- Supports cardiovascular health
- Has anti-cancer properties

Why It Works

Olive leaf contains **oleuropein**—a compound that interferes with viral replication by preventing viruses from attaching to cells. It also stimulates phagocytosis (immune cells "eating" pathogens).

How to Make It

Ingredients:

- 1 part dried olive leaf
- 5 parts vodka (80 proof) or brandy

Instructions:

1. Place dried olive leaves in a glass jar.
2. Cover with alcohol, ensuring leaves are submerged by 1–2 inches.
3. Seal jar tightly.
4. Let sit in a cool, dark place for 4–6 weeks, shaking daily.
5. Strain through cheesecloth.
6. Pour into amber dropper bottles.
7. Label with date.

How to Use It

For acute viral infections:

- 3–4 mL (about 60–80 drops), 3 times daily

For chronic viral conditions (Epstein-Barr, herpes):

- 2–3 mL, twice daily, long-term

For cardiovascular support:

- 2 mL daily

Safety Notes

- Very safe
- May lower blood pressure—monitor if on BP medications
- Generally well-tolerated

REMEDY 17: Lomatium Root Tincture (Powerful Antiviral)

What It Heals

Lomatium is a **Native American antiviral medicine** that gained fame during the 1918 flu pandemic. It:

- Fights viral respiratory infections
- Reduces severity of flu symptoms
- Supports immune function
- Has broad-spectrum antiviral activity

Why It Works

Lomatium contains **coumarins and other compounds** with proven antiviral activity. Indigenous healers used it for pneumonia, tuberculosis, and respiratory infections.

During the 1918 Spanish flu, Indigenous communities using lomatium had significantly lower death rates than those without access to it.

How to Make It

Ingredients:

- 1 part dried lomatium root
- 5 parts vodka or Everclear (60–70% alcohol)

Instructions:

1. Place dried, chopped lomatium root in a glass jar.
2. Cover with alcohol.
3. Seal jar.
4. Let sit 4–6 weeks, shaking daily.
5. Strain through cheesecloth.
6. Bottle in amber dropper bottles.
7. Label with date.

How to Use It

For acute viral infections:

- 2–3 mL, 3–4 times daily

  Start with small doses—lomatium can cause a harmless but alarming detox rash in some people (see safety notes).

Safety Notes

- **Lomatium rash:** 1–5% of people develop a red, measles-like rash when first using lomatium. It's not an allergy—it's a detox reaction. The rash is harmless and fades within days.
- To avoid: Start with very small doses (10–20 drops) and increase gradually
- Not for pregnant or nursing women
- Generally safe for short-term use

REMEDY 18: Usnea Lichen Tincture (Natural Antibiotic)

What It Heals

Usnea (also called "Old Man's Beard") is a **lichen with powerful antibiotic properties**. It:

- Kills gram-positive bacteria (Strep, Staph)
- Treats respiratory infections
- Fights urinary tract infections
- Supports lung health
- Has antifungal properties

Why It Works

Usnea contains **usnic acid**—a compound with proven antibiotic activity. Unlike conventional antibiotics, it targets gram-positive bacteria specifically (including antibiotic-resistant strains) without disrupting beneficial gut bacteria.

How to Make It

Ingredients:

- 1 part dried usnea lichen
- 5 parts high-proof alcohol (75–95%)—usnic acid requires strong alcohol extraction

Instructions:

1. Harvest or purchase dried usnea (it grows on trees—looks like wispy, grayish-green strands).
2. Chop into small pieces.
3. Place in glass jar.
4. Cover with high-proof alcohol.

5. Seal jar.
6. Let sit 4–6 weeks, shaking daily.
7. Strain through cheesecloth.
8. Bottle in amber dropper bottles.
9. Label with date.

How to Use It

For respiratory infections (bronchitis, pneumonia):

- 2–3 mL, 3–4 times daily

For strep throat:

- Gargle with diluted tincture (2 mL in ¼ cup water)

For UTIs:

- 2–3 mL, 3 times daily

Safety Notes

- Generally safe for short-term use (7–10 days)
- Not for long-term use (usnic acid can be liver-toxic in very high doses over extended periods)
- Avoid during pregnancy
- Do not exceed recommended doses

REMEDY 19: Licorice Root Immune Tea

What It Heals

Licorice root is an **antiviral, immune-modulating, and adrenal-supporting herb**. It:

- Fights viral replication (especially herpes, hepatitis, respiratory viruses)
- Soothes sore throats and coughs
- Supports stressed adrenal glands
- Reduces inflammation
- Heals gut lining

Why It Works

Licorice contains **glycyrrhizin**, which has antiviral properties and helps regulate cortisol levels. It also contains flavonoids that support immune function and protect mucous membranes.

How to Make It

Ingredients:

- 2 teaspoons dried licorice root
- 2 cups water
- Optional: peppermint, ginger, or lemon for flavor

Instructions:

1. Place licorice root in a pot with water.
2. Bring to a boil.
3. Reduce heat and simmer for 15–20 minutes.
4. Strain into a mug.
5. Add optional flavorings.
6. Drink hot.

How to Use It

For viral infections:

- Drink 2–3 cups daily during illness

For adrenal support:

- Drink 1 cup daily for up to 6 weeks

For sore throat:

- Sip slowly, letting tea coat throat

Safety Notes

- Do not use long-term (more than 6 weeks continuously) without breaks
- Can raise blood pressure in some people—monitor if you have hypertension

- Avoid in pregnancy
- Consult doctor if on corticosteroid medications

REMEDY 20: Elderflower and Peppermint Fever Tea

What It Heals

This tea is a **fever-reducing, diaphoretic blend** (induces sweating to break fevers). It:

- Reduces fever naturally
- Opens sinuses
- Relieves headaches
- Supports immune function during acute illness

Why It Works

Elderflower is a traditional fever remedy that promotes sweating, helping the body release heat and toxins.

Peppermint cools inflammation, relieves headaches, and opens respiratory passages.

Together, they support the body's natural fever response (which is part of healing) while providing comfort.

How to Make It

Ingredients:

- 2 parts dried elderflower
- 1 part dried peppermint leaf
- Optional: yarrow flower (adds additional fever-reducing properties)

Instructions:

1. Mix dried herbs together in a jar.
2. To brew: Use 2 teaspoons herb blend per cup of hot water.
3. Steep covered for 10–15 minutes.
4. Strain.
5. Drink as hot as tolerable.
6. Bundle up in blankets to encourage sweating.

How to Use It

During fever:

- Drink 1 cup every 2–3 hours
- Encourage rest and sweating
- Drink plenty of water to stay hydrated

Do not suppress fever unless it's dangerously high (over 103°F in adults, 102°F in children).

Safety Notes

- Very safe
- Appropriate for children (adjust dose by age/weight)
- Monitor hydration during fever

REMEDY 21: Cat's Claw Bark Tincture (Immune Modulator)

What It Heals

Cat's claw is an **Amazonian immune modulator and anti-inflammatory**. It:

- Balances immune function (strengthens underactivity, calms overactivity)
- Reduces autoimmune inflammation
- Fights viral and bacterial infections
- Supports gut health
- Has anti-cancer properties

Why It Works

Cat's claw contains **pentacyclic oxindole alkaloids (POAs)**—compounds that regulate immune response and reduce inflammatory cytokines.

It's particularly valuable for autoimmune conditions because it doesn't just "boost" immunity—it **modulates** it, bringing balance.

How to Make It

Ingredients:

- 1 part dried cat's claw bark
- 5 parts vodka or brandy (50–60% alcohol)

Instructions:

1. Place dried cat's claw bark in a glass jar.
2. Cover with alcohol.
3. Seal jar.
4. Let sit 4–6 weeks, shaking daily.
5. Strain through cheesecloth.
6. Bottle in amber dropper bottles.
7. Label with date.

How to Use It

For immune support:

- 2–3 mL, twice daily, long-term

For acute infections:

- 3–4 mL, 3 times daily

For autoimmune conditions:

- 2 mL, twice daily (consult herbalist for longer protocols)

Safety Notes

- Generally safe for long-term use
- Avoid during pregnancy
- May interact with immunosuppressant drugs
- Start with low doses and increase gradually

REMEDY 22: Zinc and Elderberry Lozenges

What It Heals

These lozenges combine **zinc and elderberry**—two proven immune-supporting compounds—for:

- Shortening cold duration
- Reducing sore throat pain
- Fighting viral replication in throat and mouth
- Supporting local immune response

Why It Works

Zinc inhibits viral replication and supports immune cell function. Studies show zinc lozenges can reduce cold duration by 33%.

Elderberry adds antiviral activity and pleasant flavor.

How to Make It

Ingredients:

- ½ cup elderberry syrup (see Remedy 1)
- 2 tablespoons raw honey
- 1 teaspoon zinc gluconate powder (available at health stores)
- Optional: 5 drops peppermint essential oil

Instructions:

1. Mix elderberry syrup, honey, and zinc powder in a small saucepan.
2. Heat gently over low heat, stirring constantly, until mixture thickens (do not boil).
3. Add peppermint oil if using.
4. Pour small dollops (about ½ teaspoon each) onto a parchment-lined baking sheet.
5. Let cool and harden at room temperature (or refrigerate to speed up).

6. Dust with powdered sugar or arrowroot powder to prevent sticking.
7. Store in airtight container in refrigerator.

How to Use It

At first sign of cold or sore throat:

- Dissolve 1 lozenge slowly in mouth every 2–3 hours
- Do not exceed 8 lozenges per day (too much zinc can cause nausea)

Safety Notes

- Do not use zinc lozenges for more than 7–10 days (excess zinc can interfere with copper absorption)
- Not for children under 5 (choking hazard)
- Some people experience mild nausea—take with food if needed

---

REMEDY 23: Boneset Tea (Flu Fighter)

What It Heals

Boneset is a traditional Native American remedy for **influenza and fever**. It:

- Reduces flu symptoms (body aches, fever, chills)
- Stimulates immune response
- Promotes sweating to break fevers
- Relieves deep bone pain associated with flu

Why It Works

Boneset (*Eupatorium perfoliatum*) contains sesquiterpene lactones and flavonoids that stimulate immune function and act as diaphoretics (sweat-inducers).

Its name comes from its historical use for "break-bone fever" (dengue and severe flu)—it relieves the deep aching pain characteristic of these illnesses.

How to Make It

Ingredients:

- 1–2 teaspoons dried boneset herb
- 2 cups hot water

Instructions:

1. Place boneset in a teapot or mug.
2. Pour hot water over herb.
3. Cover and steep for 15–20 minutes.
4. Strain.
5. Drink hot.

Note: Boneset tea is quite bitter. You can add honey and lemon to improve taste.

How to Use It

During flu:

- Drink 1 cup every 3–4 hours
- Expect to sweat—bundle up and rest

Do not use as a preventive—boneset is for acute illness only.

Safety Notes

- Very bitter—not pleasant tasting
- Do not use fresh boneset (it contains toxic compounds that are deactivated when dried)
- Not for children under 12
- Not for pregnant or nursing women
- Short-term use only (during active flu)

REMEDY 24: Andrographis Tincture (King of Bitters)

What It Heals

Andrographis is called the **"King of Bitters"** and is a powerful immune stimulant. It:

- Shortens duration of colds and flu
- Reduces respiratory symptoms
- Fights bacterial and viral infections
- Protects the liver
- Reduces inflammation

Why It Works

Andrographis contains **andrographolides**—bitter compounds with proven antiviral, antibacterial, and anti-inflammatory properties.

Clinical trials show it's as effective as acetaminophen (Tylenol) for reducing cold symptoms—without side effects.

How to Make It

Ingredients:

- 1 part dried andrographis leaf
- 5 parts vodka (50–60% alcohol)

Instructions:

1. Place dried andrographis in a glass jar.
2. Cover with alcohol.
3. Seal jar.
4. Let sit 4–6 weeks, shaking daily.
5. Strain through cheesecloth.
6. Bottle in amber dropper bottles.
7. Label with date.

How to Use It

For colds and flu:

- 2–3 mL, 3–4 times daily at first sign of illness
- Continue for 5–7 days

Safety Notes

- Extremely bitter (can cause nausea in sensitive individuals—take with food)
- Avoid during pregnancy
- May lower blood pressure—monitor if on BP meds
- Not for long-term use

REMEDY 25: Immune-Supportive Herbal Honey Infusion

What It Heals

This is a **multipurpose immune honey** infused with several immune-supporting herbs. It:

- Provides daily immune support
- Tastes delicious (easy for children)
- Fights infections
- Soothes sore throats
- Can be used in teas, on toast, or taken by the spoonful

Why It Works

Honey preserves and extracts medicinal compounds from herbs while providing its own antimicrobial and soothing properties.

How to Make It

Ingredients:

- 1 jar raw honey (16 oz)
- 2 tablespoons dried elderberries

- 1 tablespoon dried astragalus root (sliced thin)
- 1 tablespoon dried rose hips
- 1 teaspoon dried thyme
- 1 cinnamon stick, broken into pieces
- 3–4 slices fresh ginger
- Peel of 1 organic lemon (no white pith)

Instructions:

1. Place all dried herbs and spices in a clean pint jar.
2. Pour honey over herbs, filling jar completely.
3. Stir with a clean spoon to release air bubbles and coat all herbs.
4. Seal jar.
5. Let sit at room temperature for 2–4 weeks, turning jar upside down daily.
6. After 2–4 weeks, you can strain out herbs (or leave them in for continued infusion).
7. Store at room temperature.

How to Use It

For prevention:

- Take 1 tablespoon daily

During illness:

- Take 1 tablespoon every few hours
- Stir into hot tea
- Eat herbs along with honey (they're delicious and medicinal)

For children:

- 1 teaspoon daily (not for infants under 1 year)

Storage: Shelf-stable indefinitely. Improves with age.

Safety Notes

- Not for infants under 1 year
- Very safe for children and adults
- Diabetics should monitor blood sugar

REMEDY 26: Lymphatic Drainage Massage Oil

What It Heals

This oil supports **lymphatic drainage**—essential for immune function. It:

- Moves stagnant lymph fluid
- Reduces swelling and congestion
- Supports detoxification
- Enhances immune surveillance
- Helps clear infections

Why It Works

The lymphatic system is your body's **waste removal and immune surveillance network**. When lymph becomes stagnant, toxins accumulate and immunity weakens.

Manual lymphatic massage combined with essential oils that stimulate lymph flow helps clear congestion and activate immune response.

How to Make It

Ingredients:

- 4 oz carrier oil (sweet almond, jojoba, or fractionated coconut oil)
- 10 drops cypress essential oil (lymphatic stimulant)
- 10 drops lemon essential oil (detoxifying)
- 8 drops frankincense essential oil (anti-inflammatory)

- 8 drops tea tree essential oil (antimicrobial)

Instructions:

1. Pour carrier oil into an amber glass bottle.
2. Add all essential oils.
3. Shake well to blend.
4. Label with name and date.

How to Use It

For lymphatic massage:

1. Apply oil to neck, armpits, groin, or any area with swollen lymph nodes.
2. Using gentle pressure, massage in circular motions toward the heart.
3. Focus on areas just under the jawline, sides of neck, armpits, and groin.
4. Massage for 5–10 minutes, 1–2 times daily.

Best combined with:

- Dry brushing before shower
- Rebounding (mini trampoline)
- Hydration

Safety Notes

- Safe for topical use
- Avoid during pregnancy (cypress and frankincense)
- Do not use on open wounds

REMEDY 27: Echinacea and Goldenseal Capsules

What It Heals

This classic combination provides **powerful immune activation and antimicrobial action**. It:

- Fights bacterial and viral infections
- Activates white blood cells
- Reduces infection duration
- Supports respiratory health

Why It Works

Echinacea stimulates immune cells. **Goldenseal** kills pathogens. Together, they're a synergistic infection-fighting duo.

How to Make It

Ingredients:

- Echinacea root powder
- Goldenseal root powder
- Empty gelatin or vegetarian capsules (size 00)
- Capsule-filling machine (optional but helpful)

Instructions:

1. Mix equal parts echinacea and goldenseal powder in a bowl.
2. Fill capsules using a capsule machine or by hand.
3. Store in amber glass jar in cool, dark place.

Yield: 100 capsules (from about 2 oz powder mix)

How to Use It

At first sign of infection:

- Take 2 capsules, 3–4 times daily
- Continue for 7–10 days maximum

Do not use long-term.

Safety Notes

- Short-term use only
- Not for autoimmune conditions
- Avoid during pregnancy

- Not for children under 2 years

REMEDY 28: Chest Rub for Respiratory Infections

What It Heals

This homemade chest rub is a natural alternative to commercial vapor rubs. It:

- Opens airways
- Reduces congestion
- Eases coughing
- Supports easier breathing during respiratory infections

Why It Works

Essential oils like eucalyptus, peppermint, and thyme contain **volatile compounds** that are absorbed through skin and inhaled, delivering antimicrobial and decongestant effects directly to respiratory tissues.

How to Make It

Ingredients:

- ½ cup coconut oil (solid at room temperature)
- 2 tablespoons beeswax pellets
- 15 drops eucalyptus essential oil
- 10 drops peppermint essential oil
- 10 drops rosemary essential oil
- 8 drops thyme essential oil

Instructions:

1. Melt coconut oil and beeswax together in a double boiler.
2. Remove from heat and let cool slightly (2–3 minutes).
3. Add all essential oils and stir well.
4. Pour into small glass jars or tins.
5. Let cool and solidify completely.
6. Label with name and date.

Yield: About 4 oz (fills 2–3 small tins)

How to Use It

During respiratory illness:

- Rub onto chest, upper back, and throat
- Apply before bed and throughout the day as needed
- Cover with a warm cloth to enhance absorption

Safe for children over 2 years (reduce essential oil amounts by half for young children).

Safety Notes

- Do not use on infants under 2 years
- Avoid contact with eyes and mucous membranes
- Peppermint can be too stimulating for very young children—omit if needed

REMEDY 29: Herbal Steam Inhalation for Sinus Infections

What It Heals

This steam treatment provides **direct antimicrobial action to sinuses**. It:

- Clears sinus congestion
- Kills bacteria and viruses in nasal passages
- Reduces inflammation
- Promotes drainage

Why It Works

Steam carries antimicrobial essential oils directly to infected tissues, while heat increases circulation and loosens mucus.

How to Make It

Ingredients:

- 4 cups boiling water
- 3 drops tea tree essential oil
- 3 drops eucalyptus essential oil
- 2 drops thyme essential oil
- 1 drop peppermint essential oil
- Optional: 1 tablespoon dried rosemary or sage

Instructions:

1. Boil water and pour into a large heat-safe bowl.
2. Add essential oils (and dried herbs if using).
3. Place bowl on a stable surface.
4. Drape a towel over your head, creating a tent over the bowl.
5. Keep face 12 inches from water (test temperature first—don't burn yourself).
6. Breathe deeply through nose and mouth for 10–15 minutes.
7. Repeat 2–3 times daily during infection.

Safety Notes

- Keep face far enough from steam to avoid burns
- Not safe for children under 7 (they can't control distance safely)
- Stop if you feel dizzy

REMEDY 30: Daily Immune Tonic Tea Blend

What It Heals

This is a **gentle, daily-use immune tonic** that:

- Builds long-term immune resilience
- Nourishes and tonifies
- Tastes pleasant (not medicinal)
- Safe for all ages

Why It Works

Unlike acute remedies (echinacea, goldenseal), this blend uses **tonic herbs** that can be taken daily for months without overstimulation.

How to Make It

Ingredients (dried herbs):

- 3 parts nettle leaf (nourishing, mineral-rich)
- 2 parts red clover (lymphatic support, blood cleanser)
- 2 parts holy basil (adaptogenic, immune-modulating)
- 1 part peppermint leaf (digestive, flavor)
- 1 part rose petals (heart-opening, uplifting)
- ½ part licorice root (harmonizes blend, adds sweetness)

Instructions:

1. Mix all herbs together in a large jar.
2. Label with name and date.
3. To brew: Use 1–2 tablespoons per quart of water.
4. Pour boiling water over herbs.
5. Cover and steep 15–20 minutes (or overnight for stronger infusion).
6. Strain and drink throughout the day.

How to Use It

- Drink 2–4 cups daily as a foundational immune tonic
- Especially beneficial during seasonal transitions (fall to winter, winter to spring)
- Safe for children (adjust quantity)

Safety Notes

- Very safe for daily, long-term use
- Licorice should be monitored if you have high blood pressure

REMEDY 31: Turmeric Golden Milk (Anti-Inflammatory Immune Drink)

What It Heals

Golden milk is an **Ayurvedic immune tonic** that:

- Reduces systemic inflammation
- Supports immune function
- Improves sleep quality
- Protects against infections
- Supports joint health
- Enhances liver detoxification

Why It Works

Turmeric contains curcumin—a powerful anti-inflammatory and immune modulator. When combined with black pepper (which increases curcumin absorption by 2,000%) and healthy fats, it becomes highly bioavailable.

Warm milk (dairy or plant-based) is traditionally used in Ayurveda as a carrier for herbs and a sleep aid.

How to Make It

Golden Milk Paste (makes enough for multiple servings):

Ingredients:

- ¼ cup turmeric powder
- ½ teaspoon black pepper (freshly ground)
- ½ cup water
- 2 tablespoons coconut oil
- 1 teaspoon cinnamon powder
- ½ teaspoon ginger powder
- Pinch of cardamom (optional)

Instructions:

1. Combine all ingredients in a small saucepan.
2. Heat over low-medium heat, stirring constantly.
3. Cook until mixture forms a thick paste (about 5–7 minutes).
4. Remove from heat and let cool.
5. Store in a glass jar in refrigerator for up to 2 weeks.

To Make Golden Milk (per serving):

1. Heat 1 cup milk (dairy, almond, oat, or coconut milk).
2. Add 1 teaspoon golden milk paste.
3. Whisk until fully dissolved.
4. Add raw honey to taste (after milk cools slightly).
5. Optional: Add a pinch of ashwagandha powder for extra adaptogenic support.

How to Use It

For immune support:

- Drink 1 cup daily, preferably before bed

During illness:

- Drink 2 cups daily

For children:

- ½ cup with reduced turmeric paste (½ teaspoon)

Safety Notes

- Very safe for daily use
- Turmeric may stain clothing and surfaces
- Not for infants under 1 year (if using honey)

- May thin blood slightly—consult doctor if on anticoagulants

---

REMEDY 32: Shiitake Mushroom Immune Broth

What It Heals

Shiitake mushrooms are **culinary medicines** with powerful immune benefits. This broth:

- Enhances white blood cell production
- Fights viral and bacterial infections
- Supports cardiovascular health
- Provides deep nourishment during illness
- Contains beta-glucans for immune modulation

Why It Works

Shiitake mushrooms contain **lentinan**—a polysaccharide that activates immune cells and has been shown in studies to enhance immune response against infections and even cancer.

Unlike rare medicinal mushrooms, shiitake is widely available and delicious.

How to Make It

Ingredients:

- 1 oz dried shiitake mushrooms (or 8 oz fresh)
- 8 cups water or bone/vegetable broth
- 6 cloves garlic, smashed
- 2-inch piece ginger, sliced
- 2 carrots, chopped
- 2 celery stalks, chopped
- 1 onion, quartered
- 2 tablespoons miso paste (adds probiotics and flavor)
- 2 tablespoons tamari or coconut aminos
- Fresh cilantro or green onions for garnish
- Sea salt to taste

Instructions:

1. If using dried shiitake, soak in warm water for 20 minutes. Reserve soaking liquid.
2. Place mushrooms, soaking liquid (or fresh mushrooms), water/broth, garlic, ginger, carrots, celery, and onion in a large pot.
3. Bring to a boil, then reduce to simmer.
4. Cover and simmer for 1–2 hours.
5. Strain out vegetables and mushrooms (or leave them in for a heartier soup).
6. Remove from heat and let cool slightly.
7. Stir in miso paste (don't boil miso—it kills beneficial probiotics).
8. Add tamari and salt to taste.
9. Garnish with fresh herbs.

Yield: About 6 cups

How to Use It

- Drink 1–2 cups daily during cold/flu season
- Increase to 3 cups daily during active illness
- Use as a base for soups with added vegetables, noodles, or protein

Storage: Refrigerate for up to 5 days, or freeze in portions.

Safety Notes

- Very safe and nourishing
- Suitable for all ages
- Generally well-tolerated

REMEDY 33: Vitamin D3 + K2 Herbal Tincture

What It Heals

While not traditionally "herbal," this preparation combines **fat-soluble vitamins** with herbs for enhanced immune support. It:

- Supports immune cell function
- Enhances calcium absorption and bone health
- Reduces risk of respiratory infections
- Modulates inflammation
- Supports cardiovascular health

Why It Works

Vitamin D3 is essential for immune function—deficiency is linked to increased infections and autoimmune disease. Most people are deficient, especially in winter.

Vitamin K2 ensures calcium goes to bones (not arteries) and works synergistically with D3.

Adding immune-supportive herbs creates a comprehensive tonic.

How to Make It

Ingredients:

- 4 oz olive oil or MCT oil
- 2 tablespoons dried astragalus root
- 1 tablespoon dried reishi mushroom powder
- Vitamin D3 drops (cholecalciferol)—dosage depends on your needs (typically 1,000–5,000 IU per dose)
- Vitamin K2 drops (MK-7 form)—typically 100–200 mcg per dose

Instructions:

1. Infuse olive oil with astragalus and reishi using the folk method:
   - Place herbs in a jar.
   - Cover with oil.
   - Let sit in a warm, sunny spot for 2–4 weeks.
   - Strain through cheesecloth.
2. Add vitamin D3 and K2 drops to the infused oil according to your desired daily dose.
3. Store in amber glass dropper bottles.
4. Label with ingredients, dosage, and date.

How to Use It

- Take 1 dropper (approximately 1 mL) daily with food (fat-soluble vitamins absorb best with fats)
- Especially important during winter months (October–March in northern climates)

Note: Get your vitamin D levels tested to determine optimal dosing.

Safety Notes

- Very safe
- Do not exceed recommended vitamin D doses without testing levels
- Vitamin K2 is contraindicated with certain blood thinners (warfarin)—consult doctor

---

REMEDY 34: Horseradish and Apple Cider Vinegar Tonic

What It Heals

This is a **powerful sinus and respiratory infection fighter**. It:

- Clears stubborn sinus congestion
- Fights bacterial sinus infections
- Breaks up mucus
- Stimulates circulation

- Provides antimicrobial action

Why It Works

Horseradish contains volatile oils (especially allyl isothiocyanate) that are intensely antimicrobial and decongestant. The moment you consume it, you feel it clearing your sinuses.

Apple cider vinegar extracts medicinal compounds and adds its own antimicrobial properties.

How to Make It

Ingredients:

- 1 cup fresh horseradish root, grated
- 2 cups raw apple cider vinegar (with "the mother")
- 2 tablespoons raw honey (optional, added at end)

Instructions:

1. Place grated horseradish in a clean pint jar.
2. Cover completely with apple cider vinegar.
3. Use parchment paper or plastic under metal lid (vinegar corrodes metal).
4. Seal jar and shake well.
5. Let sit for 2–4 weeks in a cool, dark place, shaking daily.
6. Strain through cheesecloth, squeezing out all liquid.
7. Add honey if desired (makes it more palatable).
8. Bottle in glass jar or bottle.
9. Label with date.

Yield: About 2 cups

How to Use It

For sinus infections:

- Take 1 tablespoon straight (brace yourself—it's intensely strong!)
- Or dilute 1 tablespoon in ¼ cup water
- Take 2–3 times daily until infection clears

For acute congestion:

- Take 1 teaspoon as needed (you'll feel immediate sinus drainage)

Storage: Shelf-stable for 1–2 years.

Safety Notes

- Extremely potent—start with small amounts
- May irritate sensitive stomachs (take with food)
- Not for young children
- Avoid if you have ulcers or gastritis

REMEDY 35: Mullein Leaf Lung Tonic Tea

What It Heals

Mullein is a **supreme respiratory herb**. It:

- Soothes irritated lung tissue
- Clears mucus from lungs
- Supports recovery from bronchitis and pneumonia
- Reduces dry cough
- Strengthens respiratory system

Why It Works

Mullein contains **saponins and mucilage** that coat and soothe inflamed respiratory tissues while helping expel trapped mucus. It's particularly valuable for **dry, unproductive coughs** and lingering respiratory infections.

How to Make It

Ingredients:

- 2 tablespoons dried mullein leaf
- 3 cups hot water
- Optional: 1 teaspoon dried thyme or peppermint for additional antimicrobial action
- Raw honey and lemon to taste

Instructions:

1. Place mullein leaf (and optional herbs) in a teapot or jar.
2. Pour hot water over herbs.
3. Cover and steep for 15–20 minutes.
4. **Strain through a fine-mesh strainer or coffee filter** (mullein leaves have tiny hairs that can irritate throat if not strained well).
5. Add honey and lemon.
6. Drink warm.

How to Use It

For respiratory infections:

- Drink 3–4 cups daily

For chronic respiratory conditions (asthma, COPD):

- Drink 2 cups daily long-term

For smoker's cough or lung detox:

- Drink 2–3 cups daily for several weeks

Safety Notes

- Very safe
- Must be strained well (tiny leaf hairs can irritate)
- Safe for children and elderly
- Can be used long-term

REMEDY 36: Immune-Boosting Herbal Glycerite (Alcohol-Free)

What It Heals

This is an **alcohol-free immune tonic** perfect for children, recovering alcoholics, or anyone avoiding alcohol. It:

- Supports daily immune function
- Tastes sweet (easy for kids)
- Fights infections
- Builds resilience over time

Why It Works

Glycerin extracts many medicinal compounds (though not as comprehensively as alcohol) and creates a sweet, shelf-stable remedy.

How to Make It

Ingredients:

- ½ cup dried elderberries
- ¼ cup dried astragalus root (sliced thin)
- ¼ cup dried echinacea root
- 2 tablespoons dried rose hips
- 3 parts vegetable glycerin
- 1 part distilled water

Instructions:

1. Place all dried herbs in a quart jar.
2. Mix glycerin and water together.
3. Pour glycerin mixture over herbs, covering by 1–2 inches.
4. Seal jar tightly.
5. Let sit in a cool, dark place for 4–6 weeks, shaking daily.

6. Strain through cheesecloth.
7. Pour into amber dropper bottles.
8. Label with ingredients and date.

Yield: About 2–3 cups

How to Use It

For prevention:

- Adults: 1 teaspoon, 2–3 times daily
- Children (2–12 years): ½ teaspoon, 2–3 times daily

During illness:

- Adults: 2 teaspoons, 3–4 times daily
- Children: 1 teaspoon, 3–4 times daily

Storage: Refrigerate for maximum shelf life (1–2 years).

Safety Notes

- Very safe and child-friendly
- Not for infants under 1 year (some glycerites may contain trace honey-like compounds)
- Generally well-tolerated

REMEDY 37: Sacred Immune Smoke Bundle (Antimicrobial Air Purification)

What It Heals

Smoke from antimicrobial herbs has been used for millennia to **purify air and prevent disease transmission**. This practice:

- Kills airborne bacteria and viruses
- Purifies indoor air
- Supports respiratory health
- Clears stagnant energy (traditional use)
- Reduces pathogen transmission in shared spaces

Why It Works

Research shows that burning certain herbs releases **antimicrobial compounds** into the air. Studies on sage smoke, for example, found it reduced airborne bacteria by up to 94%.

Medicinal smoke from herbs like white sage, rosemary, thyme, and cedar contains volatile oils that act as natural air disinfectants.

How to Make It

Ingredients:

- Fresh or dried white sage
- Fresh or dried rosemary
- Fresh or dried thyme
- Optional: cedar, lavender, or juniper
- Cotton string or twine (natural fiber only—no synthetics)

Instructions:

1. Gather fresh or dried herb sprigs (about 6–8 inches long).
2. Bundle herbs together, mixing varieties.
3. Wrap tightly with cotton string, starting at the base and wrapping spirally to the top.
4. Tie off securely.
5. Hang bundles upside down in a dry, airy place for 1–2 weeks to fully dry (if using fresh herbs).
6. Label and store in a basket or jar.

How to Use It

To purify air during illness or prevention:

1. Light the tip of the bundle until it catches fire.
2. Blow out the flame, letting the bundle smolder and smoke.

3. Walk through your home, wafting smoke into corners, doorways, and common areas.
4. Use a fireproof dish or abalone shell to catch ashes.
5. When finished, extinguish completely in sand or water.

Use during cold/flu season, after illness in the home, or when someone visits while sick.

Safety Notes

- Never leave burning herbs unattended
- Open windows for ventilation
- Not suitable for people with asthma or respiratory sensitivities
- Keep away from children and pets during use
- Ensure complete extinguishing after use

REMEDY 38: Astragalus and Reishi Immune Elixir

What It Heals

This is a **deep, long-term immune builder** combining two of the most revered tonic herbs in Traditional Chinese Medicine. It:

- Builds foundational immune strength
- Increases resistance to illness
- Supports recovery from chronic illness or chemotherapy
- Enhances energy and vitality
- Protects against stress-induced immune suppression

Why It Works

Astragalus tonifies "Wei Qi" (protective energy) and enhances immune cell production.

Reishi modulates immune function, calms inflammation, and has adaptogenic properties.

Together, they create a synergistic, deeply nourishing immune tonic suitable for months or years of use.

How to Make It

Ingredients:

- ¼ cup dried astragalus root (sliced)
- ¼ cup dried reishi mushroom (chopped or sliced)
- 4 cups water
- 1 cup raw honey
- Optional: 1 cinnamon stick, 3–4 slices fresh ginger, 2 tablespoons schisandra berries

Instructions:

1. Place astragalus, reishi, and optional herbs in a large pot with water.
2. Bring to a boil, then reduce to lowest simmer.
3. Cover and simmer for 3–4 hours (the longer, the stronger).
4. Strain out herbs, squeezing out all liquid.
5. Return liquid to pot and simmer uncovered until reduced to about 2 cups (concentrates the medicine).
6. Let cool to below 110°F.
7. Stir in honey until fully dissolved.
8. Bottle in glass jars or bottles.
9. Label with ingredients and date.

Yield: About 2–3 cups

How to Use It

For long-term immune building:

- Take 1–2 tablespoons daily, straight or stirred into warm water or tea

During recovery from illness:

- Take 2 tablespoons, 2–3 times daily

Storage: Refrigerate for up to 6 months.

Safety Notes

- Very safe for long-term use
- Suitable for all ages (not for infants under 1 due to honey)
- Can be used during cancer treatment (consult oncologist)

REMEDY 39: Thyme Honey for Cough and Sore Throat

What It Heals

Thyme honey is a **traditional European remedy** for respiratory infections. It:

- Soothes sore throats
- Calms persistent coughs
- Kills bacteria and viruses in throat
- Reduces inflammation
- Tastes delicious

Why It Works

Thyme contains thymol and carvacrol—potent antimicrobial volatile oils. **Honey** is naturally antimicrobial, soothes irritated tissues, and acts as a cough suppressant.

Studies show honey is as effective as over-the-counter cough syrups—without side effects.

How to Make It

Ingredients:

- Fresh thyme sprigs (enough to fill a jar halfway) or ½ cup dried thyme
- Raw honey (enough to cover herbs completely)

Instructions:

1. If using fresh thyme, gently bruise leaves to release oils.
2. Fill a clean pint jar halfway with thyme.
3. Pour honey over thyme, filling jar completely.
4. Stir gently to release air bubbles.
5. Seal jar.
6. Let sit at room temperature for 2–4 weeks, turning jar upside down daily.
7. After infusion period, you can strain out thyme (or leave it in—it's edible).
8. Store in jar at room temperature.

How to Use It

For cough:

- Take 1 teaspoon every 2–3 hours as needed
- Let honey dissolve slowly in mouth for maximum throat-coating effect

For sore throat:

- Take 1 tablespoon and hold in mouth/throat before swallowing
- Or stir 1 tablespoon into warm (not hot) tea

For children (over 1 year):

- ½–1 teaspoon as needed

Storage: Shelf-stable indefinitely. Improves with age.

Safety Notes

- Not for infants under 1 year
- Very safe for children and adults
- Diabetics should monitor blood sugar

REMEDY 40: Echinacea and Elderberry Oxymel (Vinegar-Honey Extract)

What It Heals

An oxymel combines **vinegar and honey** to create a sweet-tart medicinal extract. This immune-boosting version:

- Fights viral and bacterial infections
- Activates immune response at first sign of illness
- Extracts minerals from herbs
- Tastes pleasant (easier to take than straight vinegar or tinctures)
- Supports digestion

Why It Works

Vinegar extracts minerals and certain medicinal compounds that alcohol doesn't capture as well.

Honey extracts different compounds, adds antimicrobial properties, and makes the remedy palatable.

Together, they create a **synergistic extraction medium** that's been used since ancient Greek and Roman times.

How to Make It

Ingredients:

- ½ cup dried echinacea root
- ½ cup dried elderberries
- 2 tablespoons dried ginger root
- 1 tablespoon dried rose hips
- 2 cups raw apple cider vinegar (with "the mother")
- 1 cup raw honey

Instructions:

1. Place all dried herbs in a quart jar.
2. Pour apple cider vinegar over herbs, covering completely.
3. Use parchment paper or plastic under metal lid.
4. Seal and shake well.
5. Let sit for 2–4 weeks in a cool, dark place, shaking daily.
6. Strain through cheesecloth into a clean bowl, squeezing out all liquid.
7. Add honey and stir until fully dissolved (may need gentle warming).
8. Pour into glass bottles or jars.
9. Label with ingredients and date.

Yield: About 2–3 cups

How to Use It

At first sign of illness:

- Take 1–2 tablespoons, 3–4 times daily
- Can be taken straight or diluted in water or tea

For prevention during exposure:

- Take 1 tablespoon daily

Other uses:

- Mix with olive oil for salad dressing
- Add to sparkling water for a refreshing immune tonic drink
- Drizzle over roasted vegetables

Storage: Shelf-stable for 1–2 years in a cool, dark place.

Safety Notes

- Not for infants under 1 year (due to honey)
- Safe for children over 1 year (adjust dose by weight)
- Very safe and well-tolerated

- Echinacea should not be used long-term (use for 7–10 days during acute illness)

CHAPTER 4: ANTI-INFLAMMATORY HEALING

> Focus: Arthritis, Autoimmune, Chronic Pain

REMEDY 1: Golden Paste (High-Absorption Turmeric)

What It Heals

Golden paste is the **most bioavailable form of turmeric**—combining turmeric, black pepper, and healthy fat for maximum absorption. It:

- Reduces joint pain and stiffness (arthritis)
- Calms autoimmune inflammation
- Protects cartilage from degradation
- Reduces inflammatory markers (C-reactive protein, cytokines)
- Supports brain health and protects against neurodegeneration
- Improves liver function

Why It Works

Turmeric contains curcumin—one of the most studied anti-inflammatory compounds on Earth. It inhibits multiple inflammatory pathways simultaneously:

- Blocks NF-kB (a protein complex that drives chronic inflammation)
- Inhibits COX-2 and LOX enzymes (like NSAIDs, but safer)
- Reduces inflammatory cytokines (TNF-alpha, IL-6, IL-1)
- Acts as a powerful antioxidant

The problem: Curcumin is poorly absorbed. Only about 3% makes it into your bloodstream.

The solution: Black pepper contains **piperine**, which increases curcumin absorption by **2,000%**. Fat further enhances absorption since curcumin is fat-soluble.

How to Make It

Ingredients:

- ½ cup turmeric powder (organic, non-irradiated)
- 1 cup water
- 1½ teaspoons freshly ground black pepper
- ¼ cup coconut oil (or olive oil)

Instructions:

1. Place turmeric and water in a small saucepan.
2. Heat over medium-low heat, stirring constantly.
3. Add black pepper.
4. Cook for 7–10 minutes until mixture forms a thick paste.
5. Remove from heat.
6. Add coconut oil and stir until fully incorporated.
7. Let cool.
8. Store in a glass jar in refrigerator.

Yield: About 1 cup
Shelf life: Refrigerated for up to 2 weeks

How to Use It

For chronic inflammation:

- Take 1 teaspoon, 2–3 times daily
- Can be taken straight (followed by water) or stirred into:
  - Warm milk (golden milk—see Chapter 6, Remedy 31)

- Smoothies
- Soup or stew
- Spread on toast

For acute pain flare-ups:

- Increase to 1 tablespoon, 3 times daily

Start with small amounts (¼ teaspoon) and increase gradually to assess tolerance.

Safety Notes

- Very safe for long-term use
- May cause loose stools in high doses (reduce amount if this occurs)
- Turmeric stains clothing, counters, and cutting boards—be careful!
- Mild blood-thinning effect—consult doctor if on anticoagulants
- Avoid therapeutic doses during pregnancy (culinary amounts are safe)

REMEDY 2: Boswellia (Frankincense) Tincture

What It Heals

Boswellia, also known as frankincense, is **one of the most powerful anti-inflammatory herbs for joint health**. It:

- Reduces arthritis pain and swelling
- Improves joint mobility
- Protects cartilage from breakdown
- Reduces inflammation in autoimmune conditions
- Supports gut healing (Crohn's, ulcerative colitis)
- Reduces asthma and respiratory inflammation

Why It Works

Boswellia contains **boswellic acids**—compounds that inhibit 5-LOX (5-lipoxygenase), an enzyme that produces inflammatory leukotrienes.

Unlike NSAIDs (which can damage the gut lining), boswellia actually **heals intestinal inflammation** while reducing systemic inflammation.

Clinical studies show boswellia is as effective as conventional arthritis drugs—without the side effects.

How to Make It

Ingredients:

- 1 part boswellia resin (frankincense tears)
- 5 parts high-proof alcohol (90–95% Everclear or grain alcohol)
- Optional: Small amount of glycerin (improves extraction)

Instructions:

1. Break or grind boswellia resin into small pieces (freeze first to make it easier to break).
2. Place in a glass jar.
3. Cover with alcohol (and glycerin if using).
4. Seal jar tightly.
5. Shake vigorously—boswellia is resinous and takes extra agitation.
6. Let sit for 6–8 weeks (longer than most tinctures), shaking daily.
7. Strain through cheesecloth (it will be sticky—boswellia is resin).
8. Pour into amber dropper bottles.
9. Label with date.

Note: Because boswellia is resinous, tincturing requires high-proof alcohol and longer extraction time.

How to Use It

For arthritis:

- 2–3 mL, 3 times daily, long-term

For autoimmune flares:

- 3–4 mL, 3 times daily during flare-ups

For inflammatory bowel disease:

- 2–3 mL, 3 times daily (consult herbalist or doctor)

Safety Notes

- Very safe for long-term use
- Rare mild digestive upset (take with food if needed)
- Generally well-tolerated
- Safe to combine with other anti-inflammatory herbs

REMEDY 3: White Willow Bark Decoction (Natural Pain Relief)

What It Heals

White willow bark is **nature's aspirin**—used for thousands of years for pain and inflammation. It:

- Relieves joint pain (arthritis, gout)
- Reduces back pain
- Eases headaches and migraines
- Lowers fever
- Reduces inflammation without stomach irritation

Why It Works

Willow bark contains **salicin**, which the body converts to salicylic acid (the active compound in aspirin).

Key difference from aspirin: Willow bark also contains tannins and flavonoids that **protect the stomach lining**, making it much gentler than synthetic aspirin (which commonly causes ulcers and bleeding).

How to Make It

Ingredients:

- 2 tablespoons dried white willow bark
- 4 cups water

Instructions:

1. Place willow bark in a pot with water.
2. Bring to a boil.
3. Reduce heat and simmer for 20–30 minutes.
4. Strain into a jar or mug.
5. Store extra tea in refrigerator for up to 3 days.

Yield: About 3 cups

How to Use It

For pain:

- Drink 1 cup, 2–3 times daily as needed
- Takes 1–2 hours to reach full effect (slower than aspirin but longer-lasting)

For chronic pain:

- Drink 1–2 cups daily, long-term

Flavor tip: Willow bark is quite bitter. Add honey, lemon, or mix with peppermint tea.

Safety Notes

- Do not use if allergic to aspirin

- Avoid if on blood-thinning medications (warfarin, etc.)
- Not for children or teens with viral infections (risk of Reye's syndrome, same as aspirin)
- Avoid during pregnancy
- Generally safer than aspirin for stomach, but still use caution if you have ulcers

REMEDY 4: Devil's Claw Root Tincture

What It Heals

Devil's claw is a **powerful African herb for severe pain**. It:

- Reduces severe arthritis pain (especially osteoarthritis)
- Relieves lower back pain
- Reduces gout inflammation
- Improves mobility and flexibility
- Works as effectively as pharmaceutical pain relievers in studies

Why It Works

Devil's claw contains **harpagosides**—iridoid glycosides with potent anti-inflammatory and analgesic (pain-relieving) properties. It inhibits COX-2 and reduces inflammatory cytokines.

Clinical trials show it's as effective as NSAIDs for osteoarthritis pain—without gastrointestinal side effects.

How to Make It

Ingredients:

- 1 part dried devil's claw root (chopped)
- 5 parts vodka or brandy (50–60% alcohol)

Instructions:

1. Place devil's claw root in a glass jar.
2. Cover with alcohol, ensuring root is submerged by 1–2 inches.
3. Seal jar.
4. Let sit for 4–6 weeks, shaking daily.
5. Strain through cheesecloth.
6. Bottle in amber dropper bottles.
7. Label with date.

How to Use It

For arthritis or chronic pain:

- 2–3 mL, 3 times daily, long-term

For acute pain flare-ups:

- 3–4 mL, 3 times daily

Note: Devil's claw works best with consistent use over several weeks (not instant relief).

Safety Notes

- Do not use if you have ulcers or GERD (it increases stomach acid)
- Avoid during pregnancy
- May interact with blood pressure and diabetes medications
- Do not use if you have gallstones
- Generally safe for long-term use in appropriate individuals

REMEDY 5: Ginger Compress for Acute Pain and Inflammation

What It Heals

A ginger compress provides **immediate, localized relief** for:

- Joint pain and swelling
- Muscle strains and sprains
- Arthritis flare-ups
- Stiff, painful areas
- Bruising and injury

Why It Works

Ginger contains **gingerols and shogaols**—compounds that inhibit inflammatory prostaglandins and improve circulation.

When applied topically as a hot compress, ginger's volatile oils penetrate tissues, bringing heat, increased blood flow, and anti-inflammatory action directly to the affected area.

How to Make It

Ingredients:

- 4 tablespoons fresh ginger, grated
- 4 cups water
- Clean cloth or towel

Instructions:

1. Boil water.
2. Add grated ginger.
3. Reduce heat and simmer for 10 minutes.
4. Remove from heat and let cool slightly (you want it hot but not scalding).
5. Soak a clean cloth in the ginger water.
6. Wring out excess liquid.
7. Apply hot compress to painful area.
8. Cover with a dry towel to retain heat.
9. Leave on for 15–20 minutes.
10. Repeat 2–3 times daily.

Alternative method (dry ginger compress):

1. Mix 2 tablespoons ginger powder with enough hot water to form a paste.
2. Spread paste on cloth.
3. Apply to skin (test temperature first).
4. Cover with towel.

How to Use It

For acute injury or flare-up:

- Apply 2–3 times daily until pain subsides

For chronic joint pain:

- Apply nightly before bed

Pro tip: Follow ginger compress with anti-inflammatory oil or salve for deeper penetration.

Safety Notes

- Test temperature before applying (don't burn skin)
- Can cause mild redness (this is normal—it's increased circulation)
- Discontinue if skin becomes irritated
- Safe for most people

REMEDY 6: Anti-Inflammatory Oil Blend (Topical Pain Relief)

What It Heals

This oil blend is a **multi-herb topical formula** for:

- Joint pain (knees, hands, hips, shoulders)
- Muscle aches and tension
- Nerve pain (sciatica, neuropathy)
- Arthritis
- Sports injuries

Why It Works

Combines multiple anti-inflammatory and pain-relieving herbs in an oil base that penetrates skin and delivers medicinal compounds directly to affected tissues.

How to Make It

Ingredients (dried herbs):

- 2 tablespoons arnica flowers (pain relief, bruising)
- 2 tablespoons St. John's wort flowers (nerve pain)
- 1 tablespoon cayenne powder (circulation, pain relief)
- 1 tablespoon ginger root powder (anti-inflammatory)
- 2 cups carrier oil (olive, sweet almond, or jojoba)

Instructions:

1. Place all dried herbs in a glass jar.
2. Cover with oil, ensuring herbs are submerged.
3. Seal jar.
4. Let sit in a warm, sunny spot for 3–4 weeks (or use the quick method below).
5. Strain through cheesecloth, squeezing out all oil.
6. Add essential oils (optional):
   - 20 drops peppermint essential oil (cooling, analgesic)
   - 15 drops eucalyptus essential oil (anti-inflammatory)
   - 10 drops lavender essential oil (calming, pain-relieving)
7. Pour into amber glass bottles.
8. Label with ingredients and date.

Quick method (for immediate use):

1. Place herbs and oil in a double boiler.
2. Heat on lowest setting for 2–3 hours.
3. Strain and bottle.

Yield: About 1½–2 cups

How to Use It

For pain:

- Massage oil into affected area, 2–3 times daily
- Best applied after shower when skin is warm (better absorption)

For nerve pain:

- Apply along nerve pathway (e.g., for sciatica, massage down back of leg)

Storage: Store in cool, dark place for 6–12 months.

Safety Notes

- Do not apply to broken skin
- Cayenne can be warming/hot—start with small amounts
- Wash hands after applying (avoid touching eyes)
- Arnica is for external use only (do not ingest)
- Safe for adults and children over 2 years

REMEDY 7: Turmeric and Ginger Anti-Inflammatory Tea

What It Heals

This daily tea is a **foundational anti-inflammatory tonic** that:

- Reduces systemic inflammation
- Relieves joint pain over time
- Supports digestive health

- Boosts circulation
- Protects against chronic disease

Why It Works

Combines the two most powerful anti-inflammatory roots: **turmeric** (curcumin) and **ginger** (gingerols). Together, they work synergistically to reduce inflammation throughout the body.

How to Make It

Ingredients:

- 1-inch piece fresh turmeric root, sliced (or 1 teaspoon turmeric powder)
- 1-inch piece fresh ginger root, sliced (or 1 teaspoon ginger powder)
- 3 cups water
- 1 pinch black pepper (enhances absorption)
- Raw honey and lemon to taste

Instructions:

1. Place turmeric and ginger in a pot with water.
2. Bring to a boil.
3. Reduce heat and simmer for 10–15 minutes.
4. Remove from heat and add black pepper.
5. Strain into mugs.
6. Add honey and lemon.
7. Drink warm.

Yield: About 2–3 cups

How to Use It

For chronic inflammation:

- Drink 2–3 cups daily, long-term

For acute flare-ups:

- Drink 3–4 cups daily

Pro tip: Make a large batch and store in refrigerator. Reheat as needed throughout the week.

Safety Notes

- Very safe for daily use
- May cause loose stools in high amounts (reduce if this occurs)
- Mild blood-thinning effect—monitor if on anticoagulants
- Safe for children in smaller amounts

REMEDY 8: Bromelain Pineapple Enzyme Supplement

What It Heals

Bromelain is a **proteolytic enzyme** found in pineapple that:

- Reduces inflammation and swelling
- Speeds healing of injuries
- Reduces post-surgical inflammation
- Relieves arthritis pain
- Improves digestion

Why It Works

Bromelain breaks down inflammatory proteins and reduces inflammatory markers. It's particularly effective for **acute inflammation** (injuries, surgery, flare-ups).

How to Make It

Note: Bromelain is concentrated in the **core** of fresh pineapple. While you can't "make" a supplement at home, you can maximize bromelain intake:

Fresh Pineapple Core Preparation:

1. Cut fresh pineapple and reserve the tough, fibrous core.
2. Chop core into small chunks.
3. Blend core chunks with water or juice to make a smoothie.
4. Drink on an empty stomach for maximum anti-inflammatory effect.

Alternatively: Purchase bromelain supplements (standardized extract) from health stores.

How to Use It

For inflammation:

- Eat fresh pineapple core daily or take 500–1,000 mg bromelain supplement, 2–3 times daily between meals

For digestion:

- Take bromelain with meals (helps break down protein)

Safety Notes

- Generally very safe
- Can increase bleeding risk—avoid before surgery or if on blood thinners
- May cause allergic reaction in people allergic to pineapple
- High doses can cause digestive upset

REMEDY 9: MSM and Vitamin C Joint Support Formula

What It Heals

MSM (methylsulfonylmethane) is an **organic sulfur compound** that:

- Reduces joint pain and stiffness
- Supports cartilage repair
- Reduces inflammation
- Improves flexibility
- Enhances collagen production (combined with vitamin C)

Why It Works

Sulfur is essential for connective tissue health, cartilage formation, and detoxification. Most people are deficient.

MSM provides bioavailable sulfur that supports joint structure and reduces inflammatory prostaglandins.

Vitamin C is required for collagen synthesis and enhances MSM's effects.

How to Make It

Ingredients:

- MSM powder (food-grade, available at health stores)
- Vitamin C powder (ascorbic acid or buffered)
- Optional: Rose hip powder (natural vitamin C source)

Instructions:

1. Mix equal parts MSM powder and vitamin C powder.
2. Store in airtight glass jar.
3. Label with date.

How to Use It

For joint pain:

- Mix 1 teaspoon (about 3 grams) MSM powder + ½ teaspoon vitamin C powder in water or juice
- Take 1–2 times daily with food

- Start with smaller amounts and increase gradually (some people experience detox symptoms)

Safety Notes

- Very safe
- May cause mild digestive upset initially (start low and increase)
- Drink plenty of water (supports detoxification)
- Generally well-tolerated long-term

REMEDY 10: Cayenne Salve for Deep Pain Relief

What It Heals

Cayenne salve provides **intense, penetrating heat** for:

- Arthritis pain
- Muscle soreness
- Nerve pain (shingles, neuropathy)
- Back pain
- Joint stiffness

Why It Works

Cayenne contains **capsaicin**, which depletes substance P (a neurotransmitter that carries pain signals). With repeated use, it actually **desensitizes pain receptors**, providing long-term relief.

How to Make It

Ingredients:

- 1 cup infused cayenne oil (see below)
- 2–3 tablespoons beeswax pellets (adjust for desired consistency)
- Optional: 10 drops peppermint essential oil (cooling counterbalance)

To Make Cayenne-Infused Oil:

1. Place ½ cup carrier oil (olive, coconut, or jojoba) in a jar.
2. Add 2 tablespoons cayenne powder.
3. Stir well.
4. Let sit for 2–4 weeks, shaking daily.
5. Strain through cheesecloth (wear gloves!).

To Make Salve:

1. Melt infused cayenne oil and beeswax in a double boiler.
2. Stir until beeswax is fully dissolved.
3. Remove from heat.
4. Add peppermint essential oil if using.
5. Pour into small tins or jars.
6. Let cool and solidify.
7. Label clearly: "CAYENNE SALVE—WASH HANDS AFTER USE."

How to Use It

For pain:

- Apply small amount to affected area, 2–4 times daily
- **ALWAYS wash hands thoroughly after applying**
- May cause warming/burning sensation initially (this is normal and decreases with regular use)

Safety Notes

- **DO NOT touch eyes, nose, or mucous membranes after handling**
- Wear gloves when applying if you have sensitive skin
- Can cause redness and heat (this is the mechanism of action)

- Not for broken skin or open wounds
- Keep away from children
- Test on small area first

REMEDY 11: Cat's Claw Anti-Inflammatory Tincture

What It Heals

Cat's claw (una de gato) is a **powerful Amazonian anti-inflammatory** for:

- Rheumatoid arthritis
- Osteoarthritis
- Autoimmune inflammation
- Gut inflammation (leaky gut, Crohn's)
- Chronic pain

Why It Works

Cat's claw contains **pentacyclic oxindole alkaloids (POAs)** that modulate immune function and reduce inflammatory cytokines. It's particularly valuable for **autoimmune conditions** because it doesn't just suppress inflammation—it helps **rebalance immune response**.

How to Make It

Ingredients:

- 1 part dried cat's claw bark
- 5 parts vodka or brandy (50–60% alcohol)

Instructions:

1. Place cat's claw bark in a glass jar.
2. Cover with alcohol.
3. Seal jar.
4. Let sit for 4–6 weeks, shaking daily.
5. Strain through cheesecloth.
6. Bottle in amber dropper bottles.
7. Label with date.

How to Use It

For autoimmune conditions:

- 2–3 mL, twice daily, long-term

For arthritis:

- 2–3 mL, 3 times daily

Best results with consistent use over 2–3 months.

Safety Notes

- Generally safe for long-term use
- Avoid during pregnancy
- May interact with immunosuppressant drugs (consult doctor)
- Start with low doses and increase gradually

REMEDY 12: Nettle Leaf Infusion (Mineral-Rich Anti-Inflammatory)

What It Heals

Nettle is a **deeply nourishing anti-inflammatory herb** that:

- Reduces arthritis pain and inflammation
- Provides minerals (calcium, magnesium, iron, silica)
- Supports joint health
- Reduces histamine response (helps with inflammatory allergies)
- Strengthens connective tissue

Why It Works

Nettle contains compounds that inhibit inflammatory prostaglandins and cytokines. It also provides **bioavailable minerals** that support bone and joint health.

How to Make It

Ingredients:

- ½ cup (about 1 oz) dried nettle leaf
- 1 quart (4 cups) boiling water

Instructions:

1. Place nettle leaf in a quart jar.
2. Pour boiling water over leaves, filling jar.
3. Seal jar and let steep for **4–8 hours** (or overnight).
4. Strain through a fine-mesh strainer or cheesecloth.
5. Drink throughout the day.
6. Store extra in refrigerator for up to 2 days.

Note: Long steeping time extracts maximum minerals and medicinal compounds.

How to Use It

For arthritis and inflammation:

- Drink 2–4 cups daily, long-term

For mineral support:

- Drink 1 quart daily

Flavor tip: Nettle has a mild, slightly grassy flavor. Can be enjoyed plain or mixed with peppermint or lemon.

Safety Notes

- Very safe for long-term daily use
- Generally well-tolerated
- Rare allergic reaction in people sensitive to plants in the nettle family
- Safe for children and pregnancy

REMEDY 13: Pine Bark Extract (Pycnogenol) Tincture

What It Heals

Pine bark extract is a **potent antioxidant and anti-inflammatory** that:

- Reduces arthritis pain and swelling
- Improves joint flexibility
- Protects cartilage from oxidative damage
- Reduces vascular inflammation
- Supports circulation and cardiovascular health
- Reduces muscle soreness after exercise

Why It Works

Pine bark contains **oligomeric proanthocyanidins (OPCs)**—powerful flavonoids with anti-inflammatory and antioxidant properties. Studies show it reduces inflammatory enzymes and improves blood flow to joints, accelerating healing.

It's particularly effective for **osteoarthritis** and **inflammatory joint conditions**.

How to Make It

Ingredients:

- 1 part dried pine bark (maritime pine is traditional, but other pine species work)
- 5 parts vodka or brandy (60% alcohol)

Instructions:

1. Grind or chop pine bark into small pieces.
2. Place in a glass jar.
3. Cover with alcohol, ensuring bark is submerged.

4. Seal jar.
5. Let sit for 6–8 weeks, shaking daily (bark requires longer extraction).
6. Strain through cheesecloth.
7. Bottle in amber dropper bottles.
8. Label with date.

How to Use It

For arthritis:

- 2–3 mL, 3 times daily, long-term

For circulation and vascular health:

- 2 mL, twice daily

Best results with consistent use over several months.

Safety Notes

- Very safe
- Generally well-tolerated
- May enhance effects of blood pressure medications (monitor)
- Safe for long-term use

REMEDY 14: Comfrey Salve (Bone and Joint Healer)

What It Heals

Comfrey is known as **"knitbone"** for its remarkable ability to heal:

- Broken bones (accelerates healing)
- Sprains and strains
- Arthritis pain
- Joint inflammation
- Bruises and contusions
- Muscle tears

Why It Works

Comfrey contains **allantoin**—a compound that stimulates cell proliferation and tissue regeneration. It literally speeds up the healing of bones, cartilage, tendons, and ligaments.

Important: Comfrey is for **external use only**—internal use can be toxic to the liver.

How to Make It

Ingredients:

- 1 cup comfrey-infused oil (see below)
- 2–3 tablespoons beeswax pellets
- Optional: 10 drops lavender essential oil (anti-inflammatory, pleasant scent)

To Make Comfrey-Infused Oil:

1. Fill a jar with dried comfrey leaf (or root for stronger action).
2. Cover with olive oil or sweet almond oil.
3. Let sit in a warm, sunny spot for 3–4 weeks.
4. Strain through cheesecloth.

To Make Salve:

1. Melt comfrey oil and beeswax in a double boiler.
2. Stir until beeswax is fully dissolved.
3. Test consistency by placing a drop on a cool plate (add more beeswax if too soft).
4. Remove from heat and add lavender essential oil if using.
5. Pour into tins or jars.
6. Let cool and solidify.
7. Label with date and **"External use only"**.

How to Use It

For injuries:

- Apply liberally to affected area, 3–4 times daily
- Massage gently into skin

For arthritis:

- Apply to painful joints, 2–3 times daily

Pro tip: Apply after ice or heat therapy for deeper penetration.

Safety Notes

- **EXTERNAL USE ONLY—do not ingest**
- Do not apply to open wounds or broken skin (comfrey heals so quickly it can trap infection inside)
- Safe for intact skin
- Not for use during pregnancy or nursing (topical absorption of pyrrolizidine alkaloids)
- Discontinue if skin irritation occurs

REMEDY 15: Frankincense and Myrrh Pain Relief Oil

What It Heals

This ancient biblical combination provides **deep anti-inflammatory and analgesic effects** for:

- Chronic joint pain
- Arthritis
- Nerve pain
- Muscle tension
- Inflammation
- Spiritual and emotional pain (traditional use)

Why It Works

Frankincense (Boswellia) contains boswellic acids that inhibit inflammatory enzymes.

Myrrh contains terpenoids with analgesic and anti-inflammatory properties.

Together, they create a **synergistic healing oil** used for millennia in Middle Eastern and Ayurvedic medicine.

How to Make It

Ingredients:

- 2 tablespoons frankincense resin (crushed)
- 2 tablespoons myrrh resin (crushed)
- 2 cups carrier oil (olive, jojoba, or sweet almond)
- Optional: 15 drops frankincense essential oil + 10 drops myrrh essential oil (for additional potency)

Instructions:

1. Grind or crush resins into small pieces (freeze first to make easier).
2. Place resins in a glass jar.
3. Cover with carrier oil.
4. Heat gently using one of these methods:
   - **Warm infusion:** Let jar sit in warm, sunny spot for 4–6 weeks, shaking daily
   - **Quick method:** Place jar in a double boiler or slow cooker with water. Heat on lowest setting for 4–6 hours.
5. Strain through cheesecloth (resins are sticky—this takes patience).
6. Add essential oils if using.
7. Bottle in amber glass bottles.
8. Label with date.

How to Use It

For pain:

- Massage into affected areas, 2–3 times daily
- Can be used as anointing oil for spiritual practice

For meditation or ritual:

- Apply to pulse points, third eye, or heart center

Safety Notes

- Safe for topical use
- Generally well-tolerated
- Rare allergic reactions (test on small area first)
- Not for internal use (resin-infused oils are for external application only)

REMEDY 16: Celery Seed Anti-Gout Tincture

What It Heals

Celery seed is a **traditional remedy for gout and uric acid buildup**. It:

- Reduces uric acid levels
- Relieves gout pain and swelling
- Acts as a diuretic (flushes toxins)
- Reduces arthritis inflammation
- Supports kidney function

Why It Works

Celery seed contains **3-n-butylphthalide (3nB)** and other compounds that help eliminate uric acid through the kidneys. It also has anti-inflammatory properties that reduce joint pain.

How to Make It

Ingredients:

- 1 part celery seeds (whole or crushed)
- 5 parts vodka (40–50% alcohol)

Instructions:

1. Place celery seeds in a glass jar.
2. Cover with alcohol.
3. Seal jar.
4. Let sit for 4–6 weeks, shaking daily.
5. Strain through cheesecloth.
6. Bottle in amber dropper bottles.
7. Label with date.

How to Use It

For gout:

- 2–3 mL, 3 times daily during acute attacks
- 2 mL, twice daily for prevention

For general arthritis:

- 2 mL, 2–3 times daily

Combine with cherry juice (also reduces uric acid) for enhanced effect.

Safety Notes

- Generally safe
- Acts as diuretic—ensure adequate hydration
- Avoid during pregnancy (can stimulate uterus)
- May interact with diuretic medications

REMEDY 17: Tart Cherry Concentrate (Uric Acid Reducer)

What It Heals

Tart cherries are **scientifically proven to reduce gout attacks** and:

- Lower uric acid levels
- Reduce frequency and severity of gout flares

- Decrease arthritis inflammation
- Support post-exercise recovery
- Improve sleep (contain natural melatonin)

Why It Works

Tart cherries contain **anthocyanins**—powerful anti-inflammatory compounds that reduce uric acid production and increase its excretion. Multiple studies show regular tart cherry consumption reduces gout attacks by up to 50%.

How to Make It

Ingredients:

- 4 cups fresh or frozen tart cherries (Montmorency variety is best)
- Optional: ¼ cup raw honey

Instructions:

1. Place cherries in a pot (no need to pit them).
2. Add just enough water to barely cover cherries.
3. Bring to a boil, then reduce to simmer.
4. Simmer uncovered for 1–2 hours, mashing cherries occasionally.
5. Strain through cheesecloth, squeezing out all juice.
6. Return juice to pot and continue simmering until reduced by half (creates concentrate).
7. Let cool and add honey if desired.
8. Pour into glass bottles.
9. Label with date.

Yield: About 1–2 cups concentrate

How to Use It

For gout prevention:

- Take 1–2 tablespoons concentrate daily (diluted in water or juice)

During gout attack:

- Take 2 tablespoons, 2–3 times daily

For arthritis:

- Take 1 tablespoon daily

Storage: Refrigerate for up to 2 weeks, or freeze in ice cube trays for longer storage.

Safety Notes

- Very safe
- High in natural sugars—diabetics should monitor blood sugar
- Generally well-tolerated
- Safe for long-term use

REMEDY 18: Yucca Root Anti-Inflammatory Decoction

What It Heals

Yucca is a **Native American remedy for arthritis**. It:

- Reduces arthritis pain and swelling
- Improves joint mobility
- Supports gut health (reduces toxins that trigger inflammation)
- Acts as a natural steroid alternative
- Reduces autoimmune inflammation

Why It Works

Yucca contains **saponins** that reduce intestinal inflammation and prevent absorption of toxins that trigger joint inflammation. It also has direct anti-inflammatory effects on joints.

Indigenous peoples used it for centuries for arthritis and inflammatory conditions.

How to Make It

Ingredients:

- 2 tablespoons dried yucca root (chopped)
- 4 cups water

Instructions:

1. Place yucca root in a pot with water.
2. Bring to a boil.
3. Reduce heat and simmer for 30–45 minutes.
4. Strain into a jar or mug.
5. Drink throughout the day.

Yield: About 3 cups

How to Use It

For arthritis:

- Drink 2–3 cups daily, long-term

For autoimmune inflammation:

- Drink 2 cups daily

Flavor tip: Yucca is mild and slightly soapy (due to saponins). Mix with ginger or cinnamon for better taste.

Safety Notes

- Generally safe
- High saponin content can cause digestive upset in sensitive individuals (start with small amounts)
- Avoid during pregnancy
- Safe for long-term use in most people

REMEDY 19: Green Tea EGCG Anti-Inflammatory Extract

What It Heals

Green tea is rich in **EGCG (epigallocatechin gallate)**—a powerful anti-inflammatory compound. It:

- Reduces arthritis inflammation
- Protects cartilage from breakdown
- Reduces autoimmune inflammation
- Supports brain health
- Has anti-cancer properties

Why It Works

EGCG inhibits inflammatory pathways (NF-kB, COX-2) and protects cells from oxidative damage. Studies show it can slow cartilage destruction in arthritis.

How to Make It

Concentrated Green Tea Extract:

Ingredients:

- 4 tablespoons high-quality green tea leaves (or 8–10 tea bags)
- 4 cups water
- Optional: fresh lemon juice (enhances EGCG absorption)

Instructions:

1. Heat water to 170–180°F (not boiling—boiling destroys EGCG).
2. Pour over green tea leaves.
3. Steep for 10–15 minutes (longer than normal for concentrated extraction).
4. Strain.
5. Add lemon juice if using.

6. Drink throughout the day.

For maximum EGCG: Use matcha powder (whole leaf green tea)—1 teaspoon per cup of hot water.

How to Use It

For inflammation:

- Drink 3–4 cups daily

For arthritis:

- Drink 2–3 cups daily, long-term

Or use matcha:

- 1–2 teaspoons matcha powder per day (in tea, smoothies, or lattes)

Safety Notes

- Very safe
- Contains caffeine (may affect sleep if consumed late in day)
- Generally well-tolerated
- Safe for long-term daily use

REMEDY 20: CBD Hemp Oil (Cannabinoid Anti-Inflammatory)

What It Heals

CBD (cannabidiol) from hemp is a **non-psychoactive anti-inflammatory** that:

- Reduces chronic pain
- Decreases arthritis inflammation
- Calms nerve pain
- Reduces anxiety and improves sleep (which supports healing)
- Has neuroprotective properties

Why It Works

CBD interacts with the **endocannabinoid system**—a network of receptors throughout the body that regulate pain, inflammation, and immune function. It reduces inflammatory cytokines and modulates pain perception.

How to Make It

Note: Making true CBD oil requires industrial hemp with high CBD content and specialized extraction equipment. Most people purchase high-quality CBD oil from reputable sources.

If you have access to hemp:

Hemp Flower Infused Oil:

1. Decarboxylate hemp flower (heat at 240°F for 40 minutes to activate CBD).
2. Infuse decarboxylated hemp in coconut oil or MCT oil using a double boiler (low heat for 2–3 hours).
3. Strain through cheesecloth.
4. Store in amber glass bottles.

Most reliable method: Purchase lab-tested, full-spectrum CBD oil from reputable vendors.

How to Use It

For inflammation:

- Start with 10–20 mg CBD daily (approximately 0.5 mL of 1000mg/30mL oil)
- Increase gradually until you find effective dose (typically 20–50 mg daily)
- Take sublingually (under tongue) for best absorption

For pain:

- 20–40 mg, 1–2 times daily

Topically:

- Apply CBD salve or oil directly to painful joints

Safety Notes

- Very safe
- Non-psychoactive (does not produce "high")
- May interact with certain medications (consult doctor if on prescriptions)
- Start low and increase gradually
- Choose products that provide third-party lab testing

REMEDY 21: Meadowsweet Tea (Aspirin Alternative)

What It Heals

Meadowsweet is a **gentle salicylate-containing herb** that:

- Reduces pain and inflammation
- Protects stomach lining (unlike aspirin)
- Relieves headaches
- Soothes digestive inflammation
- Reduces fever

Why It Works

Meadowsweet contains **salicylates** (like willow bark) but also has **tannins and mucilage** that protect the digestive tract. This makes it safer for people with sensitive stomachs.

It's particularly valuable for people who need anti-inflammatory relief but can't tolerate NSAIDs.

How to Make It

Ingredients:

- 2 teaspoons dried meadowsweet flowers and leaves
- 2 cups hot water
- Optional: peppermint for flavor

Instructions:

1. Place meadowsweet in a teapot or jar.
2. Pour hot water over herb.
3. Cover and steep for 10–15 minutes.
4. Strain.
5. Drink warm.

How to Use It

For pain:

- Drink 2–3 cups daily

For digestive inflammation:

- Drink 1 cup before meals

Safety Notes

- Do not use if allergic to aspirin
- Not for children with viral infections (same precaution as aspirin—Reye's syndrome risk)
- Generally safer for stomach than willow bark or aspirin
- Avoid during pregnancy

REMEDY 22: Arnica Montana Trauma Oil

What It Heals

Arnica is the **premier remedy for trauma, bruising, and muscle pain**. It:

- Reduces bruising and swelling

- Speeds healing of injuries
- Relieves muscle soreness
- Reduces inflammation from trauma
- Eases pain from sprains and strains

Why It Works

Arnica contains **sesquiterpene lactones** (helenalin) that reduce inflammation and improve microcirculation, accelerating healing and reducing bruising.

Critical: Arnica is for **external use only**—internal use can be toxic.

How to Make It

Ingredients:

- 1 cup dried arnica flowers
- 2 cups carrier oil (olive, sweet almond, or jojoba)

Instructions:

1. Place dried arnica flowers in a glass jar.
2. Cover completely with oil.
3. Let sit in a warm, sunny spot for 3–4 weeks, shaking daily.
4. Strain through cheesecloth.
5. Bottle in amber glass bottles.
6. Label clearly: "ARNICA—EXTERNAL USE ONLY"

How to Use It

For bruises:

- Apply immediately after injury and 2–3 times daily until healed

For muscle soreness:

- Massage into sore muscles after exercise

For sprains:

- Apply 3–4 times daily

Do not apply to broken skin or open wounds.

Safety Notes

- **EXTERNAL USE ONLY—highly toxic if ingested**
- Do not apply to broken skin
- Rare allergic reactions (test on small area first)
- Not for use during pregnancy
- Keep away from children

REMEDY 23: Feverfew Migraine and Inflammation Tincture

What It Heals

Feverfew is a **traditional migraine preventive** that also:

- Reduces frequency and severity of migraines
- Relieves arthritis pain
- Reduces inflammation
- Eases menstrual cramps
- Reduces fever

Why It Works

Feverfew contains **parthenolide**—a compound that inhibits inflammatory prostaglandins and reduces vascular inflammation (key in migraine prevention).

Studies show regular feverfew use can reduce migraine frequency by up to 70%.

How to Make It

Ingredients:

- 1 part dried feverfew leaves and flowers

- 5 parts vodka or brandy (50% alcohol)

Instructions:

1. Place feverfew in a glass jar.
2. Cover with alcohol.
3. Seal jar.
4. Let sit for 4–6 weeks, shaking daily.
5. Strain through cheesecloth.
6. Bottle in amber dropper bottles.
7. Label with date.

How to Use It

For migraine prevention:

- 1–2 mL, twice daily, long-term (must be taken consistently—not effective for acute migraines)

For arthritis:

- 2 mL, 2–3 times daily

Note: Feverfew requires **consistent daily use for 4–6 weeks** before effects are noticeable.

Safety Notes

- Not for use during pregnancy (can stimulate uterus)
- May cause mouth ulcers in sensitive individuals (discontinue if this occurs)
- Can increase bleeding risk—avoid before surgery
- Don't stop suddenly after long-term use (taper to avoid rebound headaches)

REMEDY 24: Castor Oil Pack (Deep Tissue Anti-Inflammatory)

What It Heals

Castor oil packs provide **deep, penetrating anti-inflammatory relief** for:

- Joint pain and arthritis
- Abdominal inflammation (endometriosis, IBS)
- Liver congestion
- Lymphatic stagnation
- Muscle tension

Why It Works

Castor oil contains **ricinoleic acid**—a unique fatty acid with profound anti-inflammatory properties. When applied topically with heat, it penetrates deeply, reducing inflammation and supporting detoxification.

How to Make It

Ingredients:

- Cold-pressed castor oil (hexane-free)
- Flannel cloth (wool or cotton)
- Plastic wrap or old towel
- Heating pad or hot water bottle

Instructions:

1. Soak flannel cloth in castor oil (enough to saturate but not dripping).
2. Place cloth on affected area (joint, abdomen, liver area).
3. Cover with plastic wrap.
4. Place heating pad on top (medium heat).
5. Leave on for 30–60 minutes.
6. Remove and cleanse skin with baking soda solution (1 tsp baking soda in water).
7. Repeat 3–4 times per week.

The same cloth can be reused many times (store in a jar between uses).

How to Use It

For arthritis:

- Apply to painful joints, 3–4 times per week

For abdominal inflammation:

- Apply to lower abdomen

For liver support:

- Apply over liver area (right upper abdomen)

Safety Notes

- Very safe
- Messy—use old sheets and towels
- Avoid during pregnancy
- Not for use during menstruation (increases flow)
- Castor oil stains fabric

REMEDY 25: Stinging Nettle Fresh Leaf Urtication (Traditional Arthritis Treatment)

What It Heals

Urtication is the **ancient practice of deliberately stinging arthritic joints with fresh nettle leaves**. It:

- Provides immediate pain relief
- Reduces inflammation
- Improves joint mobility
- Has been used for thousands of years

Why It Works

When nettle stings skin, it injects **histamine, acetylcholine, and formic acid**—compounds that create a counter-irritant effect. This stimulates circulation, reduces deeper inflammation, and triggers the body's own anti-inflammatory response.

Studies show urtication can significantly reduce arthritis pain—sometimes for weeks after a single treatment.

How to Make It

Materials:

- Fresh stinging nettle plant (wear gloves when harvesting)
- Gloves for handling

Instructions:

1. Harvest fresh nettle leaves (spring/summer).
2. Identify painful joint.
3. **Deliberately brush fresh nettle leaves against the skin over the painful area** (yes, it will sting—this is the treatment).
4. Let the stinging sensation run its course (5–10 minutes of burning/tingling is normal).
5. The area will become red and raised (like a mild allergic reaction).
6. After 30 minutes to several hours, the inflammation and pain in the deeper joint tissue will decrease significantly.

How to Use It

For arthritis:

- Perform urtication 1–2 times per week as needed
- Effects can last days to weeks

Not for the faint of heart—but remarkably effective for those willing to try.

Safety Notes

- Causes temporary intense stinging (this is the treatment)
- Skin will become red, raised, itchy (this resolves within hours)
- Not for people with severe allergies

- Avoid if you have skin conditions
- Traditional remedy with modern research support

REMEDY 26: Quercetin Supplement (Natural Antihistamine and Anti-Inflammatory)

What It Heals

Quercetin is a **powerful flavonoid** that:

- Reduces inflammatory histamine response
- Decreases arthritis pain
- Reduces exercise-induced inflammation
- Protects against oxidative stress
- Has antiviral properties

Why It Works

Quercetin stabilizes **mast cells** (which release histamine) and inhibits inflammatory enzymes. It's particularly effective for inflammation triggered by allergies or immune overactivation.

How to Make It

Note: Quercetin is best obtained through supplements or quercetin-rich foods.

Food sources:

- Onions (especially red)
- Apples (with skin)
- Capers
- Elderberries
- Kale
- Red grapes

Supplement: Purchase quercetin supplements (typically 500–1,000 mg capsules).

Quercetin-Rich Tea Blend:

Mix equal parts:

- Elderflower
- Elderberries
- Calendula flowers
- Green tea

Steep 2 teaspoons per cup, 10–15 minutes.

How to Use It

For inflammation:

- 500–1,000 mg quercetin, 2–3 times daily with food
- Or drink 2–3 cups quercetin-rich tea daily

For allergies with inflammatory component:

- 1,000 mg, twice daily

Safety Notes

- Very safe
- May interact with certain antibiotics
- Generally well-tolerated
- Safe for long-term use

REMEDY 27: Black Seed Oil (Nigella Sativa)

What It Heals

Black seed oil is a **Middle Eastern anti-inflammatory medicine** that:

- Reduces arthritis pain and swelling
- Calms autoimmune inflammation
- Supports respiratory health
- Has anti-cancer properties
- Boosts immune function

Why It Works

Black seed contains **thymoquinone**—a compound with potent anti-inflammatory, antioxidant, and immunomodulatory effects. It inhibits inflammatory prostaglandins and reduces oxidative stress.

How to Make It

Note: Black seed oil is typically cold-pressed from seeds. Most people purchase high-quality black seed oil.

Black Seed Infused Honey (easier to take):

1. Mix 1 cup raw honey with 2 tablespoons ground black seeds.
2. Store in glass jar.
3. Take 1 teaspoon daily.

How to Use It

For inflammation:

- Take 1 teaspoon black seed oil, twice daily

For arthritis:

- 1 teaspoon, 2–3 times daily

Topically:

- Can be applied to painful joints

Safety Notes

- Generally safe
- Strong flavor (can be mixed with honey to improve taste)
- May lower blood pressure and blood sugar (monitor if on medications)
- Avoid therapeutic doses during pregnancy

REMEDY 28: Holy Basil (Tulsi) Anti-Inflammatory Tea

What It Heals

Holy basil is an **adaptogenic anti-inflammatory** that:

- Reduces stress-induced inflammation
- Lowers cortisol (which drives inflammation)
- Supports respiratory health
- Reduces pain
- Balances immune function

Why It Works

Holy basil contains **eugenol, rosmarinic acid, and ursolic acid**—compounds that inhibit COX-2 and reduce inflammatory cytokines. It also modulates the stress response, preventing stress from triggering inflammation.

How to Make It

Ingredients:

- 2 teaspoons dried holy basil leaves (or 4–6 fresh leaves)
- 2 cups hot water
- Optional: ginger, lemon, honey

Instructions:

1. Place holy basil in a teapot.
2. Pour hot water over leaves.
3. Cover and steep 10–15 minutes.
4. Strain.
5. Add ginger, lemon, or honey if desired.

How to Use It

For inflammation:

- Drink 2–3 cups daily

For stress-related inflammation:

- Drink 2 cups daily, long-term

Safety Notes

- Very safe for daily use

- May lower blood sugar (monitor if diabetic)
- Generally well-tolerated
- Safe for children and pregnancy (in tea form)

REMEDY 29: Omega-3 Fish Oil (Anti-Inflammatory Essential Fatty Acids)

What It Heals

Omega-3 fatty acids (EPA and DHA) are **essential anti-inflammatory nutrients** that:

- Reduce arthritis pain and stiffness
- Decrease inflammatory markers
- Support cardiovascular health
- Protect brain function
- Reduce autoimmune inflammation

Why It Works

Omega-3s are converted into **resolvins and protectins**—compounds that actively resolve inflammation. Most people are deficient in omega-3s and excess omega-6s (from vegetable oils), creating an inflammatory state.

How to Make It

Food sources:

- Wild-caught fatty fish (salmon, mackerel, sardines, herring)
- Flaxseeds (ground)
- Chia seeds
- Walnuts
- Algae oil (for vegetarians/vegans)

Supplement: Purchase high-quality fish oil or algae oil (molecularly distilled, third-party tested for purity).

How to Use It

For inflammation:

- Eat fatty fish 3–4 times per week
- Or take 1,000–2,000 mg EPA+DHA daily (from fish oil or algae oil)

For severe arthritis:

- 2,000–3,000 mg EPA+DHA daily

Safety Notes

- Very safe
- Mild blood-thinning effect (consult doctor if on anticoagulants)
- Choose high-quality, tested sources (heavy metal and toxin-free)
- Store in refrigerator to prevent oxidation

REMEDY 30: Yarrow Poultice (Topical Anti-Inflammatory)

What It Heals

Yarrow is a **battlefield herb** traditionally used for:

- Sprains and strains
- Bruises
- Arthritis pain
- Wound healing
- Reducing swelling

Why It Works

Yarrow contains **flavonoids and sesquiterpene lactones** that reduce inflammation and improve circulation to injured tissues.

How to Make It

Fresh Yarrow Poultice:

1. Harvest fresh yarrow leaves and flowers.
2. Chew or crush leaves to release juices (or use a mortar and pestle).
3. Apply crushed herb directly to affected area.
4. Cover with clean cloth.
5. Leave on for 30–60 minutes.
6. Repeat 2–3 times daily.

Dried Yarrow Compress:

1. Make strong yarrow tea (4 tablespoons dried yarrow per 2 cups hot water).
2. Steep 20 minutes.
3. Soak clean cloth in tea.
4. Wring out and apply to painful area.
5. Leave on until cool.

How to Use It

For acute injuries:

- Apply immediately after injury and every few hours for first 48 hours

For arthritis flares:

- Apply as needed for pain relief

Safety Notes

- Very safe
- Rare allergic reactions in people sensitive to Asteraceae family
- Generally well-tolerated
- Safe for topical use

REMEDY 31: Kava Kava Muscle Relaxant Tincture

What It Heals

Kava is a **Pacific Islander herb for pain and muscle tension**. It:

- Relaxes muscles
- Reduces pain perception
- Calms anxiety (which often accompanies chronic pain)
- Induces relaxation without sedation
- Has mild euphoric effects

Why It Works

Kava contains **kavalactones**—compounds that act on GABA receptors, producing muscle relaxation and pain relief. It's particularly effective for **tension-related pain** and fibromyalgia.

How to Make It

Ingredients:

- 1 part dried kava root (powder or chopped)
- 5 parts vodka or brandy (60% alcohol—kava requires higher alcohol for extraction)

Instructions:

1. Place kava root in a glass jar.
2. Cover with alcohol.
3. Seal jar.
4. Shake vigorously (kava is dense and needs extra agitation).
5. Let sit for 4–6 weeks, shaking daily.
6. Strain through cheesecloth.
7. Bottle in amber dropper bottles.
8. Label with date.

How to Use It

For muscle tension and pain:

- 2–3 mL, 2–3 times daily as needed

For fibromyalgia:

- 2 mL, 3 times daily

Note: Effects are felt within 30–60 minutes.

Safety Notes

- **Not for long-term daily use** (concern about liver effects with excessive long-term use)
- Do not combine with alcohol
- Do not use if you have liver disease
- May cause drowsiness—don't drive after taking
- Not for use during pregnancy
- Use intermittently, not continuously

REMEDY 32: Magnesium Oil Spray (Muscle and Nerve Pain)

What It Heals

Magnesium is a **critical mineral** often deficient in people with chronic pain. It:

- Relaxes muscles
- Reduces nerve pain
- Improves sleep (which supports healing)
- Reduces inflammation
- Reduces muscle cramps and spasms

Why It Works

Magnesium regulates **neuromuscular function** and reduces inflammatory pathways. Deficiency is common and contributes to muscle tension, pain, and inflammation.

Transdermal (through-skin) application bypasses digestive issues and delivers magnesium directly to tissues.

How to Make It

Ingredients:

- ½ cup magnesium chloride flakes
- ½ cup distilled water
- Optional: 10 drops lavender essential oil (calming, enhances relaxation)

Instructions:

1. Boil distilled water.
2. Place magnesium flakes in a glass measuring cup.
3. Pour hot water over flakes.
4. Stir until completely dissolved.
5. Let cool.
6. Add lavender oil if using.
7. Pour into spray bottle.
8. Label with date.

How to Use It

For muscle pain:

- Spray onto affected muscles, 2–3 times daily
- Massage gently into skin
- Leave on for 20–30 minutes, then rinse if desired (some people experience tingling—this is normal)

For nerve pain:

- Spray along nerve pathways

Before bed:

- Spray on legs and feet to improve sleep and reduce nighttime cramping

Safety Notes

- Very safe
- May cause tingling or itching initially (dilute more if this is uncomfortable)
- Avoid on broken skin
- Generally well-tolerated
- Can be used daily

REMEDY 33: Capsaicin Cream (Intense Pain Relief)

What It Heals

Capsaicin provides **powerful topical pain relief** for:

- Arthritis
- Nerve pain (neuropathy, shingles)
- Back pain
- Chronic pain

Why It Works

Capsaicin depletes **substance P** (neurotransmitter that carries pain signals). With repeated use, it desensitizes pain receptors, providing long-term relief.

How to Make It

Ingredients:

- ½ cup infused cayenne oil (see Chapter 6, Remedy 10)
- 2 tablespoons beeswax
- 1 tablespoon shea butter or cocoa butter (for smoother texture)
- Optional: 10 drops peppermint essential oil

Instructions:

1. Melt infused cayenne oil, beeswax, and butter in double boiler.
2. Stir until fully melted and combined.
3. Remove from heat.
4. Add peppermint oil if using.
5. Pour into small jars or tins.
6. Let cool and solidify.
7. Label clearly: **"CAPSAICIN CREAM—WASH HANDS AFTER USE"**

How to Use It

For pain:

- Apply small amount to affected area, 3–4 times daily
- **ALWAYS wash hands thoroughly after applying**
- Expect warming/burning sensation (this decreases with regular use)
- **Most effective with consistent use over 2–4 weeks**

Safety Notes

- **DO NOT touch eyes, nose, or mucous membranes**
- Wear gloves if you have sensitive skin
- May cause intense heat initially
- Not for broken skin
- Keep away from children
- Discontinue if severe irritation occurs

REMEDY 34: Mangosteen Anti-Inflammatory Supplement

What It Heals

Mangosteen (especially the rind) contains **xanthones**—powerful anti-inflammatory compounds. It:

- Reduces arthritis inflammation
- Acts as a potent antioxidant
- Supports joint health
- Has anti-cancer properties
- Reduces pain

Why It Works

Xanthones inhibit multiple inflammatory pathways and have been shown in studies to reduce arthritis symptoms.

How to Make It

Note: Mangosteen rind is typically consumed as a powder or supplement.

If you have access to fresh mangosteen:

1. Remove the purple rind (pericarp).
2. Dry thoroughly (in dehydrator or oven on lowest setting).
3. Grind dried rind into powder.
4. Store in airtight jar.
5. Take ½–1 teaspoon powder daily (mixed in smoothies or encapsulated).

Most people purchase mangosteen extract supplements.

How to Use It

For inflammation:

- 500–1,000 mg mangosteen extract daily

Or:

- ½–1 teaspoon dried rind powder daily

Safety Notes

- Generally safe
- May interact with blood-thinning medications
- Generally well-tolerated
- Safe for long-term use

REMEDY 35: Collagen-Boosting Herbal Broth

What It Heals

This broth provides **building blocks for joint repair** and:

- Supports cartilage regeneration
- Reduces joint pain
- Improves flexibility
- Strengthens connective tissue
- Supports gut lining (which affects inflammation)

Why It Works

Combines **collagen-rich bone broth** with herbs that reduce inflammation and support tissue repair.

How to Make It

Ingredients:

- 2–3 lbs bones (chicken feet, beef knuckles, or fish heads—highest collagen content)
- 2 tablespoons apple cider vinegar (extracts minerals from bones)
- 8 cups water
- 2 tablespoons dried nettle leaf (mineral-rich)
- 1 tablespoon dried horsetail (silica for connective tissue)

- 6 slices dried astragalus root (immune support)
- 4 cloves garlic
- 2-inch piece ginger
- Sea salt to taste

Instructions:

1. Place bones in slow cooker or large pot.
2. Add apple cider vinegar and let sit 30 minutes (draws out minerals).
3. Add water, herbs, garlic, and ginger.
4. Bring to a boil, then reduce to lowest simmer.
5. Cover and simmer for 12–24 hours (longer = more collagen extraction).
6. Strain out bones and herbs.
7. Season with salt.
8. Store in refrigerator (broth should gel when cold—this indicates high collagen content).

Yield: About 6 cups

How to Use It

For joint health:

- Drink 1–2 cups daily
- Use as base for soups and stews

Storage: Refrigerate for up to 5 days, or freeze in portions.

Safety Notes

- Very safe and nourishing
- Suitable for all ages
- Generally well-tolerated

REMEDY 36: White Peony Root (Bai Shao) Anti-Spasm Tincture

What It Heals

White peony root is a **Traditional Chinese Medicine herb for muscle spasms and pain**. It:

- Reduces muscle cramps and spasms
- Relieves menstrual cramps
- Reduces arthritis pain
- Calms autoimmune inflammation
- Supports liver function

Why It Works

White peony contains **paeoniflorin**—a compound that relaxes smooth muscle, reduces pain, and modulates immune function. It's particularly effective for conditions involving **muscle tension and cramping**.

How to Make It

Ingredients:

- 1 part dried white peony root (sliced)
- 5 parts vodka or brandy (50–60% alcohol)

Instructions:

1. Place peony root in a glass jar.
2. Cover with alcohol.
3. Seal jar.
4. Let sit for 6–8 weeks, shaking daily (roots require longer extraction).
5. Strain through cheesecloth.
6. Bottle in amber dropper bottles.
7. Label with date.

How to Use It

For muscle spasms:

- 2–3 mL, 3 times daily

For arthritis:

- 2 mL, 2–3 times daily, long-term

For menstrual cramps:

- 3 mL, 3 times daily during menstruation

Safety Notes

- Generally safe for long-term use
- May interact with blood-thinning medications
- Avoid during pregnancy
- Generally well-tolerated

REMEDY 37: Horsetail (Shavegrass) Silica Tea

What It Heals

Horsetail is the **richest plant source of silica**—a mineral essential for:

- Connective tissue strength
- Cartilage repair
- Bone health
- Hair, skin, and nail health
- Joint flexibility

Why It Works

Silica is required for collagen production and connective tissue integrity. Deficiency contributes to weak joints, brittle bones, and poor healing.

Horsetail provides bioavailable silica that supports structural tissues.

How to Make It

Ingredients:

- 2 tablespoons dried horsetail herb
- 4 cups hot water

Instructions:

1. Place horsetail in a jar or teapot.
2. Pour hot water over herb.
3. Cover and steep for 20–30 minutes (longer extraction for minerals).
4. Strain.
5. Drink throughout the day.

Yield: About 3 cups

How to Use It

For joint health:

- Drink 2–3 cups daily, long-term

For bone and connective tissue support:

- Drink 2 cups daily

Pro tip: Combine with nettle for a powerful mineral-building blend.

Safety Notes

- Generally safe
- Do not use if you have kidney disease or heart problems (acts as diuretic)
- Not for long-term use without breaks (take 6 weeks, then break for 1 week)
- Avoid during pregnancy

REMEDY 38: Guggul (Commiphora mukul) Resin Tincture

What It Heals

Guggul is an **Ayurvedic anti-inflammatory resin** that:

- Reduces arthritis pain and swelling
- Lowers cholesterol
- Supports weight loss
- Reduces inflammation
- Improves circulation

Why It Works

Guggul contains **guggulsterones**—compounds that inhibit inflammatory pathways and have been shown in studies to be as effective as NSAIDs for arthritis.

How to Make It

Ingredients:

- 1 part guggul resin (crushed)
- 5 parts high-proof alcohol (90–95% Everclear)

Instructions:

1. Crush or grind guggul resin into small pieces.
2. Place in glass jar.
3. Cover with alcohol.
4. Seal jar tightly.
5. Shake vigorously daily (resin requires extra agitation).
6. Let sit for 6–8 weeks.
7. Strain through cheesecloth.
8. Bottle in amber dropper bottles.
9. Label with date.

How to Use It

For arthritis:

- 2–3 mL, 3 times daily with meals

For inflammation:

- 2 mL, twice daily

Safety Notes

- Generally safe for most people
- May cause digestive upset (take with food)
- Can interact with thyroid medications
- Avoid during pregnancy
- Not for people with liver or kidney disease

REMEDY 39: Birch Bark Pain Relief Salve

What It Heals

Birch bark contains **betulin and betulinic acid**—anti-inflammatory compounds. This salve:

- Reduces joint pain
- Relieves muscle soreness
- Has anti-inflammatory effects
- Supports skin healing

Why It Works

Betulinic acid inhibits inflammatory enzymes and has been studied for its anti-cancer properties. Topically, it provides pain relief and reduces inflammation.

How to Make It

Ingredients:

- 1 cup birch bark-infused oil (see below)
- 2 tablespoons beeswax

- Optional: 10 drops wintergreen essential oil (additional pain relief)

To Make Birch Bark Oil:

1. Harvest inner bark of birch (white or yellow birch).
2. Dry thoroughly.
3. Chop or powder bark.
4. Place in jar and cover with oil.
5. Let sit 4–6 weeks, shaking daily.
6. Strain.

To Make Salve:

1. Melt birch oil and beeswax in double boiler.
2. Stir until combined.
3. Remove from heat.
4. Add wintergreen oil if using.
5. Pour into tins or jars.
6. Let cool.
7. Label with date.

How to Use It

For pain:

- Apply to painful areas, 2–3 times daily

Safety Notes

- Safe for topical use
- Do not ingest
- Rare allergic reactions
- Generally well-tolerated

REMEDY 40: Full-Spectrum Anti-Inflammatory Formula (Comprehensive Blend)

What It Heals

This is a **master anti-inflammatory formula** combining the most powerful herbs in one tincture. It:

- Addresses multiple inflammatory pathways
- Provides broad-spectrum pain relief
- Supports long-term joint health
- Reduces systemic inflammation
- Works synergistically for maximum effect

Why It Works

By combining herbs with different mechanisms of action, this formula creates a **synergistic effect** more powerful than any single herb alone.

How to Make It

Ingredients (dried herbs):

- 2 parts turmeric root
- 2 parts ginger root
- 1 part boswellia resin
- 1 part devil's claw root
- 1 part white willow bark
- 1 part cat's claw bark
- ½ part black pepper (enhances turmeric absorption)
- Vodka or brandy (60% alcohol)

Instructions:

1. Mix all dried herbs together in a large bowl.
2. Place herb mixture in a half-gallon jar.

3. Cover completely with alcohol, ensuring all herbs are submerged by 1–2 inches.
4. Seal jar tightly.
5. Shake vigorously daily.
6. Let sit for 6–8 weeks (longer for maximum extraction).
7. Strain through cheesecloth, squeezing out all liquid.
8. Bottle in amber dropper bottles.
9. Label: "Full-Spectrum Anti-Inflammatory Formula" with date.

Yield: About 3–4 cups (depending on herb volume)

How to Use It

For chronic inflammation:

- 3–4 mL, 3 times daily with food, long-term

For acute pain flares:

- 4–5 mL, 3–4 times daily

For arthritis:

- 3 mL, 3 times daily (allow 4–6 weeks for full effects)

Best results with consistent daily use.

Safety Notes

- Generally safe for long-term use in most people
- Contains willow bark (salicylates)—avoid if allergic to aspirin
- Avoid during pregnancy
- May interact with blood-thinning medications
- Mild blood-thinning effect
- Take with food to prevent digestive upset

[IMAGE SUGGESTION: An elegant amber bottle labeled "Full-Spectrum Anti-Inflammatory Formula" surrounded by all the component herbs—turmeric root, ginger, boswellia resin, devil's claw, willow bark, and cat's claw—arranged artfully on a wooden apothecary table.]

CHAPTER 5: GUT & DIGESTIVE RESTORATION

Focus: IBS, Bloating, Nutrient Absorption

REMEDY 1: Slippery Elm Gruel (Gut Lining Healer)

What It Heals

Slippery elm is the **supreme remedy for damaged gut lining**. It:

- Heals leaky gut (intestinal permeability)
- Soothes IBS symptoms (cramping, diarrhea)
- Coats and protects ulcers
- Reduces acid reflux and heartburn
- Supports recovery from food poisoning or stomach flu
- Nourishes when solid food is too painful to digest

Why It Works

Slippery elm bark contains **mucilage**—a gel-like substance that coats the entire digestive tract from mouth to colon. This coating:

- Protects inflamed tissues
- Reduces pain and irritation
- Creates a barrier against stomach acid
- Provides nutrients that feed healing cells
- Promotes tissue regeneration

Native Americans used it for centuries for digestive ailments, wound healing, and as survival food.

How to Make It

Ingredients:

- 1 tablespoon slippery elm bark powder
- 1 cup warm water (not boiling)
- Optional: pinch of cinnamon, raw honey, or almond milk for flavor

Instructions:

1. Place slippery elm powder in a mug.
2. Add a small amount of warm water and stir into a paste.
3. Gradually add remaining water while stirring constantly.
4. The mixture will thicken into a gruel-like consistency.
5. Add cinnamon or honey if desired (keep it gentle—no spices if gut is very inflamed).
6. Drink slowly.

For thicker consistency (like porridge): Use less water.
For thinner consistency (like tea): Use more water.

How to Use It

For acute gut inflammation:

- Drink 1 cup, 3–4 times daily on an empty stomach (at least 30 minutes before meals)

For leaky gut repair:

- Drink 1 cup, 2–3 times daily for several weeks to months

For acid reflux:

- Drink 1 cup before meals and before bed

During fasting or gut rest:

- Slippery elm gruel provides nourishment while allowing the gut to heal

Safety Notes

- Extremely safe—even for children and pregnancy
- Can interfere with medication absorption (take medications 1–2 hours before or after slippery elm)
- Generally very well-tolerated
- One of the gentlest, safest gut remedies available

REMEDY 2: Marshmallow Root Cold Infusion

What It Heals

Marshmallow root is another **powerful demulcent** (soothing, coating herb) that:

- Heals inflamed gut lining
- Reduces IBS pain and cramping
- Soothes acid reflux and esophagitis
- Supports recovery from gastritis
- Heals ulcers (stomach and intestinal)
- Reduces urinary tract inflammation (bonus benefit)

Why It Works

Like slippery elm, marshmallow root is extremely high in **mucilage**. The cold infusion method extracts maximum mucilage without degrading it with heat.

This thick, soothing liquid coats irritated tissues and provides immediate relief.

How to Make It

Ingredients:

- 2–4 tablespoons dried marshmallow root
- 1 quart (4 cups) cold or room-temperature water

Instructions:

1. Place marshmallow root in a quart jar.
2. Cover with cold water.
3. Seal jar and place in refrigerator.
4. Let sit **overnight (8–12 hours)**.
5. Strain through a fine-mesh strainer or cheesecloth.
6. The liquid will be thick and slightly slimy (this is the healing mucilage).
7. Store in refrigerator.

Yield: About 3 cups

Shelf life: Use within 48 hours

How to Use It

For gut inflammation:

- Drink ½–1 cup, 3–4 times daily on an empty stomach

For acid reflux:

- Drink ½ cup before meals

For IBS:

- Drink 1 cup, 2–3 times daily

Pro tip: Combine marshmallow root with slippery elm for even more powerful gut healing.

Safety Notes

- Extremely safe
- Can slow absorption of medications (take meds 1–2 hours before or after)
- Safe during pregnancy and for children
- Generally very well-tolerated

REMEDY 3: Digestive Bitters Blend

What It Heals

Bitters are the **missing key in modern digestion**. They:

- Stimulate stomach acid production (most people have too little, not too much)
- Increase bile flow from gallbladder
- Stimulate digestive enzymes
- Improve nutrient absorption
- Reduce bloating and gas
- Support liver function
- Curb sugar cravings

Why It Works

When you taste something bitter, **receptors on your tongue** send signals throughout your digestive tract, triggering:

- Saliva production (begins carbohydrate digestion)
- Gastric juice secretion (stomach acid, pepsin)
- Bile release (fat digestion)
- Pancreatic enzyme release (protein, fat, carb digestion)

Modern diets lack bitterness—we've bred it out of food. The result: weak digestion, bloating, malabsorption.

Bitters restore this lost reflex.

How to Make It

Ingredients (dried herbs):

- 2 parts gentian root (extremely bitter, stimulates all digestive secretions)
- 2 parts dandelion root (liver support, mild bitter)
- 1 part orange peel (aromatic, improves flavor)
- 1 part ginger root (warming, anti-nausea)
- ½ part cardamom pods (aromatic, reduces gas)
- ½ part fennel seeds (aromatic, anti-bloating)
- Vodka or brandy (40–50% alcohol)

Instructions:

1. Mix all dried herbs together in a bowl.
2. Place herb mixture in a quart jar.
3. Cover completely with alcohol.
4. Seal jar tightly.
5. Let sit for 4–6 weeks, shaking daily.
6. Strain through cheesecloth.
7. Bottle in 2 oz amber dropper bottles.
8. Label with date.

Yield: About 2–3 cups

How to Use It

Critical: You must **taste the bitterness** for bitters to work. Don't dilute heavily or swallow quickly.

Before meals:

- Take ¼–½ teaspoon (about 20–40 drops) on the tongue
- Hold in mouth for 10–20 seconds
- Swallow
- Wait 15–30 minutes, then eat

For chronic bloating:

- Take before each meal for several weeks

For sluggish digestion:

- Take before lunch and dinner daily

Safety Notes

- Very safe for most people

- **Do not use if you have active ulcers** (bitters increase stomach acid)
- Start with small doses (bitters are intense!)
- Safe for long-term use
- Avoid during pregnancy (some bitter herbs can stimulate uterus)

REMEDY 4: DGL (Deglycyrrhizinated Licorice) for Ulcers and Reflux

What It Heals

DGL is **licorice with the blood-pressure-raising compound removed**. It:

- Heals stomach ulcers
- Reduces acid reflux and heartburn
- Protects stomach lining from damage
- Promotes mucus production in gut
- Reduces H. pylori (ulcer-causing bacteria)

Why It Works

Licorice contains compounds that **increase mucus production** and **accelerate healing** of stomach and intestinal lining. DGL is processed to remove glycyrrhizin (which can raise blood pressure), making it safe for long-term use.

Studies show DGL is as effective as pharmaceutical ulcer medications—without side effects.

How to Make It

Note: DGL requires specialized processing to remove glycyrrhizin. Most people purchase DGL tablets or powder.

DGL Paste (from purchased DGL powder):

1. Mix DGL powder with a small amount of water or honey to form a paste.
2. Store in small jar.
3. Take ½–1 teaspoon as needed.

Best form: Chewable DGL tablets (available at health stores).

How to Use It

For ulcers or reflux:

- Chew 1–2 DGL tablets (380–760 mg) 20 minutes before meals and before bed
- **Must be chewed** (not swallowed whole) to mix with saliva and coat stomach

For acute ulcer pain:

- Chew 2 tablets every 4–6 hours

Continue for 8–12 weeks for ulcer healing.

Safety Notes

- Very safe (no blood pressure effects like regular licorice)
- Safe for long-term use
- Generally well-tolerated
- Safe during pregnancy (consult practitioner)
- Do not use whole licorice root for this purpose (use DGL only for safety)

REMEDY 5: Cabbage Juice (Ulcer Healer)

What It Heals

Fresh cabbage juice is a **traditional ulcer remedy** with remarkable healing properties. It:

- Heals stomach and duodenal ulcers
- Reduces acid reflux symptoms
- Contains L-glutamine (repairs gut lining)
- Provides sulfur compounds that support detoxification

- Reduces H. pylori bacterial load

Why It Works

Cabbage contains **vitamin U (S-methylmethionine)**—a compound that heals ulcerated tissue. Studies from the 1950s showed cabbage juice healed ulcers in 7–10 days (compared to weeks with conventional treatment).

It also contains **L-glutamine**, the primary fuel for intestinal cells, supporting rapid regeneration.

How to Make It

Ingredients:

- ½–1 whole green cabbage
- Optional: 1 apple or carrot (improves flavor)

Instructions:

1. Chop cabbage into chunks that fit your juicer.
2. Juice cabbage (and apple/carrot if using).
3. Strain if desired (some people prefer pulp-free).
4. Drink immediately (fresh is most potent).
5. Store extra juice in refrigerator for up to 24 hours (potency decreases with time).

Yield: About 2–3 cups from one cabbage

How to Use It

For ulcers:

- Drink 1 cup, 3–4 times daily on an empty stomach
- Continue for 7–10 days (many people see dramatic improvement in this time)

For reflux or gastritis:

- Drink 1 cup, 2 times daily

Flavor tip: Cabbage juice is quite strong. Mix with apple, carrot, or celery juice to improve taste.

Safety Notes

- Very safe
- May cause gas in sensitive individuals (start with small amounts)
- Can interfere with thyroid function if consumed in very large amounts long-term (contains goitrogens—not a concern for short-term healing protocols)
- Safe for most people

REMEDY 6: Aloe Vera Juice (Soothing, Anti-Inflammatory)

What It Heals

Pure aloe vera juice (from the inner gel, not the latex) is a **gentle gut soother** that:

- Reduces inflammation throughout digestive tract
- Soothes IBS symptoms
- Supports healing of ulcers
- Acts as a gentle laxative (mild)
- Supports liver function
- Reduces acid reflux

Why It Works

Aloe contains **polysaccharides and glycoproteins** that reduce inflammation, support immune function, and promote tissue repair.

Critical: You must use **inner leaf gel** (clear), NOT the yellow latex (found just under the skin), which is a harsh laxative.

How to Make It

From fresh aloe:

1. Cut a mature aloe leaf (at least 3 years old for maximum benefits).
2. Stand leaf upright in a cup for 10–15 minutes to drain yellow latex.
3. Rinse leaf thoroughly.
4. Peel away the thick green skin.
5. Scoop out the clear inner gel.
6. Blend gel with water (1 part gel to 3 parts water).
7. Strain if desired.
8. Store in glass jar in refrigerator for up to 5 days.

Or purchase: High-quality, pure aloe vera juice (look for 99–100% inner leaf gel with no added sugars or preservatives).

How to Use It

For gut inflammation:

- Drink ¼–½ cup, 2–3 times daily before meals

For constipation:

- Drink ½ cup in the morning on an empty stomach

Start with small amounts and increase gradually.

Safety Notes

- Generally safe when using pure inner leaf gel
- **Avoid aloe latex** (yellow substance—harsh laxative, can cause cramping)
- Can lower blood sugar (monitor if diabetic)
- May have mild laxative effect (reduce amount if loose stools occur)
- Not for use during pregnancy

REMEDY 7: Triphala Bowel Tonic (Gentle Regularity)

What It Heals

Triphala is an **Ayurvedic formula** of three fruits that:

- Promotes regular, comfortable bowel movements
- Gently tones the colon
- Reduces bloating and gas
- Supports detoxification
- Does not create dependency (unlike harsh laxatives)
- Provides antioxidants and supports overall health

Why It Works

Triphala combines three dried fruits:

- **Amalaki** (Indian gooseberry) – antioxidant, rejuvenating
- **Bibhitaki** – detoxifying, supports respiratory and digestive health
- **Haritaki** – gentle laxative, "king of medicines" in Ayurveda

Together, they **tonify the bowel** rather than irritate it (like senna or cascara), making them safe for long-term use.

How to Make It

Note: Triphala is typically purchased as a powder or tablets (the three fruits are hard to source individually).

Triphala Tea:

1. Mix ½–1 teaspoon triphala powder in 1 cup warm water.
2. Let steep for 5–10 minutes.
3. Drink before bed (works overnight).

Or take as powder:

- Stir ½–1 teaspoon into water or juice.

How to Use It

For constipation:

- Take ½–1 teaspoon powder before bed
- Start with smaller amount and increase as needed

For general bowel toning:

- Take ½ teaspoon daily, long-term

For detoxification:

- Take 1 teaspoon daily for 4–6 weeks

Safety Notes

- Generally very safe for long-term use
- May cause loose stools if dose is too high (reduce amount)
- Not for use during pregnancy or nursing
- Safe for most adults

REMEDY 8: Psyllium Husk Fiber (Bulk and Binding)

What It Heals

Psyllium is a **soluble fiber** that:

- Relieves constipation (adds bulk to stool)
- Relieves diarrhea (absorbs excess water)
- Reduces bloating
- Supports healthy cholesterol levels
- Feeds beneficial gut bacteria
- Improves bowel regularity

Why It Works

Psyllium husk **absorbs water and swells**, creating soft, bulky stools that move easily through the intestines. It works for both constipation AND diarrhea by normalizing stool consistency.

It also acts as a **prebiotic**, feeding beneficial bacteria.

How to Make It

Ingredients:

- 1 teaspoon psyllium husk powder (or 1 tablespoon whole husks)
- 8–12 oz water (adequate water is critical)

Instructions:

1. Mix psyllium into water.
2. Stir vigorously (it thickens quickly).
3. Drink immediately (before it gels).
4. Follow with another full glass of water.

Start with small amounts (½ teaspoon) and increase gradually.

How to Use It

For constipation:

- Take 1 teaspoon powder in water, 1–2 times daily

For diarrhea:

- Take 1 teaspoon powder in water, 2–3 times daily

For bowel regularity:

- Take 1 teaspoon daily

Critical: Always drink plenty of water with psyllium (at least 8–12 oz per dose). Without adequate water, psyllium can cause blockage.

Safety Notes

- Very safe when taken with adequate water
- Start with small amounts (can cause gas initially as gut bacteria adjust)

- **Must drink plenty of water**
- Can interfere with medication absorption (take meds 1–2 hours before or after)
- Safe for long-term use

REMEDY 9: Ginger Digestive Tea

What It Heals

Ginger is a **warming digestive stimulant** that:

- Relieves nausea (morning sickness, motion sickness, post-surgery)
- Reduces bloating and gas
- Stimulates digestive enzymes
- Reduces inflammation in gut
- Improves motility (moves food through system)
- Relieves cramping

Why It Works

Ginger contains **gingerols and shogaols**—compounds that stimulate saliva, bile, and gastric secretions. It also relaxes intestinal smooth muscle, reducing cramping and improving motility.

How to Make It

Ingredients:

- 1–2 inches fresh ginger root, sliced or grated
- 2 cups water
- Optional: lemon, honey, peppermint

Instructions:

1. Place ginger in a pot with water.
2. Bring to a boil.
3. Reduce heat and simmer for 10–15 minutes.
4. Strain into a mug.
5. Add lemon or honey if desired.
6. Drink warm.

How to Use It

For nausea:

- Sip slowly as needed

For bloating and gas:

- Drink 1 cup after meals

For general digestive support:

- Drink 1–2 cups daily

For morning sickness:

- Sip small amounts throughout the day

Safety Notes

- Very safe
- High doses may cause heartburn in sensitive individuals
- Generally safe during pregnancy (in tea form)
- Safe for children

REMEDY 10: Peppermint Tea (IBS Relief)

What It Heals

Peppermint is a **carminative and antispasmodic** that:

- Relieves IBS symptoms (cramping, bloating, gas)
- Relaxes intestinal smooth muscle
- Reduces nausea
- Stimulates bile flow
- Cools inflammation

Why It Works

Peppermint contains **menthol**—a compound that relaxes smooth muscle in the digestive tract, reducing spasms and pain. It also has antimicrobial properties that help balance gut flora.

How to Make It

Ingredients:

- 1–2 teaspoons dried peppermint leaves (or 6–8 fresh leaves)
- 1 cup hot water

Instructions:

1. Place peppermint in a mug or teapot.
2. Pour hot water over leaves.
3. Cover and steep for 10 minutes.
4. Strain.
5. Drink warm (not hot—can aggravate reflux).

How to Use It

For IBS:

- Drink 1 cup, 2–3 times daily between meals

For bloating:

- Drink 1 cup after meals

For nausea:

- Sip slowly as needed

Pro tip: For severe IBS, consider enteric-coated peppermint oil capsules (available at health stores)—these release in the intestines rather than stomach, providing targeted relief.

Safety Notes

- Generally very safe
- Can worsen acid reflux in some people (relaxes lower esophageal sphincter)
- Avoid during pregnancy in therapeutic doses (tea form is generally safe)
- Can reduce milk supply in nursing mothers
- Safe for children over 3 years

REMEDY 11: Chamomile Gut-Soothing Tea

What It Heals

Chamomile is a **gentle anti-inflammatory and nervine** that:

- Soothes irritated gut lining
- Reduces IBS-related cramping
- Calms stress-induced digestive upset
- Reduces gas and bloating
- Supports healing of ulcers
- Relieves nervous stomach

Why It Works

Chamomile contains **apigenin** (anti-inflammatory flavonoid) and **bisabolol** (anti-inflammatory volatile oil) that relax smooth muscle, reduce inflammation, and calm the nervous system.

The **gut-brain connection** is powerful—stress directly impacts digestion. Chamomile addresses both the physical inflammation and the emotional/nervous component.

How to Make It

Ingredients:

- 2 teaspoons dried chamomile flowers (or 2 chamomile tea bags)
- 1 cup hot water
- Optional: fennel seeds (reduce gas), lemon balm (additional calming)

Instructions:

1. Place chamomile in a mug or teapot.
2. Pour hot water over flowers.

3. Cover and steep for 10–15 minutes.
4. Strain.
5. Drink warm.

How to Use It

For IBS:

- Drink 1 cup, 2–3 times daily

For stress-related digestive upset:

- Drink 1 cup as needed

Before meals (for nervous stomach):

- Drink 1 cup 20–30 minutes before eating

Before bed:

- Drink 1 cup to soothe gut and promote restful sleep

Safety Notes

- Extremely safe
- Rare allergic reactions in people sensitive to Asteraceae family
- Safe for children and pregnancy
- Can be used long-term

REMEDY 12: Fennel Seed Anti-Gas Tea

What It Heals

Fennel is a **carminative** (gas-relieving herb) that:

- Eliminates gas and bloating
- Reduces intestinal cramping
- Stimulates digestive enzymes
- Relieves colic (safe for babies)
- Supports healthy bowel movements

Why It Works

Fennel contains **anethole**—a volatile oil that relaxes intestinal smooth muscle, allowing trapped gas to move and be expelled. It also stimulates digestive secretions.

Fennel has been used for thousands of years across cultures for digestive complaints—especially gas.

How to Make It

Ingredients:

- 1 teaspoon fennel seeds (crushed or whole)
- 1 cup hot water

Instructions:

1. Lightly crush fennel seeds (releases essential oils).
2. Place in a mug.
3. Pour hot water over seeds.
4. Cover and steep for 10 minutes.
5. Strain (or chew the seeds—they're edible and beneficial).
6. Drink warm.

How to Use It

For bloating and gas:

- Drink 1 cup after meals or as needed

For IBS:

- Drink 2–3 cups daily

For colic (infants):

- Give weak, diluted fennel tea (1 teaspoon tea mixed with formula or breast milk)

Traditional practice: Chew ½ teaspoon fennel seeds after meals as a digestive aid.

Safety Notes

- Very safe
- Generally well-tolerated by all ages
- Safe for babies (in proper dilution)
- Safe during pregnancy and nursing
- Has mild estrogenic properties (not a concern at normal doses)

REMEDY 13: L-Glutamine Powder (Leaky Gut Repair)

What It Heals

L-glutamine is an **amino acid that is the primary fuel for intestinal cells**. It:

- Repairs leaky gut (intestinal permeability)
- Heals ulcers
- Supports recovery from inflammatory bowel disease
- Reduces sugar and alcohol cravings
- Supports immune function in the gut

Why It Works

Intestinal cells (enterocytes) use glutamine as their primary energy source. When you're deficient (common during stress, illness, or gut dysfunction), the gut lining deteriorates.

Supplementing with L-glutamine provides the raw material these cells need to regenerate and maintain tight junctions (preventing leaky gut).

How to Make It

Note: L-glutamine is purchased as a powder or capsules (available at health stores).

L-Glutamine Gut Repair Drink:

1. Mix 5 grams (about 1 teaspoon) L-glutamine powder in 8 oz water or juice.
2. Stir until dissolved.
3. Drink on an empty stomach.

How to Use It

For leaky gut:

- Take 5 grams, 2–3 times daily (especially first thing in morning and before bed)
- Continue for 8–12 weeks

For ulcers or IBD:

- Take 5 grams, 3 times daily

For general gut support:

- Take 5 grams daily

Best absorbed on an empty stomach (30 minutes before meals or 2 hours after).

Safety Notes

- Very safe for most people
- High doses can cause mild digestive upset (reduce if needed)
- People with liver or kidney disease should consult doctor
- Generally well-tolerated
- Safe for long-term use

REMEDY 14: Bone Broth (Gut-Healing Collagen and Gelatin)

What It Heals

Bone broth is **liquid medicine** for the gut. It:

- Heals leaky gut
- Provides collagen and gelatin (seal intestinal lining)

- Supplies amino acids (proline, glycine, glutamine) for tissue repair
- Reduces inflammation
- Supports immune function
- Provides easily absorbable minerals

Why It Works

When bones simmer for hours, **collagen breaks down into gelatin and amino acids** that are easily absorbed. These compounds literally **seal gaps in the intestinal lining**, restoring barrier function.

Gelatin also attracts water into the gut, supporting healthy digestion and bowel movements.

How to Make It

Ingredients:

- 2–3 lbs bones (chicken feet, beef knuckles, or fish heads—high in collagen)
- 2 tablespoons apple cider vinegar (extracts minerals)
- 8–10 cups water
- Optional: onion, carrots, celery, garlic, herbs

Instructions:

1. Place bones in slow cooker or large pot.
2. Add apple cider vinegar and let sit 30 minutes.
3. Add water and vegetables if using.
4. Bring to a boil, then reduce to lowest simmer.
5. Cover and simmer:
   - **Chicken/fish:** 12–24 hours
   - **Beef/lamb:** 24–48 hours
6. Strain out bones and vegetables.
7. Let cool—broth should gel when refrigerated (indicates high collagen content).
8. Store in refrigerator for up to 5 days or freeze.

Yield: About 6–8 cups

How to Use It

For leaky gut:

- Drink 1–2 cups daily, warm

For IBD or severe gut damage:

- Drink 2–3 cups daily

For general gut support:

- Use as base for soups and stews

During gut healing protocols:

- Some people do bone broth-only fasts (3–5 days) to give the gut deep rest while providing nutrients

Safety Notes

- Very safe and nourishing
- Use organic, grass-fed bones when possible (conventional bones may contain antibiotics/hormones)
- Generally well-tolerated by all ages
- Suitable for most dietary restrictions

REMEDY 15: Activated Charcoal (Gas and Toxin Absorber)

What It Heals

Activated charcoal is a **powerful adsorbent** that:

- Eliminates gas and bloating
- Absorbs toxins and pathogens
- Relieves food poisoning
- Reduces symptoms of SIBO (small intestinal bacterial overgrowth)
- Provides emergency detoxification

Why It Works

Activated charcoal has an **enormous surface area**—one teaspoon has about the surface area of a football field. This porous structure binds to gas, toxins, bacteria, and chemicals in the digestive tract, preventing their absorption.

It's used in emergency rooms for poisoning and drug overdoses.

How to Make It

Note: Activated charcoal must be purchased (food-grade or pharmaceutical-grade). Do not use charcoal briquettes!

Available forms:

- Powder
- Capsules
- Tablets

How to Use It

For gas and bloating:

- Take 500–1,000 mg (2–4 capsules) with water before gas-producing meals
- Or take after meals if bloating occurs

For food poisoning:

- Take 1,000–2,000 mg immediately when symptoms begin
- Repeat every 2–3 hours until symptoms subside

For SIBO (during treatment):

- Take 500 mg, 2–3 times daily between meals

Critical: Take charcoal **2 hours away from food, supplements, and medications**—it will bind to everything, including nutrients and drugs.

Safety Notes

- Very safe for short-term, occasional use
- **Do not use daily or long-term** (will bind nutrients and cause deficiencies)
- Will turn stool black (this is normal)
- Can cause constipation if not taken with adequate water
- **Keep away from medications** (binds to them, making them ineffective)
- Not for use during pregnancy without medical supervision

REMEDY 16: Apple Cider Vinegar Digestive Tonic

What It Heals

Apple cider vinegar (with "the mother") is a **traditional digestive aid** that:

- Increases stomach acid production (most people are low, not high)
- Improves protein digestion
- Reduces bloating after meals
- Supports blood sugar balance
- Stimulates bile flow
- Has antimicrobial properties

Why It Works

Contrary to popular belief, most digestive issues are caused by LOW stomach acid, not high. Symptoms of low acid mimic high acid (bloating, reflux, indigestion).

Apple cider vinegar provides acetic acid that:

- Signals the stomach to produce more acid
- Helps break down protein
- Creates an inhospitable environment for harmful bacteria

How to Make It

Ingredients:

- 1–2 tablespoons raw, unfiltered apple cider vinegar (with "the mother")
- 8 oz water
- Optional: 1 teaspoon raw honey, squeeze of lemon

Instructions:

1. Mix apple cider vinegar in water.
2. Add honey and lemon if desired.
3. Drink before meals.

How to Use It

For low stomach acid:

- Drink 1 tablespoon in water, 15–20 minutes before meals

For bloating:

- Drink 1–2 tablespoons in water after meals

For blood sugar balance:

- Drink before carbohydrate-heavy meals

Start with 1 teaspoon and increase to 1–2 tablespoons as tolerated.

Safety Notes

- Generally safe
- Always dilute (undiluted vinegar can damage tooth enamel and esophagus)
- **Do not use if you have active ulcers** (will aggravate)
- May worsen reflux in people with hiatal hernia
- Rinse mouth with water after drinking (protects enamel)
- Can lower potassium in very high doses long-term

REMEDY 17: Papaya Enzyme Supplement

What It Heals

Papaya contains **papain**—a proteolytic enzyme that:

- Improves protein digestion
- Reduces bloating after meals
- Eases indigestion
- Reduces intestinal parasites
- Supports gut healing

Why It Works

Papain breaks down protein into smaller peptides and amino acids, reducing the burden on the stomach and pancreas. This is especially helpful for people with low stomach acid or pancreatic insufficiency.

How to Make It

Fresh Papaya:

1. Eat ½–1 cup fresh, ripe papaya before or after meals.
2. Focus on eating fruit when slightly under-ripe (higher enzyme content).

Papaya Seeds (antiparasitic bonus):

1. Scoop out papaya seeds.
2. Rinse and dry.
3. Chew 1 teaspoon seeds daily (they're spicy—similar to black pepper).
4. Or grind and add to smoothies.

Supplement: Purchase papaya enzyme tablets (chewable or capsules).

How to Use It

For digestive support:

- Chew 1–2 papaya enzyme tablets after protein-heavy meals

For parasites:

- Eat 1 teaspoon papaya seeds daily for 1–2 weeks

For general support:

- Eat fresh papaya regularly

Safety Notes

- Very safe
- May have mild anticoagulant effect (caution with blood thinners)
- Generally well-tolerated
- Safe for most people

REMEDY 18: Wormwood Antiparasitic Tincture

What It Heals

Wormwood is a **powerful antiparasitic and antimicrobial** that:

- Eliminates intestinal parasites (worms, protozoa)
- Kills harmful bacteria and fungi
- Stimulates digestion (bitter)
- Reduces SIBO symptoms
- Supports liver detoxification

Why It Works

Wormwood contains **thujone** and other compounds that are toxic to parasites. It's been used for centuries to expel worms and treat parasitic infections.

It also stimulates bile and digestive secretions due to its intense bitterness.

How to Make It

Ingredients:

- 1 part dried wormwood leaf and flower
- 5 parts vodka (40–50% alcohol)

Instructions:

1. Place wormwood in a glass jar.
2. Cover with alcohol.
3. Seal jar.
4. Let sit for 4–6 weeks, shaking daily.
5. Strain through cheesecloth.
6. Bottle in amber dropper bottles.
7. Label with date and **"Use short-term only"**.

How to Use It

For parasites:

- Take 10–20 drops in water, 2–3 times daily for 2–4 weeks
- Best combined with black walnut hull and cloves (traditional antiparasitic trio)

For digestive stimulation:

- Take 5–10 drops before meals

Important: Wormwood is **not for long-term use** (thujone can be neurotoxic in high doses over extended periods).

Safety Notes

- **Short-term use only** (2–4 weeks maximum)
- Do not exceed recommended doses
- Not for use during pregnancy or nursing
- Not for people with seizure disorders

- Can be very bitter—start with low doses
- Consult practitioner for parasite protocols

REMEDY 19: Black Walnut Hull Tincture (Antiparasitic)

What It Heals

Black walnut hull is another **traditional antiparasitic** that:

- Kills intestinal parasites
- Eliminates fungal infections (Candida)
- Has antimicrobial properties
- Supports bowel regularity

Why It Works

Black walnut hull contains **juglone**—a compound toxic to parasites, fungi, and certain bacteria. It's a key component of traditional parasite cleanses.

How to Make It

Ingredients:

- 1 part dried black walnut hulls (green/unripe hulls, dried)
- 5 parts vodka or brandy (40–50% alcohol)

Instructions:

1. Place black walnut hulls in a glass jar.
2. Cover with alcohol.
3. Seal jar.
4. Let sit for 6–8 weeks, shaking daily.
5. Strain through cheesecloth.
6. Bottle in amber dropper bottles.
7. Label with date.

Note: Black walnut hull tincture will be very dark (almost black).

How to Use It

For parasites:

- Take 20–30 drops in water, 2–3 times daily for 2–4 weeks
- Often combined with wormwood and cloves

For Candida:

- Take 20 drops, twice daily for 4–6 weeks

Safety Notes

- Generally safe for short-term use
- Can cause nausea if taken on empty stomach (take with food)
- Stains everything (be careful with clothes and surfaces)
- Not for use during pregnancy
- Short-term use recommended

REMEDY 20: Clove Antiparasitic Tea

What It Heals

Cloves complete the **antiparasitic trinity** (wormwood, black walnut, cloves). They:

- Kill parasite eggs
- Eliminate intestinal worms
- Have powerful antimicrobial properties
- Reduce gas and bloating
- Stimulate digestion

Why It Works

Cloves contain **eugenol**—an antimicrobial compound that kills parasite eggs (which wormwood and black walnut don't always reach). This prevents re-infestation.

How to Make It

Clove Tea:

Ingredients:

- 1 teaspoon whole cloves (or ½ teaspoon ground)
- 2 cups water

Instructions:

1. Crush whole cloves slightly.
2. Add to water in a pot.
3. Bring to a boil, then reduce to simmer.
4. Simmer for 10–15 minutes.
5. Strain.
6. Drink warm.

Clove Tincture:

Follow standard tincture method (1 part cloves to 5 parts alcohol, 4–6 weeks).

How to Use It

For parasites:

- Drink 1 cup clove tea, 2–3 times daily for 2–4 weeks
- Or take 10–20 drops clove tincture, 3 times daily

For digestion:

- Chew 1–2 whole cloves after meals

Safety Notes

- Generally safe in normal doses
- Clove oil is very concentrated—do not take undiluted
- Can irritate mucous membranes in high doses
- Not for use during pregnancy in medicinal amounts
- Safe as culinary spice

REMEDY 21: Berberine Antimicrobial Supplement

What It Heals

Berberine is a **yellow alkaloid found in several plants** (goldenseal, Oregon grape, barberry) that:

- Kills harmful bacteria, viruses, fungi, and parasites
- Treats SIBO (small intestinal bacterial overgrowth)
- Improves blood sugar and insulin sensitivity
- Supports healthy gut flora
- Reduces intestinal inflammation

Why It Works

Berberine has **broad-spectrum antimicrobial activity** proven in numerous studies. It disrupts bacterial biofilms, making it effective against stubborn infections.

It also **improves gut barrier function** and reduces inflammation.

How to Make It

Note: Berberine is typically purchased as a supplement (extracted from goldenseal, Oregon grape, or barberry).

Berberine-Rich Herbs:

- Goldenseal root tincture (see Chapter 6)
- Oregon grape root tincture
- Barberry root tincture

How to Use It

For SIBO or dysbiosis:

- Take 500 mg berberine supplement, 3 times daily with meals
- Continue for 4–8 weeks

For blood sugar support:

- Take 500 mg, 2–3 times daily with meals

Or use tinctures:

- Goldenseal or Oregon grape tincture: 2–3 mL, 3 times daily

Safety Notes

- Generally safe for short-term use (4–12 weeks)
- Can cause digestive upset (take with food)
- May lower blood sugar (monitor if diabetic)
- Can be hard on beneficial bacteria with long-term use (take breaks, use probiotics)
- Not for use during pregnancy or nursing

REMEDY 22: Saccharomyces Boulardii (Beneficial Yeast Probiotic)

What It Heals

S. boulardii is a **beneficial yeast** (not bacteria) that:

- Treats and prevents diarrhea (antibiotic-associated, C. diff, traveler's)
- Reduces symptoms of Crohn's and ulcerative colitis
- Fights pathogenic yeasts (Candida)
- Supports gut barrier integrity
- Reduces inflammation

Why It Works

Unlike bacterial probiotics (which can be killed by stomach acid and antibiotics), **S. boulardii is a hardy yeast** that survives stomach acid and antibiotics.

It **outcompetes pathogenic organisms**, produces compounds that strengthen the gut lining, and modulates immune function.

How to Make It

Note: S. boulardii is purchased as a supplement (available at health stores and pharmacies).

Look for: Supplements with at least 5–10 billion CFU per capsule.

How to Use It

For diarrhea:

- Take 5–10 billion CFU, 2–3 times daily until resolved

For antibiotic-associated diarrhea (prevention):

- Take 5–10 billion CFU daily while on antibiotics and for 1–2 weeks after

For IBD:

- Take 5–10 billion CFU, twice daily, long-term

For Candida overgrowth:

- Take 10 billion CFU, twice daily for 4–8 weeks

Safety Notes

- Very safe for most people
- **Do not use if immunocompromised or have central venous catheter** (rare risk of fungal infection)
- Generally well-tolerated
- Can be taken with antibiotics (unlike most probiotics)

REMEDY 23: Soil-Based Probiotic Supplement

What It Heals

Soil-based organisms (SBOs) are **spore-forming probiotics** that:

- Survive stomach acid (reach intestines intact)
- Support microbiome diversity
- Reduce SIBO symptoms
- Improve immune function
- Reduce leaky gut

Why It Works

Unlike most probiotics (lactobacillus, bifidobacterium), **soil-based probiotics are spore-forming**. They form protective shells that survive harsh stomach acid and bile, germinating in the intestines.

Our ancestors consumed these organisms naturally from soil on vegetables. Modern sanitation has eliminated this exposure.

How to Make It

Note: Soil-based probiotics are purchased as supplements.

Look for strains:

- Bacillus subtilis
- Bacillus coagulans
- Bacillus clausii

How to Use It

For general gut health:

- Take 1–2 capsules daily with food

For SIBO:

- Take 2 capsules daily (soil-based probiotics are less likely to worsen SIBO than lactobacillus strains)

For immune support:

- Take 1 capsule daily

Safety Notes

- Generally very safe
- Well-tolerated by most people
- Less likely to cause gas/bloating than other probiotics
- Safe for long-term use

REMEDY 24: Fermented Vegetables (Natural Probiotics)

What It Heals

Fermented vegetables provide **naturally occurring probiotics** that:

- Repopulate beneficial gut bacteria
- Support digestion
- Provide enzymes that aid nutrient absorption
- Improve immune function
- Support mental health (gut-brain connection)

Why It Works

Fermentation creates **billions of beneficial bacteria** (lactobacillus species) that colonize the gut. Fermented foods also contain **enzymes** that predigest food, making nutrients more bioavailable.

Traditional cultures consumed fermented foods daily—sauerkraut, kimchi, pickles, kvass, etc.

How to Make It

Simple Sauerkraut:

Ingredients:

- 1 medium head green cabbage, shredded
- 1–1½ tablespoons sea salt
- Optional: caraway seeds, garlic, ginger

Instructions:

1. Place shredded cabbage in a large bowl.
2. Sprinkle with salt.
3. Massage vigorously for 10–15 minutes until cabbage releases liquid.
4. Pack cabbage tightly into a clean quart jar.
5. Pour released liquid over cabbage (cabbage must be submerged).
6. If needed, add filtered water to cover.
7. Weight down cabbage (use a small glass jar or fermentation weight to keep it submerged).
8. Cover jar with cloth or loose lid (gases need to escape).
9. Let sit at room temperature for **5–10 days**, checking daily.
10. Taste after 5 days—when it reaches desired tanginess, move to refrigerator.

Yield: About 1 quart

How to Use It

For gut health:

- Eat 1–2 tablespoons fermented vegetables with meals daily

Start small (1 teaspoon) and increase gradually—fermented foods can cause gas initially as gut bacteria adjust.

Storage: Refrigerated sauerkraut lasts months (continues fermenting slowly).

Safety Notes

- Very safe when made properly
- Start with small amounts (can cause gas/bloating initially)
- Ensure vegetables stay submerged during fermentation (prevents mold)
- If mold appears on surface, discard batch
- Generally safe for most people

REMEDY 25: Kombucha (Fermented Tea Probiotic)

What It Heals

Kombucha is a **fermented tea** that:

- Provides probiotics
- Supports liver detoxification
- Improves digestion
- Provides B vitamins
- Has antimicrobial properties

Why It Works

Kombucha is fermented using a **SCOBY** (symbiotic culture of bacteria and yeast). The fermentation process creates probiotics, organic acids, and enzymes.

The organic acids support liver detox and digestion.

How to Make It

Ingredients:

- 1 SCOBY (obtain from friend or purchase online)
- 1 cup starter liquid (kombucha from previous batch)

- 8 cups water
- ½ cup sugar (feeds fermentation—most is consumed by SCOBY)
- 4 tea bags (black or green tea)

Instructions:

1. Boil water.
2. Add tea bags and sugar. Steep 10–15 minutes.
3. Remove tea bags and let tea cool completely.
4. Pour tea into a gallon glass jar.
5. Add starter liquid.
6. Gently place SCOBY on top (it will float).
7. Cover jar with cloth secured with rubber band.
8. Let sit at room temperature for **7–14 days** (taste daily after day 7).
9. When it reaches desired tanginess, bottle in glass bottles.
10. Optional: Add fruit juice for second fermentation (carbonation).
11. Reserve SCOBY and 1 cup kombucha for next batch.

Yield: About 7 cups

How to Use It

For gut health:

- Drink 4–8 oz daily

Start with small amounts (2–4 oz) and increase gradually.

Safety Notes

- Generally safe when made properly
- Contains small amount of alcohol (from fermentation—typically <0.5%)
- Can be too acidic for people with active ulcers or severe reflux
- Ensure proper sanitation during brewing
- Start with small amounts

REMEDY 26: Beet Kvass (Probiotic Tonic)

What It Heals

Beet kvass is a **traditional Russian fermented drink** that:

- Provides probiotics
- Supports liver detoxification
- Improves digestion
- Provides minerals and antioxidants
- Supports blood health

Why It Works

Beets are **rich in betaine**—a compound that supports liver function. Fermentation adds probiotics and makes nutrients more bioavailable.

How to Make It

Ingredients:

- 3 medium beets, peeled and chopped into chunks
- 1 tablespoon sea salt
- Filtered water (non-chlorinated)

Instructions:

1. Place beet chunks in a half-gallon jar (fill about ¼ full).
2. Add salt.
3. Fill jar with filtered water, leaving 2 inches headspace.
4. Cover with cloth or loose lid.
5. Let sit at room temperature for **3–5 days**.

6. Taste—should be slightly salty, earthy, and tangy.
7. Strain out beets (can be used to make a second, weaker batch).
8. Refrigerate liquid.

Yield: About 6 cups

How to Use It

For digestive and liver support:

- Drink 2–4 oz daily (small amounts—it's potent)

Best consumed:

- Before meals (stimulates digestion)
- First thing in morning (supports detox)

Safety Notes

- Very safe
- Start with small amounts (1–2 oz)
- Can have mild laxative effect
- Earthy flavor—not for everyone
- Stains surfaces (beets are messy)

REMEDY 27: Licorice Root DGL and Aloe Gut Repair Formula

What It Heals

This combination provides **comprehensive gut lining repair** for:

- Leaky gut
- Ulcers
- Gastritis
- IBS
- Acid reflux
- Inflammatory bowel disease

Why It Works

Combines **DGL** (increases protective mucus) with **aloe vera** (anti-inflammatory, healing) and **marshmallow root** (soothing demulcent) for synergistic gut repair.

How to Make It

Ingredients:

- 2 tablespoons DGL powder
- 2 tablespoons slippery elm powder
- 1 tablespoon marshmallow root powder
- ¼ cup aloe vera inner leaf gel (fresh or purchased pure gel)

Instructions:

1. Mix all powdered herbs in a bowl.
2. Add aloe gel and stir into a paste.
3. Store in glass jar in refrigerator.

Or make as a drink:

1. Mix 1 tablespoon of powder blend in 8 oz water.
2. Add 2 tablespoons aloe juice.
3. Stir well and drink.

How to Use It

For gut repair:

- Take 1 tablespoon paste (or 1 cup drink), 2–3 times daily on empty stomach

Continue for 8–12 weeks for leaky gut healing.

Safety Notes

- Very safe
- Ensure aloe is inner leaf gel only (not latex)
- Generally well-tolerated
- Safe for long-term use

REMEDY 28: Zinc Carnosine (Gut Lining Protector)

What It Heals

Zinc carnosine is a **chelated zinc supplement** that:

- Heals ulcers
- Repairs leaky gut
- Protects stomach lining from NSAID damage
- Reduces inflammation
- Supports immune function in gut

Why It Works

Zinc carnosine **adheres to the stomach and intestinal lining**, providing sustained release of zinc directly to damaged tissues. It promotes cell regeneration and strengthens tight junctions.

Studies show it heals ulcers as effectively as pharmaceutical drugs.

How to Make It

Note: Zinc carnosine is purchased as a supplement (available at health stores).

Look for: 75 mg zinc carnosine per capsule.

How to Use It

For ulcers or leaky gut:

- Take 75–150 mg, twice daily on an empty stomach
- Continue for 8–12 weeks

For NSAID protection:

- Take 75 mg before taking NSAIDs

Safety Notes

- Very safe
- Do not exceed recommended doses (excess zinc can interfere with copper absorption)
- Generally well-tolerated
- Safe for long-term healing protocols (8–12 weeks)

REMEDY 29: Mastic Gum (H. Pylori Fighter)

What It Heals

Mastic gum is a **resin from the mastic tree** that:

- Kills H. pylori bacteria (causes ulcers)
- Heals stomach ulcers
- Reduces acid reflux
- Has antimicrobial properties
- Freshens breath

Why It Works

Mastic gum contains compounds that **specifically target H. pylori**, disrupting its cell membrane. Studies show it can reduce or eliminate H. pylori in many people.

It's been used in Mediterranean medicine for thousands of years.

How to Make It

Note: Mastic gum is purchased as capsules or as raw gum (available at health stores or Greek markets).

Raw mastic gum:

- Can be chewed (like gum)—releases medicinal compounds

Supplement form:

- Typically 500 mg capsules

How to Use It

For H. pylori:

- Chew ½–1 teaspoon raw mastic gum daily for several minutes, then swallow
- Or take 500 mg capsules, 2–3 times daily
- Continue for 4–8 weeks

For ulcers:

- Take 1 gram daily, divided into 2–3 doses

Safety Notes

- Generally very safe
- Rare allergic reactions
- Can cause mild digestive upset initially
- Safe for most people

REMEDY 30: Digestive Enzyme Supplement Blend

What It Heals

Digestive enzymes **support breakdown of food** when your body's production is insufficient. They:

- Reduce bloating and gas
- Improve nutrient absorption
- Reduce food sensitivities (incomplete digestion creates immune reactions)
- Support pancreatic function
- Relieve indigestion

Why It Works

Many people have **insufficient enzyme production** due to stress, aging, or pancreatic insufficiency. Supplementing with enzymes bridges the gap.

How to Make It

Note: Digestive enzymes are typically purchased as supplements.

Look for full-spectrum blends containing:

- **Protease** (protein digestion)
- **Amylase** (carbohydrate digestion)
- **Lipase** (fat digestion)
- **Lactase** (dairy digestion—if needed)
- **Cellulase** (plant fiber)

Naturally enzyme-rich foods:

- Pineapple (bromelain)
- Papaya (papain)
- Kiwi
- Mango
- Raw honey
- Fermented foods

How to Use It

With meals:

- Take 1–2 enzyme capsules at beginning of each meal

For protein-heavy meals:

- Emphasize protease-rich formulas

For fat-heavy meals:

- Emphasize lipase-rich formulas

Safety Notes

- Very safe for most people
- Start with low doses (can cause digestive upset if too strong initially)
- Not necessary for everyone (some people produce adequate enzymes)

- Safe for long-term use if needed

REMEDY 31: Iberogast (9-Herb Digestive Formula)

What It Heals

Iberogast is a **German herbal formula** (available over-the-counter) that:

- Reduces IBS symptoms (cramping, bloating, pain)
- Improves gut motility
- Reduces nausea
- Relaxes intestinal muscle
- Reduces acid reflux

Why It Works

Contains **9 synergistic herbs** that work on multiple digestive pathways simultaneously:

- Iberis (bitter candytuft)
- Angelica root
- Chamomile
- Caraway
- Milk thistle
- Lemon balm
- Peppermint
- Celandine
- Licorice

Multiple clinical studies support its effectiveness for functional dyspepsia and IBS.

How to Make It

Note: Iberogast is a proprietary formula—purchased as liquid (available at health stores and online).

To make a similar blend at home:

Combine equal parts tinctures:

- Chamomile
- Peppermint
- Lemon balm
- Caraway seed
- Licorice root

How to Use It

For IBS or dyspepsia:

- Take 20 drops in water, 3 times daily before meals

For nausea:

- Take 20 drops as needed

Safety Notes

- Generally very safe
- Well-studied and clinically validated
- Rare allergic reactions
- Safe for long-term use

REMEDY 32: Oregano Oil (Antimicrobial)

What It Heals

Oregano oil is a **powerful broad-spectrum antimicrobial** that:

- Kills harmful bacteria, viruses, fungi, and parasites
- Treats SIBO
- Eliminates Candida overgrowth
- Reduces intestinal infections
- Supports immune function

Why It Works

Oregano oil contains **carvacrol and thymol**—compounds with proven antimicrobial activity against a wide range of pathogens.

It's as effective as some antibiotics—without promoting resistance.

How to Make It

Note: True medicinal-strength oregano essential oil requires steam distillation. Most people purchase high-quality oregano essential oil.

Look for: At least 70% carvacrol content.

See Chapter 6, Remedy 8 for infused oil method (milder than essential oil).

How to Use It

For SIBO or dysbiosis:

- Dilute 2–3 drops essential oil in 1 tablespoon carrier oil (olive, coconut)
- Take in capsule or under tongue, 2–3 times daily
- Continue for 2–4 weeks

For Candida:

- Take 2–3 drops diluted essential oil, twice daily for 4–6 weeks

Topically:

- Dilute heavily and apply to fungal infections

Safety Notes

- **Very potent—always dilute**
- Can irritate mucous membranes if too concentrated
- Short-term use only (2–4 weeks—can disrupt beneficial bacteria with prolonged use)
- Not for children under 2
- Avoid during pregnancy

REMEDY 33: Artichoke Leaf Extract (Bile Stimulant)

What It Heals

Artichoke leaf is a **choleretic** (stimulates bile production) that:

- Improves fat digestion
- Reduces bloating after fatty meals
- Supports liver function
- Lowers cholesterol
- Reduces nausea

Why It Works

Artichoke contains **cynarin and silymarin**—compounds that increase bile production and flow. **Bile is essential for fat digestion**—insufficient bile causes bloating, nausea, and fat malabsorption.

How to Make It

Artichoke Leaf Tea:

Ingredients:

- 2 teaspoons dried artichoke leaf
- 2 cups hot water

Instructions:

1. Place artichoke leaf in teapot.
2. Pour hot water over leaves.
3. Steep 10–15 minutes.
4. Strain.
5. Drink before meals.

Artichoke Leaf Tincture:

Follow standard tincture method (1 part dried leaf to 5 parts alcohol, 4–6 weeks).

Or purchase: Artichoke extract supplements.

How to Use It

For fat digestion:

- Drink 1 cup tea before fatty meals
- Or take 300–600 mg extract before meals

For liver support:

- Take 300 mg extract, twice daily

Safety Notes

- Very safe
- May cause increased bowel movements (bile is a natural laxative)
- Avoid if you have gallstones or bile duct obstruction
- Generally well-tolerated

REMEDY 34: Cumin, Coriander, Fennel Tea (CCF Tea - Ayurvedic Digestive)

What It Heals

CCF tea is a **traditional Ayurvedic digestive blend** that:

- Reduces gas and bloating
- Improves digestion
- Balances all three doshas (Ayurvedic constitution types)
- Gently detoxifies
- Reduces inflammation

Why It Works

This gentle blend combines three **carminative seeds** that work synergistically to support digestion without being harsh or depleting.

It's safe for daily, long-term use.

How to Make It

Ingredients:

- 1 teaspoon cumin seeds
- 1 teaspoon coriander seeds
- 1 teaspoon fennel seeds
- 3 cups water

Instructions:

1. Combine all seeds in a pot with water.
2. Bring to a boil.
3. Reduce heat and simmer 5–10 minutes.
4. Strain into a thermos.
5. Sip throughout the day.

Can be made fresh daily or in larger batches.

How to Use It

For general digestive support:

- Sip 1–3 cups throughout the day (Ayurveda recommends room temperature)

For bloating:

- Drink 1 cup after meals

For detox:

- Drink 3–4 cups daily

Safety Notes

- Extremely safe
- Suitable for all ages and constitutions
- Safe for pregnancy and nursing
- Can be used daily long-term

REMEDY 35: Okra Mucilage Drink (Gut Soother)

What It Heals

Okra is a **mucilaginous vegetable** that:

- Soothes inflamed gut lining
- Reduces acid reflux
- Supports regular bowel movements
- Provides prebiotic fiber
- Binds toxins

Why It Works

Okra is extremely high in **mucilage**—similar to marshmallow root and slippery elm. When soaked in water, it releases a gel-like substance that coats and soothes the digestive tract.

How to Make It

Ingredients:

- 4–5 fresh okra pods
- 2 cups water

Instructions:

1. Wash okra pods.
2. Cut off ends and slice in half lengthwise.
3. Place in a jar with water.
4. Cover and refrigerate overnight.
5. In the morning, the water will be thick and gel-like.
6. Strain out okra (or eat it).
7. Drink the mucilaginous water.

How to Use It

For gut inflammation:

- Drink okra water first thing in morning on empty stomach

For acid reflux:

- Drink ½ cup before meals

Safety Notes

- Very safe
- Generally well-tolerated
- Some people dislike the texture
- Safe for daily use

REMEDY 36: Chia Seed Mucilage Gel

What It Heals

Chia seeds create a **soothing gel** that:

- Soothes gut lining
- Provides soluble fiber (supports bowel movements)
- Feeds beneficial bacteria (prebiotic)
- Reduces inflammation
- Supports hydration

Why It Works

When soaked, chia seeds release **mucilage** that coats the gut. They also provide omega-3 fatty acids (anti-inflammatory) and fiber.

How to Make It

Ingredients:

- 2 tablespoons chia seeds
- 1 cup water or non-dairy milk

Instructions:

1. Mix chia seeds into liquid.
2. Stir well.
3. Let sit 10–15 minutes (seeds will swell and create gel).

4. Stir again before consuming.

Can add:

- Honey
- Cinnamon
- Fruit
- Vanilla

How to Use It

For gut health:

- Eat chia gel 1–2 times daily

For constipation:

- Eat chia gel in morning with plenty of water

Safety Notes

- Very safe
- **Must drink adequate water** (chia absorbs a lot of liquid)
- Start with small amounts (can cause gas initially)
- Safe for daily use

REMEDY 37: Manuka Honey (Antimicrobial Gut Healer)

What It Heals

Manuka honey is **medical-grade honey** from New Zealand that:

- Kills H. pylori bacteria
- Heals ulcers
- Has powerful antimicrobial properties
- Soothes inflamed tissues
- Supports wound healing internally and externally

Why It Works

Manuka honey contains **methylglyoxal (MGO)**—a compound with unique antimicrobial properties not found in other honeys. It's been clinically proven to kill antibiotic-resistant bacteria.

How to Make It

Note: Manuka honey must be purchased (from specific New Zealand tea trees).

Look for:

- **UMF (Unique Manuka Factor) rating of 10+ for medicinal use**
- UMF 15+ or MGO 400+ for strong antimicrobial action

How to Use It

For H. pylori or ulcers:

- Take 1 tablespoon raw manuka honey (UMF 15+), 3 times daily on empty stomach
- Hold in mouth briefly before swallowing (coats throat and esophagus)

For general gut healing:

- Take 1 teaspoon manuka honey daily

For sore throat:

- Let dissolve slowly in mouth

Safety Notes

- Very safe
- Not for infants under 1 year
- Diabetics should monitor blood sugar
- Generally well-tolerated

REMEDY 38: Cabbage Poultice for External Gut Pain

What It Heals

A cabbage poultice applied externally can **reduce abdominal pain and inflammation** from:

- IBS cramping
- Inflammatory bowel disease
- Gastritis
- Ulcers
- Abdominal bloating

Why It Works

The same compounds in cabbage that heal internal ulcers also work topically through the skin. Cabbage has **drawing and anti-inflammatory properties**.

This is a traditional folk remedy used across cultures.

How to Make It

Instructions:

1. Take 2–3 fresh cabbage leaves.
2. Remove thick center stem.
3. Pound or roll leaves with rolling pin to bruise and release juices.
4. Warm leaves slightly (place in warm water or microwave briefly—test temperature).
5. Place warm, bruised leaves over painful area of abdomen.
6. Cover with cloth or towel.
7. Leave on for 30–60 minutes.
8. Repeat 2–3 times daily as needed.

How to Use It

For acute cramping:

- Apply fresh poultice and rest

For chronic pain:

- Apply nightly before bed

Safety Notes

- Very safe
- External use only
- Generally well-tolerated
- May have cabbage smell

REMEDY 39: Bentonite Clay Internal Detox Drink

What It Heals

Bentonite clay is a **powerful detoxifying clay** that:

- Binds toxins and heavy metals
- Absorbs harmful bacteria
- Supports gut healing
- Reduces bloating
- Cleanses digestive tract

Why It Works

Bentonite clay has a **negative electrical charge** that attracts and binds positively-charged toxins, heavy metals, and pathogens. It then carries them out of the body.

It's been used for centuries for internal cleansing.

How to Make It

Ingredients:

- 1 teaspoon food-grade bentonite clay

- 8 oz water (filtered or distilled)

Instructions:

1. Mix bentonite clay into water (use glass or wooden spoon—not metal).
2. Stir well and let sit 5 minutes.
3. Stir again before drinking.
4. Drink on empty stomach.
5. Follow with another glass of water.

Important: Only use **food-grade bentonite clay** (not industrial clay).

How to Use It

For detoxification:

- Drink 1 cup clay water in morning on empty stomach
- Wait 30 minutes before eating
- Use for 1–2 weeks at a time (not continuously)

For acute food poisoning:

- Take 1 teaspoon clay in water, 2–3 times daily until symptoms resolve

Safety Notes

- Generally safe for short-term use
- **Can cause constipation**—drink plenty of water
- Take **2 hours away from food and medications** (binds to everything)
- Not for long-term daily use (can bind nutrients)
- Use only food-grade clay

REMEDY 40: Full-Spectrum Gut Healing Protocol (Comprehensive 4-Week Reset)

What It Heals

This is a **complete gut restoration protocol** combining the most effective remedies into a structured healing plan for:

- Leaky gut
- IBS
- SIBO
- IBD
- Chronic bloating and digestive dysfunction

Why It Works

Healing the gut requires a **multi-phase approach**:

1. **Remove** (eliminate pathogens, toxins, inflammatory foods)
2. **Replace** (digestive enzymes, stomach acid)
3. **Reinoculate** (beneficial bacteria)
4. **Repair** (heal gut lining)
5. **Rebalance** (support ongoing health)

This protocol addresses all five phases.

CHAPTER 6: LIVER & DETOX REMEDIES

Focus: Cellular Cleansing and Energy

REMEDY 1: Milk Thistle Tincture (Liver Regenerator)

What It Heals

Milk thistle is the **king of liver herbs**. It:

- Regenerates damaged liver cells
- Protects liver from toxins (alcohol, medications, chemicals, heavy metals)
- Treats fatty liver disease
- Supports recovery from hepatitis and cirrhosis
- Increases glutathione production (master antioxidant)
- Reduces liver inflammation
- Improves liver enzyme levels

Why It Works

Milk thistle contains **silymarin**—a complex of flavonolignans with extraordinary liver-protective properties. Silymarin:

- **Blocks toxins from entering liver cells** (sits on cell membranes, preventing penetration)
- **Stimulates protein synthesis** (helps liver regenerate new tissue)
- **Acts as a powerful antioxidant** (protects cells from free radical damage)
- **Increases glutathione by up to 35%** (the body's most important detox molecule)
- **Reduces fibrosis** (scarring of liver tissue)

Studies show milk thistle can **reverse liver damage** from alcohol, medications, hepatitis, and fatty liver disease.

How to Make It

Ingredients:

- 1 part freshly ground milk thistle seeds
- 5 parts vodka or brandy (60% alcohol)

Instructions:

1. Grind milk thistle seeds in a coffee grinder (must be fresh—pre-ground seeds lose potency quickly).
2. Place ground seeds in a glass jar immediately.
3. Cover with alcohol, ensuring seeds are submerged.
4. Seal jar tightly.
5. Shake vigorously daily.
6. Let sit for 4–6 weeks.
7. Strain through cheesecloth.
8. Bottle in amber dropper bottles.
9. Label with date.

Important: Milk thistle seeds must be ground fresh—silymarin degrades rapidly once seeds are broken.

Yield: Varies by jar size

How to Use It

For liver protection (prevention):

- Take 2–3 mL (40–60 drops), 3 times daily with meals

For liver damage or disease:

- Take 3–4 mL (60–80 drops), 3 times daily

- Continue for several months

For alcohol or medication use:

- Take 3 mL before and after alcohol or medication exposure

Can also use:

- Freshly ground seeds: 1–2 teaspoons daily in smoothies or sprinkled on food
- Standardized extract: 200–400 mg silymarin, 3 times daily

Safety Notes

- Extremely safe—even for long-term use
- Rare mild digestive upset (take with food if needed)
- May have mild laxative effect initially (bile stimulation)
- Safe during pregnancy and nursing (consult practitioner)
- Generally well-tolerated

REMEDY 2: Dandelion Root Liver Decoction

What It Heals

Dandelion root is a **gentle but powerful liver and kidney tonic**. It:

- Stimulates bile production (essential for fat digestion and toxin elimination)
- Supports liver detoxification
- Acts as a mild diuretic (flushes kidneys)
- Reduces liver inflammation
- Supports healthy cholesterol levels
- Improves digestion
- Provides minerals (potassium, calcium, iron)

Why It Works

Dandelion root contains **bitter compounds (taraxacin) and inulin** (prebiotic fiber) that:

- Stimulate bile flow from liver and gallbladder
- Support Phase 2 liver detoxification
- Feed beneficial gut bacteria
- Provide gentle, sustained detoxification without harsh reactions

It's called dandelion because the leaves look like "dent de lion" (lion's teeth)—and this "weed" is more valuable than most plants in your garden.

How to Make It

Ingredients:

- 2 tablespoons dried dandelion root (chopped or powdered)
- 4 cups water

Instructions:

1. Place dandelion root in a pot with water.
2. Bring to a boil.
3. Reduce heat and simmer for 20–30 minutes.
4. Strain into a jar or mug.
5. Drink throughout the day.

Yield: About 3 cups

Roasted dandelion "coffee":

1. Roast dried dandelion root in oven at 350°F for 20–30 minutes until dark brown.
2. Grind and brew like coffee.
3. Delicious, caffeine-free liver tonic.

How to Use It

For liver support:

- Drink 2–3 cups daily, long-term

For detoxification:

- Drink 3–4 cups daily for 4–6 weeks

For digestion (bitter action):

- Drink 1 cup before meals

As coffee substitute:

- Drink roasted dandelion coffee in morning

Safety Notes

- Very safe for long-term use
- Mild diuretic effect (stay hydrated)
- May increase bowel movements (bile stimulation)
- Avoid if you have gallstones or bile duct obstruction (consult practitioner)
- Safe during pregnancy

REMEDY 3: Burdock Root Blood Purifier

What It Heals

Burdock is a **deep blood cleanser and lymphatic mover**. It:

- Cleanses blood of metabolic waste
- Supports liver detoxification
- Clears skin conditions (acne, eczema, psoriasis)
- Moves lymphatic fluid (reduces swelling)
- Supports kidney function
- Reduces inflammation
- Contains powerful antioxidants

Why It Works

Burdock contains **inulin, polyacetylenes, and arctigenin** that:

- Support Phase 2 liver detoxification
- Bind toxins in the bloodstream
- Stimulate lymphatic drainage
- Reduce inflammatory markers

Traditional herbalists call it an "alterative"—an herb that **gradually restores proper function** to the body by supporting elimination.

How to Make It

Burdock Root Decoction:

Ingredients:

- 2 tablespoons dried burdock root (chopped)
- 4 cups water

Instructions:

1. Place burdock root in pot with water.
2. Bring to a boil.
3. Reduce heat and simmer 30–40 minutes.
4. Strain.
5. Drink throughout the day.

Burdock Root Tincture:

Follow standard tincture method (1 part root to 5 parts alcohol, 50–60%, 4–6 weeks).

How to Use It

For blood cleansing:

- Drink 2–3 cups decoction daily for 4–6 weeks
- Or take 2–3 mL tincture, 3 times daily

For skin conditions:

- Drink 3 cups daily, long-term (skin improvement may take 4–8 weeks)

For lymphatic congestion:

- Combine internal use with dry brushing and movement

Safety Notes

- Very safe for long-term use
- Mild diuretic—stay hydrated
- Can increase urination and bowel movements
- Rare allergic reactions (related to Asteraceae family)
- Safe during pregnancy

REMEDY 4: Liver Flush Protocol (Gallstone and Congestion Cleanse)

What It Heals

A liver flush is a **traditional cleanse** that:

- Expels gallstones and liver stones
- Clears bile duct congestion
- Improves fat digestion
- Increases energy
- Reduces right shoulder pain (referred from liver)
- Improves skin clarity

Why It Works

The liver produces bile constantly. When bile becomes thick and sludgy (from poor diet, toxins, stress), it can form stones in the liver and gallbladder. These stones block bile flow, impairing detoxification.

The flush uses **olive oil, citrus juice, and Epsom salts** to:

- Dilate bile ducts
- Stimulate massive bile release
- Flush out stones and sludge

This is controversial in conventional medicine but has been used successfully by herbalists and naturopaths for decades.

How to Make It

Classic Liver Flush (2-Day Protocol):

Preparation (Days 1–5 before flush):

- Eat light, whole foods
- Drink apple juice or take malic acid supplement (softens stones)
- Avoid fats, dairy, fried foods

Day of Flush:

Morning to 2 PM:

- Eat light breakfast and lunch (no fats)
- After 2 PM: nothing to eat

6 PM:

- Drink 1 tablespoon Epsom salts dissolved in ¾ cup water

8 PM:

- Drink 1 tablespoon Epsom salts dissolved in ¾ cup water

9:45 PM:

- Mix: ½ cup olive oil + ½ cup fresh-squeezed grapefruit juice (or lemon/orange)
- Shake vigorously
- Drink entire mixture quickly (within 5 minutes)
- Lie down immediately on right side with knees to chest for 20 minutes

Next Morning:

6 AM:

- Drink 1 tablespoon Epsom salts in ¾ cup water

8 AM:

- Drink 1 tablespoon Epsom salts in ¾ cup water

10 AM:

- May eat light fruit or juice

Expected: Multiple bowel movements throughout morning/afternoon. Look for green, tan, or brown stones (pea-sized to marble-sized) in stool.

How to Use It

Frequency:

- Perform flush 1–2 times per year (or as needed)
- Some practitioners recommend doing flushes every 2–4 weeks until no more stones are expelled

After flush:

- Eat light, easy-to-digest foods for 2–3 days
- Support liver with herbs and supplements

Safety Notes

- **Do not attempt if you have active gallbladder disease or large gallstones** (risk of stone lodging in bile duct—requires medical intervention)
- Not for pregnant or nursing women
- Can cause nausea and discomfort
- Expect multiple bowel movements
- Controversial—some doctors dispute effectiveness
- Consider working with experienced practitioner
- Stay home and near bathroom during flush

REMEDY 5: Castor Oil Pack (External Liver Support)

What It Heals

Castor oil packs applied over the liver provide **deep detoxification support**. They:

- Stimulate liver function
- Increase lymphatic drainage
- Reduce liver inflammation
- Improve circulation to liver
- Support bile flow
- Relieve right-sided abdominal pain
- Improve sleep and relaxation

Why It Works

Castor oil contains **ricinoleic acid**—a unique fatty acid that penetrates deeply through skin, increasing lymphatic flow and reducing inflammation.

Applied with heat over the liver area, it creates a **therapeutic effect** that supports the liver's natural detoxification processes.

This ancient remedy was popularized by Edgar Cayce and is used by naturopaths worldwide.

How to Make It

Materials:

- Cold-pressed, hexane-free castor oil
- Flannel cloth (wool or cotton, large enough to cover liver area)
- Plastic wrap or old towel
- Heating pad or hot water bottle
- Old sheets/towels (castor oil stains)

Instructions:

1. Lie on back on protected surface.
2. Saturate flannel cloth with castor oil (enough to be wet but not dripping).
3. Place cloth over liver area (right upper abdomen, under ribcage).
4. Cover with plastic wrap.
5. Place heating pad on top (medium heat).

6. Relax for 45–60 minutes.
7. Remove pack and clean skin with baking soda solution (1 teaspoon baking soda in 2 cups water).
8. Store cloth in jar (can reuse many times—just add more oil as needed).

How to Use It

For liver support:

- Apply 3–4 times per week

During detox protocols:

- Apply nightly

For deep cleansing:

- Use daily for 3–4 weeks

Best time: Evening before bed (promotes deep relaxation and sleep)

Safety Notes

- Very safe
- Messy—use old sheets and towels
- Avoid during menstruation (increases flow)
- Not during pregnancy
- Not over open wounds or broken skin
- Generally well-tolerated

REMEDY 6: Lemon Water Liver Flush (Daily Morning Ritual)

What It Heals

Starting the day with lemon water provides **gentle, daily liver stimulation**. It:

- Stimulates bile production
- Alkalizes the body
- Supports liver detoxification
- Provides vitamin C
- Improves digestion
- Hydrates after overnight fast
- Supports immune function

Why It Works

Lemon juice stimulates the liver to produce bile—your body's natural detergent for breaking down fats and eliminating toxins.

Drinking it first thing in the morning (before food) **primes your digestive system** and supports the liver's natural detoxification that occurs overnight.

Despite being acidic, lemon becomes **alkaline** once metabolized, supporting pH balance.

How to Make It

Ingredients:

- ½–1 fresh lemon
- 8–12 oz warm water (not hot—preserves vitamin C)
- Optional: pinch of cayenne pepper (increases circulation)

Instructions:

1. Squeeze fresh lemon into warm water.
2. Add cayenne if using.
3. Drink on empty stomach first thing in the morning.
4. Wait 15–30 minutes before eating breakfast.

Upgrade: Add 1 teaspoon raw apple cider vinegar and 1 teaspoon raw honey for additional benefits.

How to Use It

Daily ritual:

- Drink every morning upon waking

During detox:

- Drink 2–3 times daily (morning, midday, evening)

Long-term practice:

- Safe for indefinite daily use

Safety Notes

- Very safe
- Can damage tooth enamel—rinse mouth with water after or drink through a straw
- May worsen acid reflux in sensitive individuals (though it often helps)
- Safe during pregnancy
- Start with half a lemon if sensitive

REMEDY 7: Turmeric Liver Tonic

What It Heals

Turmeric is a **powerful liver protector and anti-inflammatory**. It:

- Protects liver cells from toxins
- Reduces liver inflammation
- Supports bile production
- Aids fat digestion
- Protects against fatty liver disease
- Supports liver regeneration
- Acts as powerful antioxidant

Why It Works

Curcumin (turmeric's active compound) increases bile production, protects liver cells from damage, and reduces inflammatory markers throughout the body.

Studies show turmeric can **reverse early-stage fatty liver disease** and protect against chemical-induced liver damage.

How to Make It

Turmeric Liver Tonic (Daily Drink):

Ingredients:

- 1 teaspoon turmeric powder (or 1 tablespoon fresh grated turmeric)
- ¼ teaspoon black pepper (increases absorption 2,000%)
- 1 tablespoon coconut oil or olive oil
- 1 cup warm water or non-dairy milk
- Raw honey to taste
- Optional: 1 teaspoon cinnamon, pinch of ginger

Instructions:

1. Mix turmeric, black pepper, and oil in a mug.
2. Add warm liquid and stir well.
3. Add honey and optional spices.
4. Drink daily.

Or use golden paste (see Chapter 7, Remedy 1) in warm water or milk.

How to Use It

For liver protection:

- Drink 1 cup daily

During detox or exposure to toxins:

- Drink 2 cups daily

With alcohol or medication use:

- Drink 1 cup before and after exposure

Safety Notes

- Very safe for daily use

- May cause loose stools in high doses
- Stains everything—be careful
- Mild blood-thinning effect
- Therapeutic doses: avoid during pregnancy (culinary amounts safe)

REMEDY 8: Schisandra Berry Liver Tonic

What It Heals

Schisandra is called the **"five-flavor berry"** in Chinese medicine. It:

- Protects liver from toxins
- Increases liver enzymes that detoxify chemicals
- Supports Phase 1 and Phase 2 detoxification
- Reduces liver inflammation
- Improves mental clarity and focus
- Acts as adaptogen (stress support)
- Enhances physical endurance

Why It Works

Schisandra contains **lignans (schisandrin, schisandrol)** that induce production of glutathione-S-transferase and other Phase 2 detox enzymes.

It's been extensively studied in Russia and China for **protecting liver from chemical exposure** (including alcohol and medications).

How to Make It

Schisandra Tea:

Ingredients:

- 1 tablespoon dried schisandra berries
- 3 cups water

Instructions:

1. Place berries in pot with water.
2. Bring to a boil.
3. Reduce heat and simmer 20–30 minutes.
4. Strain (or leave berries in—they're edible).
5. Drink throughout the day.

Schisandra Tincture:

Follow standard tincture method (1 part berries to 5 parts alcohol, 50–60%, 4–6 weeks).

How to Use It

For liver protection:

- Drink 2–3 cups tea daily or take 2–3 mL tincture, twice daily

For detox support:

- Take 3 mL tincture, 3 times daily during exposure to toxins

For energy and focus:

- Drink 1 cup tea in morning

Safety Notes

- Very safe for long-term use
- Mild stimulant effect (some people feel energized)
- Can cause mild digestive upset initially
- Generally well-tolerated
- Safe during pregnancy (consult practitioner)

REMEDY 9: Artichoke and Milk Thistle Liver Repair Formula

What It Heals

This synergistic blend combines **two of the most powerful liver herbs**. It:

- Regenerates liver tissue

- Stimulates bile production
- Protects from toxins
- Reduces liver inflammation
- Lowers cholesterol
- Improves fat digestion
- Supports recovery from liver disease

Why It Works

Milk thistle regenerates liver cells and protects from damage.
Artichoke stimulates bile flow and improves liver function.

Together, they create a **comprehensive liver healing formula**.

How to Make It

Ingredients:

- Equal parts milk thistle seed tincture
- Equal parts artichoke leaf tincture
- Or combine dried herbs for tea

Tincture Blend:

1. Mix equal amounts of both tinctures in a bottle.
2. Label and date.

Tea Blend:

Ingredients:

- 1 tablespoon freshly ground milk thistle seeds
- 1 tablespoon dried artichoke leaf
- 4 cups water

Instructions:

1. Simmer artichoke leaf in water for 15 minutes.
2. Remove from heat.
3. Add milk thistle seeds.
4. Steep 10 minutes.
5. Strain.

How to Use It

For liver disease or damage:

- Take 3 mL tincture blend, 3 times daily
- Or drink 3 cups tea daily

For prevention:

- Take 2 mL tincture, twice daily
- Or drink 2 cups tea daily

Safety Notes

- Very safe
- Generally well-tolerated
- May increase bowel movements (bile stimulation)
- Safe for long-term use

REMEDY 10: Chlorella Heavy Metal Chelator

What It Heals

Chlorella is a **freshwater algae** that:

- Binds heavy metals (mercury, lead, cadmium, arsenic)
- Supports liver detoxification
- Provides complete protein and nutrients
- Boosts immune function
- Increases glutathione production
- Binds environmental toxins

Why It Works

Chlorella has a **unique cell wall structure** that binds to heavy metals and toxins in the digestive tract, preventing reabsorption and carrying them out of the body.

It's one of the most effective natural chelators available.

How to Make It

Note: Chlorella must be purchased as powder or tablets (it's an algae, not a plant you can grow at home).

Look for:

- "Broken cell wall" chlorella (better absorption)
- Organic, tested for purity

How to Use It

For heavy metal detox:

- Take 3–6 grams (about 1–2 teaspoons powder or 10–20 tablets) daily
- Gradually increase dose over several weeks

During dental work (mercury filling removal):

- Take 6 grams before and after procedure

For general detox:

- Take 3 grams daily, long-term

Can add to:

- Smoothies
- Juice
- Water

Safety Notes

- Very safe
- Start with small amounts (can cause detox symptoms—headache, fatigue—if started too quickly)
- Some people experience digestive upset initially
- May turn stool dark green (normal)
- Generally well-tolerated
- Safe for long-term use

REMEDY 11: Cilantro Heavy Metal Mobilizer

What It Heals

Cilantro (coriander leaf) is a **powerful heavy metal mobilizer**. It:

- Mobilizes mercury, lead, and aluminum from tissues (especially brain and nervous system)
- Crosses the blood-brain barrier (unique among herbs)
- Supports liver detoxification
- Provides antioxidants
- Reduces inflammation
- Supports cardiovascular health

Why It Works

Cilantro contains **compounds that chelate heavy metals** from deep tissues—particularly the brain and central nervous system where most chelators can't reach.

Critical pairing: Cilantro MUST be combined with a **binder** (chlorella, activated charcoal, bentonite clay) because it mobilizes metals into circulation. Without a binder, metals can redistribute and cause harm.

How to Make It

Cilantro Heavy Metal Detox Protocol:

Method 1: Fresh Cilantro Juice/Smoothie

Ingredients:

- 1 cup fresh cilantro (packed)
- 1 apple or pear
- 1 cup water or coconut water

- Juice of ½ lime
- Optional: cucumber, celery

Instructions:

1. Blend all ingredients until smooth.
2. Drink immediately (on empty stomach for best absorption).
3. Wait 30 minutes, then take chlorella (3–6 grams) to bind mobilized metals.

Method 2: Cilantro Tincture

Ingredients:

- 1 part fresh cilantro (chopped)
- 2 parts vodka (40% alcohol)

Instructions:

1. Pack fresh cilantro in jar.
2. Cover with alcohol.
3. Let sit 2–3 weeks, shaking daily.
4. Strain and bottle.

How to Use It

For heavy metal detox:

- Drink cilantro smoothie daily for 2–4 weeks
- ALWAYS follow with chlorella 30 minutes later
- Or take 2–3 mL cilantro tincture, twice daily, followed by chlorella

Cycle: 2–4 weeks on, 1 week off, repeat as needed

Safety Notes

- **Must combine with binder** (chlorella, activated charcoal)—cilantro mobilizes but doesn't eliminate
- Can cause detox reactions (headache, fatigue, irritability) if done too aggressively
- Start slowly and increase gradually
- Not for pregnant or nursing women
- Support detox with plenty of water, rest, and liver support herbs

---

REMEDY 12: Spirulina Protein and Detox Superfood

What It Heals

Spirulina is a **blue-green algae** that:

- Binds heavy metals (especially arsenic)
- Provides complete protein (60–70% protein by weight)
- Supports liver detoxification
- Boosts immune function
- Provides B vitamins, iron, and trace minerals
- Reduces oxidative stress
- Has anti-inflammatory properties

Why It Works

Spirulina contains **phycocyanin**—a blue pigment with powerful antioxidant and detoxifying properties. Studies show it's particularly effective at reducing **arsenic toxicity** (common water contaminant).

It also provides **complete nutrition** during detox when appetite may be reduced.

How to Make It

Note: Spirulina is purchased as powder or tablets.

Look for: Organic, tested for purity (avoid spirulina from contaminated waters).

Spirulina Detox Smoothie:

Ingredients:

- 1 teaspoon spirulina powder

- 1 banana
- 1 cup berries
- 1 tablespoon almond butter
- 1 cup non-dairy milk or coconut water
- Handful of spinach
- Optional: 1 teaspoon chlorella

Instructions:

1. Blend all ingredients until smooth.
2. Drink for breakfast or post-workout.

How to Use It

For detoxification:

- Take 3–5 grams (about 1 teaspoon) daily in smoothies or water

For arsenic exposure:

- Take 5–10 grams daily during exposure or detox

For nutrition:

- Add to smoothies, juice, or mix into energy balls

Safety Notes

- Very safe
- Strong taste (earthy, seaweed-like)—blend with fruit to mask
- May turn stool slightly greenish
- Rare allergic reactions (discontinue if rash occurs)
- Can contain iodine—those with thyroid conditions should consult practitioner
- Generally well-tolerated

REMEDY 13: NAC (N-Acetyl Cysteine) Glutathione Booster

What It Heals

NAC is an **amino acid precursor to glutathione**—your body's master antioxidant. It:

- Increases glutathione production (primary liver detoxifier)
- Protects liver from acetaminophen (Tylenol) overdose
- Supports Phase 2 detoxification
- Breaks up mucus (respiratory support)
- Protects brain from oxidative damage
- Reduces inflammation
- Supports recovery from addiction

Why It Works

Glutathione is the liver's most important detoxification molecule—it binds to toxins and carries them out. When glutathione is depleted (from toxin overload, stress, poor nutrition), detoxification fails.

NAC provides the **building blocks** your body needs to make more glutathione.

It's used in emergency rooms for **acetaminophen poisoning**—it literally saves lives by preventing liver failure.

How to Make It

Note: NAC is purchased as a supplement (amino acid, not a plant).

Available forms:

- Capsules (typically 600–1,000 mg)
- Powder

How to Use It

For liver support and detoxification:

- Take 600–1,200 mg, 1–2 times daily on empty stomach

For acetaminophen use or exposure to toxins:

- Take 1,200 mg before and after exposure

For respiratory support:

- Take 600 mg, 2–3 times daily

For addiction recovery:

- Take 1,200–2,400 mg daily (consult practitioner)

Safety Notes

- Very safe
- May cause mild digestive upset (take with food if needed)
- Rare allergic reactions
- Can thin mucus (beneficial for most, may feel unusual initially)
- Consult doctor if on nitroglycerin or blood thinners
- Generally well-tolerated

REMEDY 14: Alpha Lipoic Acid (Universal Antioxidant)

What It Heals

Alpha lipoic acid (ALA) is called the **"universal antioxidant"** because it works in both water and fat. It:

- Supports liver detoxification
- Chelates heavy metals (mercury, arsenic, lead)
- Protects nerve cells (treats diabetic neuropathy)
- Regenerates other antioxidants (vitamin C, vitamin E, glutathione)
- Reduces inflammation
- Supports blood sugar balance
- Protects brain and nervous system

Why It Works

ALA is **both fat-soluble and water-soluble**, so it works throughout the entire body—crossing the blood-brain barrier and entering fat tissue.

It **chelates heavy metals** and regenerates depleted antioxidants, creating a comprehensive detoxification and protection system.

How to Make It

Note: Alpha lipoic acid is purchased as a supplement.

Look for: R-lipoic acid (more bioavailable form) if available.

How to Use It

For detoxification:

- Take 300–600 mg daily with food

For heavy metal chelation:

- Take 600 mg, twice daily (under practitioner guidance for heavy metal protocols)

For diabetic neuropathy:

- Take 600 mg, 2–3 times daily

For general antioxidant support:

- Take 300 mg daily

Safety Notes

- Very safe
- Can lower blood sugar (monitor if diabetic)
- Take with food (better absorbed and reduces nausea)

- May cause mild body odor in some people (temporary)
- Generally well-tolerated

REMEDY 15: Liver-Supporting Green Juice

What It Heals

Fresh green juice provides **concentrated nutrients and chlorophyll** that:

- Alkalize the body
- Support liver detoxification
- Provide enzymes, vitamins, and minerals
- Reduce inflammation
- Increase energy
- Support cellular repair
- Bind and eliminate toxins

Why It Works

Chlorophyll (the green pigment in plants) has a molecular structure similar to hemoglobin. It:

- Binds to toxins and heavy metals
- Oxygenates cells
- Supports liver function
- Provides magnesium

Fresh juice is **pre-digested** (fiber removed), so nutrients are rapidly absorbed without requiring digestive energy.

How to Make It

Liver-Loving Green Juice Recipe:

Ingredients:

- 3–4 stalks celery
- 1 cucumber
- 1 green apple (or pear)
- 2 cups leafy greens (spinach, kale, or romaine)
- ½ lemon (peeled)
- 1-inch piece ginger
- Optional: handful parsley or cilantro (liver cleansers)

Instructions:

1. Wash all produce thoroughly.
2. Run through juicer.
3. Drink immediately (within 15 minutes for maximum enzyme activity).
4. Drink on empty stomach for best absorption.

Yield: About 16 oz

How to Use It

For detoxification:

- Drink 16 oz fresh green juice every morning on empty stomach

During juice cleanse:

- Drink 3–4 green juices daily (replace meals)

For maintenance:

- Drink 8–16 oz, 3–4 times per week

Pro tip: Drink slowly—"chew" your juice to mix with saliva for better digestion.

Safety Notes

- Very safe
- High in vitamin K (consult doctor if on blood thinners)
- Can be too cleansing if started aggressively (detox symptoms)
- Start with 8 oz and increase gradually

- May cause increased bowel movements (this is beneficial)
- Safe for most people

REMEDY 16: Coffee Enema (Advanced Liver Detox)

What It Heals

Coffee enemas are a **powerful liver detoxification tool** used in the Gerson Therapy. They:

- Stimulate bile flow dramatically (increases bile production up to 600%)
- Open bile ducts
- Support Phase 2 liver detoxification
- Reduce toxicity during cancer treatment
- Relieve pain (produces glutathione)
- Clear toxins during intensive detox protocols
- Provide immediate relief from toxic overload

Why It Works

When coffee is absorbed through the **rectal wall**, it travels directly to the **liver via the hemorrhoidal vein**. This creates an intense stimulus that:

- Causes bile ducts to open and release stored toxins
- Increases production of glutathione-S-transferase (master detox enzyme)
- Produces a parasympathetic response (relaxation, pain relief)

This is NOT about the caffeine—it's about specific compounds (palmitates) that stimulate liver detoxification.

How to Make It

Coffee Enema Preparation:

Ingredients:

- 2–3 tablespoons organic, light-roast coffee (NOT instant, NOT decaf)
- 1 quart (4 cups) filtered or distilled water
- Enema kit (available at pharmacies or online)

Instructions:

1. Boil water.
2. Add coffee and simmer 10–15 minutes.
3. Strain out grounds.
4. Let cool to body temperature (test on wrist—should be lukewarm, NOT hot).
5. Pour into enema bag.
6. Lubricate enema tip with coconut oil.
7. Lie on right side on towel on bathroom floor.
8. Insert tip gently into rectum.
9. Release clamp and allow coffee to flow in slowly.
10. Hold for 12–15 minutes (if possible).
11. Release into toilet.

How to Use It

During intensive detox:

- Perform 1–2 times daily

For chronic illness or cancer support:

- Perform 1–4 times daily (under practitioner guidance)

For maintenance:

- Perform 1–2 times per week

Best time: Morning, after bowel movement

Safety Notes

- Generally safe when done correctly

- **Do not use if you have:** hemorrhoids (active/bleeding), diverticulitis, recent abdominal surgery, rectal/colon cancer
- Use organic coffee only
- **Temperature is critical**—too hot can cause burns
- Can cause electrolyte imbalances if done excessively (replenish with minerals)
- Not for children
- Consult practitioner if new to this practice

REMEDY 17: Activated Charcoal Toxin Binder

What It Heals

Activated charcoal is a **powerful emergency detoxifier**. It:

- Binds toxins, chemicals, and poisons
- Reduces alcohol and food poisoning effects
- Absorbs mold toxins
- Reduces gas and bloating
- Supports liver by reducing toxic burden
- Used in emergency rooms for poisoning

Why It Works

Activated charcoal has an **enormous surface area**—one teaspoon has the surface area of a football field. This porous structure **binds to toxins in the digestive tract**, preventing absorption into the bloodstream and carrying them out in stool.

How to Make It

Note: Activated charcoal must be purchased (food-grade or pharmaceutical-grade).

Available forms:

- Powder
- Capsules
- Tablets

How to Use It

For acute poisoning or toxic exposure:

- Take 1,000–2,000 mg (25–50 grams for severe poisoning) immediately
- Follow with water

For food poisoning or alcohol overindulgence:

- Take 1,000 mg as soon as symptoms appear
- Repeat every 2–3 hours until symptoms resolve

For mold exposure:

- Take 500–1,000 mg, 2–3 times daily for 2–4 weeks

For general detox:

- Take 500 mg before bed, 2–3 times per week

Critical: Take **2 hours away from food, supplements, and medications**—charcoal binds to everything.

Safety Notes

- Very safe for short-term, occasional use
- **Do not use daily or long-term** (will bind nutrients and cause deficiencies)
- Will turn stool black (normal)
- Can cause constipation—drink plenty of water
- **Keep away from medications** (makes them ineffective)
- Not for long-term daily use

REMEDY 18: Red Clover Blood Cleanser

What It Heals

Red clover is a **traditional blood purifier and lymphatic cleanser**. It:

- Cleanses blood and lymph
- Supports liver detoxification
- Clears skin conditions (acne, eczema, psoriasis)
- Has mild estrogenic effects (hormonal balance)
- Reduces inflammation
- Supports respiratory health
- Provides minerals

Why It Works

Red clover contains **isoflavones and coumarins** that support liver detoxification, thin lymphatic fluid, and support elimination of metabolic waste.

It's been used traditionally for **cancer prevention and support** (especially hormone-related cancers).

How to Make It

Red Clover Infusion:

Ingredients:

- ¼ cup (about 1 oz) dried red clover blossoms
- 1 quart (4 cups) hot water

Instructions:

1. Place red clover in quart jar.
2. Pour hot water over flowers.
3. Cover and steep 4–8 hours (or overnight).
4. Strain.
5. Drink throughout the day.

Red Clover Tincture:

Follow standard tincture method (1 part flower to 5 parts alcohol, 40–50%, 4–6 weeks).

How to Use It

For blood cleansing:

- Drink 2–4 cups infusion daily for 4–6 weeks

For skin conditions:

- Drink 3 cups daily, long-term

For lymphatic support:

- Drink 2 cups daily

Safety Notes

- Generally safe
- Mild estrogenic effects—use caution with hormone-sensitive conditions
- May thin blood—consult doctor if on blood thinners
- Not for use during pregnancy
- Generally well-tolerated

REMEDY 19: Yellow Dock Root Iron Tonic and Liver Cleanser

What It Heals

Yellow dock is a **blood builder and liver cleanser**. It:

- Provides bioavailable iron (treats anemia)
- Stimulates bile production
- Supports liver detoxification
- Acts as gentle laxative
- Clears skin conditions
- Supports lymphatic drainage

- Reduces inflammation

Why It Works

Yellow dock contains **anthraquinones** (stimulate bowel movements) and **iron** in a form that's easily absorbed without causing constipation like iron supplements do.

It's an excellent **alterative** (blood purifier) that gradually improves overall health.

How to Make It

Yellow Dock Decoction:

Ingredients:

- 2 tablespoons dried yellow dock root (chopped)
- 4 cups water

Instructions:

1. Place yellow dock root in pot with water.
2. Bring to a boil.
3. Reduce heat and simmer 20–30 minutes.
4. Strain.
5. Drink throughout the day.

Yellow Dock Tincture:

Follow standard tincture method (1 part root to 5 parts alcohol, 50–60%, 4–6 weeks).

How to Use It

For anemia:

- Drink 3 cups decoction daily or take 2–3 mL tincture, 3 times daily

For constipation:

- Drink 1–2 cups decoction or take 2–3 mL tincture before bed

For liver support:

- Drink 2 cups daily or take 2 mL tincture, twice daily

Safety Notes

- Generally safe
- Can have laxative effect (reduce dose if stools become too loose)
- High in oxalates—avoid if prone to kidney stones
- Not for use during pregnancy
- Safe for most people in appropriate doses

REMEDY 20: Beetroot Liver Support Juice

What It Heals

Beets are **liver-supporting superstars**. They:

- Support Phase 2 liver detoxification
- Thin bile (improves fat digestion)
- Provide betaine (protects liver cells)
- Increase glutathione production
- Lower blood pressure
- Improve athletic performance
- Support healthy blood formation

Why It Works

Beets contain **betaine (trimethylglycine)**, a compound that:

- Supports methylation (critical detox pathway)
- Protects liver cells from toxins
- Reduces fat accumulation in liver
- Stimulates bile flow

They're also rich in **betalains**—powerful antioxidant pigments.

How to Make It

Liver-Cleansing Beet Juice:

Ingredients:

- 2 medium beets
- 2 carrots
- 1 apple
- 1-inch piece ginger
- ½ lemon
- 1 cucumber

Instructions:

1. Wash all produce.
2. Run through juicer.
3. Drink immediately.

Or make Beet Kvass (fermented beet tonic—see Chapter 8, Remedy 26).

Roasted Beets:

1. Roast whole beets at 400°F for 45–60 minutes until tender.
2. Peel and eat regularly.

How to Use It

For liver support:

- Drink 8–16 oz beet juice, 3–4 times per week
- Or eat cooked beets daily
- Or drink 2–4 oz beet kvass daily

During detox:

- Drink beet juice daily

Safety Notes

- Very safe
- Will turn urine and stool pink/red (harmless—called "beeturia")
- High in oxalates—moderate intake if prone to kidney stones
- Can lower blood pressure (beneficial for most)
- Start with small amounts (can have mild laxative effect)
- Generally well-tolerated

REMEDY 21: Parsley Kidney and Liver Flush Tea

What It Heals

Parsley is a **diuretic and kidney cleanser** that also supports liver. It:

- Flushes kidneys (eliminates water retention)
- Supports liver detoxification
- Provides chlorophyll (blood cleanser)
- Rich in vitamins A, C, K
- Acts as breath freshener
- Reduces inflammation
- Supports urinary tract health

Why It Works

Parsley contains **apiol and myristicin**—volatile oils that increase urine production and support kidney function. This assists the liver by ensuring toxins are eliminated efficiently through urine.

How to Make It

Parsley Tea:

Ingredients:

- ¼ cup fresh parsley (or 2 tablespoons dried)
- 2 cups hot water

Instructions:

1. Place parsley in teapot or jar.

2. Pour hot water over herb.
3. Cover and steep 10–15 minutes.
4. Strain.
5. Drink warm or cold.

Fresh Parsley Juice:

Add handful of fresh parsley to green juice recipes (strong flavor—use sparingly).

How to Use It

For kidney and liver support:

- Drink 2–3 cups tea daily

For water retention:

- Drink 2 cups daily

For detoxification:

- Add fresh parsley to juices and smoothies daily

Safety Notes

- Generally safe
- Strong diuretic—stay hydrated
- Very high in vitamin K (consult doctor if on blood thinners)
- Avoid therapeutic doses during pregnancy (culinary amounts safe)
- Can irritate kidneys in very high doses—use moderately
- Generally well-tolerated

REMEDY 22: Glutathione Liposomal Supplement

What It Heals

Glutathione is the **master detoxifier**—your body's most important antioxidant. Supplementing increases:

- Liver detoxification capacity
- Cellular antioxidant protection
- Heavy metal chelation
- Immune function
- Skin health (reduces melanin production)
- Recovery from toxic exposure
- Energy levels

Why It Works

Glutathione is **produced in the liver** and is essential for Phase 2 detoxification. When levels are low (from toxin overload, stress, poor nutrition, aging), detoxification fails.

Liposomal glutathione wraps glutathione in fat bubbles, protecting it from digestion and increasing absorption dramatically.

How to Make It

Note: True liposomal glutathione requires specialized equipment. Most people purchase high-quality liposomal glutathione supplements.

Look for:

- Liposomal delivery (much better absorption than regular glutathione)
- Reduced form (GSH)

How to Use It

For detoxification:

- Take 500–1,000 mg liposomal glutathione daily on empty stomach

During toxic exposure:

- Take 1,000 mg, twice daily

For skin lightening:

- Take 500 mg daily (takes 3–6 months for visible effects)

For immune support:

- Take 500 mg daily

Safety Notes

- Very safe
- Some people report mild digestive upset
- Take on empty stomach for best absorption
- Expensive compared to precursors (NAC)—but more direct
- Generally well-tolerated

REMEDY 23: Cupping Therapy for Liver (External Detox Support)

What It Heals

Cupping creates **suction on the skin** that:

- Increases blood flow to liver
- Supports lymphatic drainage
- Releases toxins from tissues
- Reduces muscle tension
- Improves circulation
- Supports detoxification processes

Why It Works

Cupping creates **negative pressure** that draws blood to the surface, increasing circulation and lymphatic flow in the area. When applied over the liver, it supports the organ's detoxification functions.

How to Make It

Materials:

- Cupping set (silicone cups or traditional fire cups)
- Massage oil (for glide cupping)

Instructions:

1. Apply thin layer of oil to skin over liver area (right upper abdomen).
2. Apply cup(s) to create suction.
3. Leave in place for 5–10 minutes (stationary cupping).
4. Or gently glide cups across area (massage cupping).
5. Remove cups.
6. Red circular marks are normal (fade in 3–7 days).

How to Use It

For liver support:

- Apply cupping over liver area 1–2 times per week

During detox:

- Apply 2–3 times per week

Can combine with castor oil pack for enhanced effect.

Safety Notes

- Generally safe when done correctly
- Will cause temporary red circular marks (not painful)
- Don't cup over broken skin, moles, or varicose veins
- Avoid during pregnancy (over abdomen)
- Start with gentle suction and short duration
- Generally well-tolerated

REMEDY 24: Selenium Supplement (Glutathione Cofactor)

What It Heals

Selenium is a **trace mineral essential for glutathione production**. It:

- Supports glutathione peroxidase (major antioxidant enzyme)
- Protects liver from oxidative damage
- Supports thyroid function
- Has anti-cancer properties
- Boosts immune function
- Protects against heavy metal toxicity

Why It Works

Selenium is a **cofactor for glutathione peroxidase**—one of the body's most important antioxidant enzymes. Without adequate selenium, glutathione can't function properly.

Many people are deficient (depleted soils).

How to Make It

Food sources:

- Brazil nuts (1–2 nuts daily provides adequate selenium)
- Seafood
- Organ meats
- Sunflower seeds

Supplement:

- Purchase selenium supplement (selenomethionine form preferred)

How to Use It

For liver support and detoxification:

- Eat 2 Brazil nuts daily
- Or take 200 mcg selenium supplement daily

Do not exceed 400 mcg daily (toxicity can occur with excess).

Safety Notes

- Safe in appropriate doses
- **Toxic in excess**—do not exceed recommended amounts
- Symptoms of excess: hair loss, brittle nails, garlic breath
- Generally very safe at 200 mcg daily
- Consult practitioner if taking multiple supplements (may contain selenium)

REMEDY 25: Infrared Sauna Detox

What It Heals

Infrared sauna therapy supports **detoxification through sweat**. It:

- Eliminates heavy metals through sweat
- Removes environmental toxins (BPA, phthalates)
- Supports liver by reducing toxic burden
- Improves circulation
- Reduces inflammation
- Supports cardiovascular health
- Promotes relaxation

Why It Works

Infrared saunas penetrate deeper than traditional saunas, raising **core body temperature** and inducing profuse sweating. Studies show **sweat can eliminate heavy metals** (lead, mercury, cadmium) and environmental chemicals.

This reduces the burden on the liver.

How to Make It

Note: Infrared saunas are purchased or available at wellness centers.

DIY option: Near-infrared lamp (much less expensive—creates similar effect).

How to Use It

For detoxification:

- Sauna 3–5 times per week
- Start with 15–20 minutes, work up to 30–45 minutes
- Temperature: 120–150°F for infrared (lower than traditional sauna)

Protocol:

1. Hydrate well before and after.
2. Shower before entering (clean skin absorbs better).
3. Dry brush skin before sauna (opens pores).
4. Sauna for 20–45 minutes.
5. Shower immediately after to rinse off toxins.
6. Rehydrate with water + electrolytes.

During intensive detox:

- Sauna daily for 2–4 weeks

Safety Notes

- Generally safe for most people
- **Contraindications:** pregnancy, cardiovascular disease, certain medications
- Stay hydrated (drink extra water and electrolytes)
- Can cause detox symptoms initially (headache, fatigue)
- Start slowly and build tolerance
- Consult doctor if you have health conditions

REMEDY 26: Epsom Salt Bath Detox

What It Heals

Epsom salt baths provide **magnesium and sulfate** that:

- Support Phase 2 liver detoxification (sulfation pathway)
- Relax muscles and reduce tension
- Draw toxins out through skin
- Reduce inflammation
- Improve sleep
- Relieve pain
- Support recovery from illness

Why It Works

Epsom salts are **magnesium sulfate**. When dissolved in warm water:

- Magnesium absorbs through skin (most people are deficient)
- Sulfate supports liver's sulfation detox pathway
- Heat opens pores and promotes sweating
- Creates osmotic pressure that draws toxins out

How to Make It

Detox Bath Recipe:

Ingredients:

- 2 cups Epsom salts
- 1 cup baking soda (alkalizing, skin-soothing)
- 10 drops essential oil (lavender, eucalyptus, or frankincense)
- Optional: 1 cup bentonite clay (additional detox)

Instructions:

1. Fill bathtub with warm water (not too hot—opens pores but shouldn't stress cardiovascular system).
2. Add Epsom salts and baking soda.
3. Stir to dissolve.
4. Add essential oils.
5. Soak for 20–40 minutes.
6. Rinse with cool shower.
7. Rest afterward (detox baths can be tiring).

How to Use It

For detoxification:

- Take 2–3 detox baths per week

During illness or toxic exposure:

- Take daily for 1–2 weeks

For relaxation and sleep:

- Take before bed 2–3 times per week

Safety Notes

- Very safe
- Drink water before and after (can be dehydrating)
- Can cause dizziness if water too hot or soak too long
- May cause temporary fatigue (rest afterward)
- Not for people with open wounds or severe skin conditions
- Generally well-tolerated

REMEDY 27: Bentonite Clay Internal Cleanse

What It Heals

We covered this in Chapter 8, but it's critical for liver support too. Bentonite clay:

- Binds toxins in digestive tract (prevents reabsorption)
- Supports liver by reducing toxic burden
- Absorbs heavy metals
- Binds mold toxins
- Supports gut healing
- Alkalizes body

Why It Works

Bentonite clay has **negative ionic charge** that attracts positively-charged toxins. By binding them in the gut, it prevents the liver from having to process them repeatedly (enterohepatic recirculation).

How to Make It

See **Chapter 8, Remedy 39** for full instructions.

Quick protocol:

- 1 teaspoon food-grade bentonite clay
- 8 oz water
- Stir and drink on empty stomach
- Follow with another glass of water
- Take 2 hours away from food and medications

How to Use It

During liver detox:

- Take once daily for 1–2 weeks

For toxic exposure:

- Take 2 times daily for 1 week

Safety Notes

- See Chapter 8, Remedy 39 for complete safety information
- Not for long-term daily use
- Take away from medications and supplements

REMEDY 28: Curcumin Supplement (Concentrated Turmeric)

What It Heals

Curcumin supplements provide **concentrated liver protection**. They:

- Protect liver cells from toxins
- Reduce liver inflammation
- Support bile production
- Prevent and reverse fatty liver
- Protect against liver disease
- Act as powerful anti-inflammatory throughout body

Why It Works

While turmeric powder is excellent, **standardized curcumin extracts** provide much higher doses of the active compound—allowing for therapeutic effects in liver disease.

How to Make It

Note: High-potency curcumin requires extraction. Most people purchase supplements.

Look for:

- Standardized to 95% curcuminoids
- Enhanced absorption formulas (with piperine, phosphatidylcholine, or other absorption enhancers)

How to Use It

For liver protection:

- Take 500–1,000 mg curcumin (standardized extract) daily with black pepper

For fatty liver or liver disease:

- Take 1,000 mg, 2–3 times daily

For inflammation:

- Take 500–1,000 mg daily, long-term

Safety Notes

- Very safe
- Take with food and fat for best absorption
- May thin blood slightly
- Can cause digestive upset in high doses
- Generally well-tolerated

REMEDY 29: Dandelion Leaf Diuretic Tea

What It Heals

Dandelion leaf (as opposed to root) is a **potassium-sparing diuretic** that:

- Flushes kidneys (supports toxin elimination)
- Reduces water retention
- Provides potassium (unlike pharmaceutical diuretics which deplete it)
- Supports liver by ensuring waste elimination
- Provides vitamins A, C, K
- Reduces blood pressure gently

Why It Works

Most diuretics cause potassium loss. **Dandelion leaf provides potassium while increasing urine output**, making it safe for long-term use.

This supports the liver by ensuring toxins are eliminated through urine efficiently.

How to Make It

Dandelion Leaf Infusion:

Ingredients:

- 2 tablespoons dried dandelion leaf (or ½ cup fresh)

- 2 cups hot water

Instructions:

1. Place dandelion leaf in teapot or jar.
2. Pour hot water over leaves.
3. Cover and steep 10–15 minutes.
4. Strain.
5. Drink warm or cool.

How to Use It

For water retention:

- Drink 2–3 cups daily

For kidney and liver support:

- Drink 2 cups daily, long-term

During detox:

- Drink 3 cups daily

Safety Notes

- Very safe for long-term use
- Increases urination (stay hydrated)
- Rare allergic reactions (Asteraceae family)
- Safe during pregnancy
- Generally well-tolerated

REMEDY 30: Liver-Supporting Smoothie Protocol

What It Heals

A daily liver-supportive smoothie provides **comprehensive nutrition and detox support**. It:

- Provides nutrients for Phase 1 and 2 detoxification
- Supplies antioxidants
- Supports glutathione production
- Provides fiber (binds toxins)
- Alkalizes body
- Increases energy
- Supports cellular repair

Why It Works

Combines multiple liver-supporting foods in one easy, delicious drink—making daily liver support simple and sustainable.

How to Make It

Ultimate Liver-Love Smoothie:

Ingredients:

- 1 cup leafy greens (spinach, kale, or mixed)
- ½ cup blueberries (or mixed berries)
- ½ green apple (with skin)
- 1 tablespoon ground flaxseed or chia seeds
- 1 teaspoon spirulina or chlorella
- ½ teaspoon turmeric powder
- Pinch black pepper
- 1 tablespoon almond butter (healthy fat)
- 1 cup coconut water or non-dairy milk
- Optional: handful fresh parsley or cilantro, ½-inch ginger

Instructions:

1. Add all ingredients to blender.
2. Blend until smooth.
3. Drink for breakfast.

How to Use It

For liver support:

- Drink daily for breakfast

During detox:

- Drink 1–2 smoothies daily

For maintenance:

- Drink 4–5 times per week

Safety Notes

- Very safe
- Highly nutritious
- Start with smaller amounts of greens and superfoods if not accustomed
- Can replace breakfast
- Generally well-tolerated

REMEDY 31: Reishi Mushroom Liver Protector

What It Heals

Reishi is called the **"mushroom of immortality"** and is a powerful liver protector. It:

- Protects liver cells from toxins
- Reduces liver inflammation
- Supports Phase 2 detoxification
- Has anti-cancer properties (especially liver cancer)
- Modulates immune function
- Reduces oxidative stress
- Supports sleep and stress resilience

Why It Works

Reishi contains **triterpenes (ganoderic acids)** that:

- Protect hepatocytes (liver cells) from damage
- Reduce liver enzyme elevation (ALT, AST)
- Support liver regeneration
- Have direct anti-tumor activity in liver cancer cells

Studies show reishi can **reverse fatty liver disease** and protect against chemical-induced liver damage.

How to Make It

Reishi Decoction:

Ingredients:

- 2 tablespoons dried reishi mushroom (sliced or broken into pieces)
- 4 cups water

Instructions:

1. Place reishi in pot with water.
2. Bring to a boil.
3. Reduce to lowest simmer.
4. Cover and simmer for 2–3 hours (reishi requires long extraction).
5. Strain (save mushroom pieces—can re-simmer 1–2 more times).
6. Drink throughout the day.

Reishi Tincture:

Requires dual extraction (alcohol + water) for complete compound extraction.

1. Soak dried reishi in alcohol (60–70%) for 4–6 weeks.
2. Strain, reserving alcohol extract.
3. Simmer spent mushrooms in water for 2–3 hours.
4. Strain water extract.
5. Combine both extracts in equal parts.

Or purchase: High-quality reishi extract powder or tincture.

How to Use It

For liver protection:

- Drink 1–2 cups decoction daily
- Or take 3–5 mL tincture, twice daily
- Or take 1–2 grams extract powder daily

During toxic exposure or liver disease:

- Increase to 2–3 servings daily

Long-term tonic:

- Use daily for months to years (very safe)

Safety Notes

- Extremely safe for long-term use
- May have mild blood-thinning effect
- Can cause dry mouth initially (temporary)
- Generally very well-tolerated
- Safe for most people

REMEDY 32: Molybdenum Supplement (Sulfite Detox Support)

What It Heals

Molybdenum is a **trace mineral essential for detoxification enzymes**. It:

- Supports sulfite oxidase (breaks down sulfites)
- Supports aldehyde oxidase (breaks down alcohol and chemicals)
- Helps detoxify environmental chemicals
- Reduces sulfite sensitivity
- Supports liver Phase 1 detoxification
- Aids in uric acid processing

Why It Works

Many people are **deficient in molybdenum** (depleted soils) and can't properly detoxify sulfites (common food preservatives) or aldehydes (produced by Candida and chemical exposure).

Supplementing restores these critical detox pathways.

How to Make It

Food sources:

- Lentils, beans, peas
- Whole grains
- Leafy greens
- Organ meats

Supplement:

- Purchase molybdenum supplement (typically 150–300 mcg)

How to Use It

For sulfite sensitivity:

- Take 150–300 mcg daily

During Candida or chemical detox:

- Take 300 mcg, 1–2 times daily

For general detox support:

- Take 150 mcg daily

Safety Notes

- Very safe
- Toxicity is extremely rare
- Recommended upper limit: 2,000 mcg daily (far above therapeutic doses)
- Can cause copper deficiency if taken in very high amounts long-term
- Generally well-tolerated

REMEDY 33: Globe Artichoke Whole Food Liver Medicine

What It Heals

Fresh artichoke (the vegetable) is **concentrated liver medicine**. It:

- Stimulates bile production dramatically
- Protects liver cells
- Regenerates liver tissue
- Lowers cholesterol
- Improves fat digestion
- Provides antioxidants
- Supports gallbladder function

Why It Works

Globe artichoke contains the same **cynarin and silymarin** found in artichoke leaf extract—but in whole food form with additional nutrients and fiber.

Eating artichoke provides **food as medicine** in the most bioavailable form.

How to Make It

Steamed Artichoke (Medicinal Preparation):

Ingredients:

- 2 large globe artichokes
- Water
- Lemon
- Olive oil (optional, for dipping)

Instructions:

1. Cut off artichoke stems and tips of leaves.
2. Place in steamer basket over boiling water.
3. Cover and steam 30–45 minutes until leaves pull off easily.
4. Serve with lemon and olive oil for dipping.
5. Eat leaves by pulling through teeth to scrape off flesh.
6. Eat the heart (most nutritious part).

Artichoke Tea (from leaves/stems):

1. Simmer artichoke trimmings (leaves, stems) in water for 20 minutes.
2. Strain and drink (very bitter—indicates therapeutic compounds).

How to Use It

For liver support:

- Eat 1–2 fresh artichokes per week

For gallbladder support:

- Eat artichoke before fatty meals

For detox:

- Eat 3–4 artichokes per week during cleanse protocols

Safety Notes

- Very safe
- Can increase bile flow (beneficial but may cause temporary digestive changes)
- Avoid if you have gallstones or bile duct obstruction
- Generally well-tolerated

REMEDY 34: Liver Qi Stagnation TCM Formula (Bupleurum)

What It Heals

In Traditional Chinese Medicine, **liver Qi stagnation** causes anger, frustration, PMS, and digestive issues. Bupleurum-based formulas:

- Move stagnant liver Qi (energy)
- Reduce liver inflammation
- Balance hormones
- Relieve stress and irritability
- Support digestion
- Reduce PMS symptoms
- Protect liver cells

Why It Works

Bupleurum (Chai Hu) contains **saikosaponins**—compounds that:

- Reduce liver inflammation
- Protect hepatocytes
- Regulate immune function
- Support adrenal function

TCM views the liver as responsible for the **smooth flow of Qi** (energy) throughout the body. When stagnant, symptoms arise.

How to Make It

Classic TCM Formula: Xiao Yao San (Free and Easy Wanderer)

Ingredients:

- Bupleurum root
- White peony root
- Angelica root (Dong Quai)
- Atractylodes
- Poria mushroom
- Licorice root
- Fresh ginger
- Mint

Note: This is a complex formula best purchased as prepared pills or from TCM practitioner.

Simple Bupleurum Tea:

Ingredients:

- 1 tablespoon dried bupleurum root
- 3 cups water

Instructions:

1. Simmer bupleurum in water for 20–30 minutes.
2. Strain and drink.

How to Use It

For liver Qi stagnation (stress, irritability, PMS):

- Take prepared formula as directed (typically 3–6 pills, 3 times daily)
- Or drink 2 cups bupleurum tea daily

For hormonal balance:

- Take daily for 1–3 months

Safety Notes

- Generally safe
- Best used under guidance of TCM practitioner for complex formulas
- Can cause digestive upset in sensitive individuals
- Not for use during pregnancy without professional guidance
- Generally well-tolerated

REMEDY 35: Apple Cider Vinegar and Honey Liver Tonic

What It Heals

This simple daily tonic provides **gentle liver support**. It:

- Stimulates bile production
- Supports liver detoxification
- Balances pH
- Improves digestion
- Provides enzymes
- Supports gut health
- Easy and inexpensive

Why It Works

Apple cider vinegar stimulates digestive secretions and bile flow. **Raw honey** provides enzymes, antioxidants, and antimicrobial compounds.

Together, they create a **daily liver tonic** that's easy to maintain.

How to Make It

Daily Liver Tonic:

Ingredients:

- 1 tablespoon raw apple cider vinegar (with "the mother")
- 1 teaspoon raw honey
- 8 oz warm water
- Optional: pinch of cayenne, squeeze of lemon

Instructions:

1. Mix all ingredients in warm water.
2. Stir until honey dissolves.
3. Drink on empty stomach.

How to Use It

For daily liver support:

- Drink every morning, 15–20 minutes before breakfast

During detox:

- Drink 2–3 times daily (morning, midday, evening)

For digestion:

- Drink before meals

Safety Notes

- Very safe
- Always dilute vinegar (undiluted can damage tooth enamel)
- Rinse mouth with water after drinking
- Not for infants under 1 year (honey)
- Generally well-tolerated

[IMAGE SUGGESTION: A glass of amber-colored apple cider vinegar and honey tonic beside a bottle of raw apple cider vinegar, a jar of honey with dipper, and fresh lemon on a wooden surface.]

REMEDY 36: Liver-Cleansing Herbal Tea Blend

What It Heals

This multi-herb tea provides **comprehensive liver support** in one cup. It:

- Stimulates bile production
- Supports detoxification
- Protects liver cells
- Improves digestion

- Provides antioxidants
- Tastes pleasant (important for compliance)
- Can be used daily long-term

Why It Works

Combines multiple liver-supporting herbs for **synergistic effect**—each herb contributing different protective and regenerative properties.

How to Make It

Liver Love Tea Blend:

Ingredients (dried herbs):

- 2 parts dandelion root (bile stimulant)
- 2 parts burdock root (blood cleanser)
- 1 part milk thistle seeds (liver regenerator)
- 1 part peppermint leaf (digestive, flavor)
- 1 part licorice root (harmonizer, sweetness)
- ½ part ginger root (circulation, flavor)
- ½ part turmeric root (anti-inflammatory)

Instructions:

1. Mix all dried herbs together in a bowl.
2. Store in airtight jar.
3. To brew: Use 2 tablespoons blend per quart of water.
4. Simmer (roots) for 20 minutes, then add leaves and steep 10 minutes.
5. Strain and drink throughout the day.

Or make as overnight infusion (for gentler extraction).

How to Use It

For liver support:

- Drink 2–3 cups daily, long-term

During detox:

- Drink 1 quart daily for 4–6 weeks

For maintenance:

- Drink 1–2 cups, 3–4 times per week

Safety Notes

- Very safe for long-term use
- Generally well-tolerated
- May increase bowel movements (bile stimulation—beneficial)
- Safe for most people

REMEDY 37: Omega-3 Fatty Acids (Anti-Inflammatory Liver Support)

What It Heals

Omega-3s are **essential for liver health**. They:

- Reduce liver inflammation
- Reverse fatty liver disease
- Lower liver enzymes (ALT, AST)
- Improve insulin sensitivity
- Reduce triglycerides
- Support cell membrane health
- Protect against liver fibrosis

Why It Works

The liver needs **healthy fats** to function. Omega-3s (EPA and DHA):

- Reduce inflammatory pathways in liver
- Improve insulin signaling (prevents fat accumulation)
- Support cell membrane fluidity
- Reduce oxidative stress

Studies show omega-3 supplementation can **significantly improve fatty liver disease**.

How to Make It

Food sources:

- Wild-caught fatty fish (salmon, mackerel, sardines, herring)
- Flaxseeds (ground)
- Chia seeds
- Walnuts
- Algae oil (vegan source of EPA/DHA)

Supplement:

- Purchase high-quality fish oil or algae oil

How to Use It

For liver health:

- Eat fatty fish 3–4 times per week
- Or take 1,000–2,000 mg EPA+DHA daily

For fatty liver disease:

- Take 2,000–3,000 mg EPA+DHA daily

For general health:

- Take 1,000 mg daily

Safety Notes

- Very safe
- Mild blood-thinning effect (beneficial for most)
- Choose quality brands (tested for heavy metals and contaminants)
- Store in refrigerator
- Generally well-tolerated

REMEDY 38: Liver Massage (Self-Care Technique)

What It Heals

Gentle liver massage provides **mechanical support** for detoxification. It:

- Stimulates liver function
- Increases bile flow
- Supports lymphatic drainage
- Reduces liver congestion
- Relieves right-sided abdominal discomfort
- Improves circulation to liver

Why It Works

Mechanical stimulation of the liver through massage:

- Increases blood flow to the organ
- Encourages release of stored toxins
- Stimulates bile production
- Supports lymphatic movement

This ancient practice is used in many traditional healing systems.

How to Make It

Liver Massage Technique:

Instructions:

1. Lie on your back in a comfortable position.
2. Place both hands over your liver area (right side, below ribcage).
3. Take several deep breaths, expanding belly with each inhale.
4. On exhale, gently press into liver area with fingertips.

5. Make small circular motions, gradually covering entire liver area.
6. Continue for 5–10 minutes.
7. Practice daily, especially in the evening.

Enhanced version:

- Use massage oil with essential oils (frankincense, rosemary, or lemon)
- Apply castor oil before massage for additional benefit

How to Use It

For liver support:

- Perform massage daily, especially before bed

During detox:

- Perform twice daily (morning and evening)

Can combine with:

- Deep breathing
- Castor oil pack
- Herbal tea

Safety Notes

- Very safe
- Use gentle pressure—liver is delicate
- Avoid if you have liver disease or acute liver pain (consult doctor)
- Generally well-tolerated
- Can cause slight discomfort initially if liver is congested

---

REMEDY 39: Vitamin E Antioxidant (Liver Cell Protector)

What It Heals

Vitamin E is a **fat-soluble antioxidant** critical for liver health. It:

- Protects liver cell membranes from oxidative damage
- Reverses fatty liver disease (proven in studies)
- Reduces liver inflammation
- Prevents progression to cirrhosis
- Supports immune function
- Protects against cancer

Why It Works

Vitamin E **protects fat-rich cell membranes** from free radical damage. Since the liver is constantly exposed to toxins, its cells are under constant oxidative stress.

Studies show vitamin E supplementation (especially natural mixed tocopherols) can **significantly improve NAFLD** (non-alcoholic fatty liver disease) and prevent progression to NASH (non-alcoholic steatohepatitis).

How to Make It

Food sources:

- Sunflower seeds
- Almonds
- Hazelnuts
- Spinach
- Avocado
- Olive oil

Supplement:

- Purchase natural vitamin E (d-alpha-tocopherol, or better yet, mixed tocopherols)
- Avoid synthetic vitamin E (dl-alpha-tocopherol—less effective)

How to Use It

For liver protection:

- Take 400–800 IU natural vitamin E daily with food (fat-soluble—needs fat for absorption)

For fatty liver disease:

- Take 800 IU daily (studies show significant improvement at this dose)

For general antioxidant support:

- Take 400 IU daily

Safety Notes

- Generally safe
- High doses (over 1,000 IU) may increase bleeding risk
- Take with fat for absorption
- Natural forms more effective than synthetic
- Consult doctor if on blood thinners

REMEDY 40: Complete Liver Detox Protocol (4-Week Comprehensive Reset)

What It Heals

This is a **complete liver restoration program** combining the most effective remedies into a structured protocol. It:

- Regenerates liver tissue
- Clears toxins and congestion
- Restores optimal liver function
- Increases energy dramatically
- Clears skin
- Improves digestion
- Balances hormones
- Provides foundation for long-term health

Why It Works

True liver healing requires a **multi-phase approach**:

1. **Prepare** (reduce toxic burden)
2. **Support** (provide nutrients for detoxification)
3. **Activate** (stimulate detox pathways)
4. **Bind and Eliminate** (ensure toxins leave the body)
5. **Regenerate** (rebuild liver tissue)
6. **Maintain** (ongoing support)

This protocol addresses all phases systematically.

CHAPTER 7: HORMONES & WOMEN'S LONGEVITY

Focus: Cycle Balance, Fertility, Menopause

REMEDY 1: Vitex (Chaste Tree Berry) - Master Hormone Regulator

What It Heals

Vitex regulates the entire cycle by working on the pituitary gland: irregular cycles, PMS (irritability, breast tenderness, bloating), PMDD, infertility (luteal phase defects), low progesterone, perimenopause symptoms, hormonal acne.

Why It Works

Vitex doesn't contain hormones—it teaches your body to produce proper amounts at the right times. Acts on dopamine receptors in the pituitary, normalizing FSH, LH, and prolactin. Result: consistent ovulation, improved progesterone, balanced cycles.

How to Make It

Ingredients:

- 1 part dried vitex berries
- 5 parts vodka (50%)

Instructions:

1. Place berries in jar.
2. Cover with alcohol (1-2 inches above berries).
3. Seal tightly, label with date.
4. Let sit 6 weeks, shaking daily.
5. Strain through cheesecloth.
6. Bottle in amber dropper bottles.

How to Use It

For cycle regulation/PMS: 2-3 mL every morning on empty stomach. Consistency is critical. Continue 3-6 months minimum (works slowly and cumulatively).

For fertility: 3 mL every morning until pregnancy confirmed.

Timing matters: Take first thing in morning—works with circadian hormone rhythms.

Safety Notes

Not during pregnancy. Can be used during nursing. Requires 3-6 months for full effects. May cause temporary cycle changes (normal). Don't use with hormonal birth control. Generally very safe long-term.

REMEDY 2: Red Raspberry Leaf - Uterine Tonic

What It Heals

Ultimate uterine tonic: reduces menstrual cramping, tones uterine muscles (prevents excessive bleeding), supports healthy pregnancy and labor, aids postpartum recovery, strengthens pelvic floor.

Why It Works

Contains **fragarine**—alkaloid that tones and relaxes uterine smooth muscle. Also provides iron, calcium, magnesium, B vitamins, vitamin C. Midwives use for centuries for pregnancy and labor support.

How to Make It

Ingredients:

- 2 tablespoons dried red raspberry leaf
- 1 quart hot water

Instructions:

1. Place leaf in quart jar.
2. Pour hot water, filling jar.
3. Seal tightly.
4. Steep 4-8 hours (or overnight).
5. Strain, store in refrigerator.

Yield: 3 cups

How to Use It

For cramping: 2-3 cups daily long-term, increase to 3-4 cups during menstruation.

For pregnancy: First trimester 1 cup daily, second trimester 2 cups, third trimester 3-4 cups (prepares for labor).

Postpartum: 3-4 cups daily for 4-6 weeks after birth.

Safety Notes

Extremely safe—one of safest herbs for pregnancy. Safe throughout entire pregnancy. No drug interactions. Can be used daily for years. Pleasant, mild taste.

REMEDY 3: Black Cohosh - Menopause Relief

What It Heals

Clinically proven as effective as HRT for menopause: hot flashes (reduces frequency/intensity dramatically), night sweats, vaginal dryness, mood swings, irritability, anxiety, painful periods, hormonal headaches.

Why It Works

Acts on serotonin receptors (5-HT7), affecting temperature regulation. Mild estrogenic effects without pharmaceutical risks. Contains triterpene glycosides (reduce inflammation, stabilize mood). Studies show 50%+ reduction in hot flashes within 4-8 weeks.

How to Make It

Ingredients:

- 1 part dried black cohosh root
- 5 parts vodka (60%)

Instructions:

1. Place root in jar.
2. Cover with alcohol.
3. Seal, label with date.
4. Let sit 6 weeks, shaking daily.
5. Strain, bottle in amber bottles.

How to Use It

For menopause/perimenopause: 2-3 mL tincture, 2-3 times daily. Most effective with consistent use for 4-12 weeks.

For hot flashes (acute): 3 mL when hot flash begins, repeat every 2-3 hours.

Safety Notes

Not during pregnancy. Avoid if liver disease. Hormone-sensitive cancer contraindication is debated—consult oncologist. Rare side effects: digestive upset, headache. Generally well-tolerated.

REMEDY 4: Dong Quai - Female Ginseng

What It Heals

Called "female ginseng" in TCM: anemia from heavy bleeding, painful cramping, irregular/absent periods, menopausal symptoms, hormonal fatigue, poor circulation.

Why It Works

Emmenagogue (promotes flow), blood tonic, mild estrogenic effects. Contains ferulic acid (antispasmodic), ligustilide (relaxes smooth muscle), polysaccharides (blood-building). In TCM: "nourishes blood and moves Qi."

How to Make It

Ingredients:

- 2 tablespoons dried dong quai root
- 4 cups water

Instructions:

1. Place root in pot with water.
2. Bring to boil.
3. Simmer covered 30-40 minutes.
4. Strain into jar.

How to Use It

For blood building: 2-3 cups daily for 10-14 days after period ends. Or 2-3 mL tincture, 3 times daily during this phase.

For cramping: 2 cups daily starting few days before expected period.

Safety Notes

Not during pregnancy. Avoid during heavy bleeding (wait until flow stops). Photosensitizing—increases sun sensitivity. Mild blood-thinning effect. Not for long-term continuous use—take cyclically.

REMEDY 5: Wild Yam Cream - Progesterone Support

What It Heals

May help: low progesterone symptoms (PMS, short luteal phase), menopausal symptoms, sleep disturbances, anxiety, mood swings, vaginal dryness.

Why It Works

Contains diosgenin—plant steroid structurally similar to progesterone. Body cannot convert diosgenin to progesterone, but many women report benefits from topical application. Mechanism unclear but potentially provides mild hormonal effects.

How to Make It

Infused Oil:

1. Place 1 cup dried wild yam root in jar.
2. Cover with 2 cups coconut oil.
3. Let sit 3-4 weeks, shaking daily.
4. Strain through cheesecloth.

Cream:

1. Melt 1 cup infused oil, 2 tablespoons beeswax, 2 tablespoons shea butter in double boiler.
2. Stir until combined.
3. Add 10 drops lavender oil (optional).
4. Pour into jars, let cool.

How to Use It

For progesterone support: Apply ¼ teaspoon to soft skin (inner arms, thighs, abdomen) twice daily during luteal phase (day 14-28). Rotate application sites.

Safety Notes

Very safe topically. Don't take internally expecting progesterone effects. If you need progesterone, work with practitioner for bioidentical form. Rare allergic reactions—test small area first.

REMEDY 6: Red Clover - Gentle Phytoestrogen

What It Heals

Mild estrogenic support: menopausal symptoms, bone health (osteoporosis protection), cardiovascular health, hormonal acne, breast tenderness, lymphatic congestion.

Why It Works

Contains isoflavones—phytoestrogens that bind estrogen receptors and provide mild estrogenic effects. Also blood purifier and lymphatic cleanser supporting overall detoxification.

How to Make It

Ingredients:

- ¼-½ cup dried red clover blossoms
- 1 quart hot water

Instructions:

1. Place blossoms in quart jar.
2. Pour hot water, filling jar.
3. Seal tightly.
4. Steep 4-8 hours (or overnight).
5. Strain, store in refrigerator.

How to Use It

For menopause: 2-4 cups daily, long-term.

For skin health: 2 cups daily for several months (results take time).

Can be used long-term (safe for years).

Safety Notes

Generally very safe. Mild estrogenic effects—some caution with hormone-sensitive cancers (consult oncologist). May have mild blood-thinning effect. Pleasant, nourishing tonic.

REMEDY 7: Maca Root - Energy and Libido

What It Heals

Peruvian root for: low libido (significant aphrodisiac effects), hormonal fatigue, menopausal symptoms, fertility issues, depression/low mood, lack of stamina.

Why It Works

Adaptogen working on entire hypothalamic-pituitary-adrenal-gonadal axis. Doesn't contain hormones—supports body's hormone production and balance. Studies show: increases libido significantly, reduces menopause symptoms, improves mood and energy.

How to Make It

Note: Purchased as powder (dried ground root). Eaten as food.

Maca Smoothie:

- 1-2 teaspoons maca powder
- 1 banana, 1 cup berries
- 1 tablespoon nut butter
- 1 cup non-dairy milk
- Blend until smooth

Or add to: oatmeal, warm milk, yogurt, energy balls.

How to Use It

For libido/energy: 1-2 teaspoons (3-6 grams) daily, morning or early afternoon (energizing).

Start small (½-1 teaspoon) and increase gradually.

Safety Notes

Very safe. Can be energizing—take morning/afternoon, not evening. Start with low dose. Safe long-term. Pleasant, nutty, malty flavor.

REMEDY 8: Evening Primrose Oil - PMS and Skin

What It Heals

Seed oil rich in GLA (gamma-linolenic acid): PMS (especially breast tenderness, mood swings), hormonal acne, dry skin, eczema, inflammation, menopause, PCOS.

Why It Works

GLA converts to DGLA, producing anti-inflammatory prostaglandins. Specifically reduces PGE2 (inflammatory prostaglandin causing cramping, breast pain) and prolactin levels (breast tenderness).

How to Make It

Note: Requires commercial pressing. Purchase EPO capsules.

Look for: Cold-pressed, organic, high GLA (8-10%), 1,000-1,500 mg per capsule.

How to Use It

For PMS: 1,000-1,500 mg daily throughout month, or 1,500-3,000 mg during luteal phase (day 14-28).

For hormonal acne: 1,500 mg daily for 3-6 months.

Best with food.

Safety Notes

Very safe. May have mild blood-thinning effect. Takes 4-6 weeks for full effects. Safe long-term.

REMEDY 9: Motherwort - Emotional Balance

What It Heals

Nervine and uterine tonic: anxiety (hormonal—perimenopause, PMS), heart palpitations (menopausal/stress-related), painful cramping, delayed menstruation, postpartum depression/anxiety, irritability.

Why It Works

Contains leonurine (relaxes smooth muscle—reduces cramping/palpitations), flavonoids (antioxidant), iridoids (cardiovascular support). Both calming to nervous system and stimulating to uterus (gently promotes flow if delayed).

How to Make It

Ingredients:

- 1 part fresh motherwort flowering tops (or dried)
- 2 parts vodka (fresh) or 5 parts vodka (dried, 50%)

Instructions:

1. Chop fresh plant, pack in jar.
2. Cover with alcohol, seal.
3. Let sit 3-4 weeks, shaking daily.
4. Strain, bottle in amber bottles.

Note: Fresh plant tincture significantly more effective.

How to Use It

For anxiety/palpitations: 2-3 mL as needed, repeat every 2-3 hours.

For delayed menstruation: 3 mL, 3 times daily until flow begins.

For perimenopause: 2 mL, 2-3 times daily, long-term.

Safety Notes

Not during pregnancy (stimulates uterus). Safe during nursing. Very safe for non-pregnant women. Generally well-tolerated.

REMEDY 10: Lady's Mantle - Bleeding Stopper

What It Heals

Astringent herb for: heavy menstrual bleeding (menorrhagia), flooding and clotting, postpartum hemorrhage, bleeding between periods, uterine prolapse.

Why It Works

Contains tannins—astringent compounds that constrict blood vessels, tone and tighten tissues, reduce inflammation. Used since medieval times for "women's troubles."

How to Make It

Ingredients:

- 2 tablespoons dried lady's mantle
- 2 cups hot water

Instructions:

1. Place herb in teapot.
2. Pour hot water, cover.
3. Steep 15-20 minutes.
4. Strain, drink warm.

How to Use It

For heavy bleeding: 3 cups daily during menstruation. Or 3 mL tincture, 3-4 times daily.

For flooding: 1 cup every 2-3 hours until bleeding slows.

Safety Notes

Very safe. No known contraindications. Generally well-tolerated. Pleasant, mild taste.

REMEDY 11: Shatavari - Ayurvedic Women's Rejuvenative

What It Heals

Called "she who possesses 100 husbands" in Sanskrit: fertility support, low libido, vaginal dryness, menopausal symptoms, stress-related hormonal imbalance, supports natural lubrication.

Why It Works

Adaptogenic and rejuvenative for female reproductive system. Contains saponins (shatavarin) that support hormone balance, reproductive health, and reduce stress impact on hormones. Deeply nourishing to tissues.

How to Make It

Note: Shatavari is purchased as powder (Ayurvedic herb shops or online).

Shatavari Moon Milk:

- 1-2 teaspoons shatavari powder
- 1 cup warm milk (dairy or non-dairy)
- 1 teaspoon honey
- Pinch cardamom or cinnamon

Instructions:

1. Heat milk gently (don't boil).
2. Whisk in shatavari powder.
3. Add honey and spice.
4. Drink slowly.

How to Use It

For fertility/libido: 1-2 teaspoons powder in warm milk or water, twice daily (morning and evening).

For menopause: 1 teaspoon twice daily, long-term.

For vaginal dryness: 1-2 teaspoons daily for several weeks.

Safety Notes

Very safe. Nourishing tonic for long-term use. May increase breast size slightly (estrogenic effect). Generally well-tolerated. Sweet, pleasant taste.

REMEDY 12: Nettle Leaf - Mineral-Rich Blood Builder

What It Heals

Mineral-dense herb for: anemia from heavy periods, fatigue, weak bones, poor hair/skin/nails, general depletion, supports overall vitality.

Why It Works

Extremely rich in bioavailable iron, calcium, magnesium, silica, vitamin K—minerals depleted by menstruation. Long infusion extracts maximum minerals. Also contains chlorophyll (blood-building) and vitamin C (improves iron absorption).

How to Make It

Ingredients:

- ½ cup dried nettle leaf
- 1 quart hot water

Instructions:

1. Place nettle in quart jar.
2. Pour hot water, filling jar.
3. Seal tightly.
4. Steep 4-8 hours (or overnight).
5. Strain, store in refrigerator.

Yield: About 3 cups

How to Use It

For anemia/depletion: 2-4 cups daily, long-term (several months minimum).

For general health: 1-2 cups daily as ongoing tonic.

Best taken: On empty stomach or between meals for maximum mineral absorption.

Safety Notes

Extremely safe. Nourishing long-term tonic. Very high vitamin K (consult if on blood thinners). Generally universally well-tolerated. Pleasant, mild green taste.

REMEDY 13: Shepherd's Purse - Emergency Hemorrhage Stopper

What It Heals

Emergency remedy for: severe heavy menstrual bleeding, postpartum hemorrhage, acute bleeding emergencies, uncontrolled flow, flooding.

Why It Works

Powerful hemostatic (stops bleeding) and astringent. Contains tyramine, choline, and acetylcholine—compounds that increase uterine contractions and constrict blood vessels. Works rapidly. Used by midwives for centuries for hemorrhage.

How to Make It

Ingredients:

- 1 part fresh shepherd's purse (whole plant)
- 2 parts vodka (50%)

Instructions:

1. Harvest fresh plant (most potent when flowering).
2. Chop, pack tightly in jar.
3. Cover with alcohol, seal.

4. Let sit 3-4 weeks, shaking daily.
5. Strain, bottle.

Note: Fresh plant preferred. Dried works but less effective.

How to Use It

For severe bleeding: 3-5 mL every 30 minutes until bleeding slows to normal flow.

For postpartum hemorrhage: 5 mL immediately, repeat every 15-30 minutes until bleeding controlled (seek medical attention simultaneously).

This is for emergency use only—not a daily tonic.

Safety Notes

Very safe for acute use. Not for long-term daily use (only when needed for bleeding). Not during pregnancy except in case of hemorrhage. Can cause uterine contractions (this is the mechanism).

REMEDY 14: Ashwagandha - Thyroid and Adrenal Support

What It Heals

Adaptogen for: hypothyroidism (if not autoimmune), adrenal fatigue, stress-related hormonal imbalance, low energy, anxiety affecting cycles, cortisol dysregulation.

Why It Works

Adaptogen supporting thyroid function (increases T3 and T4 production) and reduces cortisol (high cortisol disrupts reproductive hormones). Contains withanolides that support endocrine system. Studies show significant improvement in thyroid function and stress markers.

How to Make It

Note: Purchased as powder or extract.

Ashwagandha Golden Milk:

- 1 teaspoon ashwagandha powder
- 1 teaspoon turmeric powder
- 1 cup warm milk
- 1 teaspoon honey
- Pinch black pepper

Instructions:

1. Heat milk gently.
2. Whisk in powders and pepper.
3. Add honey.
4. Drink before bed (promotes sleep).

How to Use It

For thyroid support: 300-600 mg extract or 1-2 teaspoons powder, twice daily.

For stress/hormones: 1 teaspoon powder in morning, 1 teaspoon evening.

Continue for 2-3 months minimum for full effects.

Safety Notes

Very safe long-term. **Avoid with hyperthyroidism** (can increase thyroid hormones). May cause drowsiness in high doses—start low. Generally well-tolerated. Not during pregnancy.

REMEDY 15: Cramp Bark - Severe Cramp Relief

What It Heals

Powerful antispasmodic for: severe menstrual cramps, uterine spasms, threatened miscarriage, labor pains, muscle tension (anywhere in body).

Why It Works

Contains scopoletin and viopudial—compounds that directly relax smooth muscle in uterus. One of strongest herbal antispasmodics available. Works within 15-30 minutes. Related to black haw (similar properties).

How to Make It

Ingredients:

- 2 teaspoons dried cramp bark
- 2 cups water

Instructions:

1. Place bark in pot with water.
2. Bring to boil.
3. Simmer 15-20 minutes.
4. Strain, drink warm.

Or make tincture: 1 part bark to 5 parts vodka (60%), 6 weeks.

How to Use It

For severe cramping: Drink 1 cup decoction as needed during menstruation. Or 3-5 mL tincture every 2-3 hours.

For threatened miscarriage: 5 mL tincture every 2-4 hours (seek medical attention simultaneously).

For labor: Under midwife/doctor guidance.

Safety Notes

Very safe. Gentle muscle relaxant. Can be used as needed. No known contraindications. Works well combined with ginger (increases circulation and effectiveness).

REMEDY 16: Fenugreek Seeds - Lactation Support

What It Heals

Traditional galactagogue (milk production support): low milk supply, supports establishment of breast milk production, increases volume and flow.

Why It Works

Contains diosgenin (phytoestrogen) and compounds that stimulate prolactin production and milk secretion. Most studied galactagogue herb. Can increase milk production within 24-72 hours in many women.

How to Make It

Fenugreek Tea:

Ingredients:

- 1-2 teaspoons fenugreek seeds
- 1 cup hot water

Instructions:

1. Lightly crush seeds.
2. Place in mug.
3. Pour hot water, cover.
4. Steep 10-15 minutes.
5. Strain, drink.

Or take as capsules: 1-2 grams, 3 times daily.

How to Use It

For low milk supply: 1-2 teaspoons seeds as tea, 3 times daily. Or capsules: 2-3 capsules (500-600 mg each), 3 times daily.

Expect results: Within 24-72 hours if effective for you.

Often combined with blessed thistle for synergistic effect.

Safety Notes

Safe during nursing. May cause maple syrup smell in urine/sweat (harmless). Can lower blood sugar—monitor if diabetic. May cause gas/digestive upset (reduce dose). Not effective for everyone.

REMEDY 17: Blessed Thistle - Lactation Enhancer

What It Heals

Galactagogue often combined with fenugreek: supports milk production, enhances milk quality, digestive support (bitter properties aid nutrient absorption).

Why It Works

Stimulates prolactin and milk production. Also digestive bitter—improves nutrient absorption (important for milk production). Works synergistically with fenugreek.

How to Make It

Ingredients:

- 1-2 teaspoons dried blessed thistle
- 1 cup hot water

Instructions:

1. Place herb in mug.
2. Pour hot water, cover.
3. Steep 10-15 minutes.
4. Strain, drink.

Very bitter—add honey or mix with peppermint for flavor.

How to Use It

For lactation: 1 cup tea, 3 times daily. Or tincture: 2-3 mL, 3 times daily.

Often combined with fenugreek: Drink both teas together or alternate.

Safety Notes

Safe during nursing. Very bitter (some find unpalatable). Generally well-tolerated. No known serious side effects.

REMEDY 18: Fennel Seeds - Milk Production and Colic Relief

What It Heals

Gentle galactagogue: supports lactation, reduces infant colic (passes through breast milk), relieves maternal gas and bloating, mild estrogenic support.

Why It Works

Contains anethole—compound with mild estrogenic effects supporting milk production. Carminative oils relieve gas (both mother and baby). One of safest galactagogues.

How to Make It

Fennel Seed Tea:

Ingredients:

- 1 teaspoon fennel seeds
- 1 cup hot water

Instructions:

1. Lightly crush seeds.
2. Place in mug, pour hot water.
3. Steep 10 minutes.
4. Strain (or chew softened seeds).

How to Use It

For lactation: Chew 1 teaspoon seeds after nursing sessions. Or drink tea 2-3 times daily.

For infant colic: Mother drinks fennel tea—compounds pass through breast milk to baby.

Safety Notes

Very safe for nursing mothers and babies. Pleasant licorice-like flavor. Can be used long-term. Generally well-tolerated.

REMEDY 19: Damiana - Libido and Mood Enhancer

What It Heals

Traditional aphrodisiac: low libido, sexual dysfunction, mild depression, anxiety, hormonal fatigue, enhances pleasure and sensation.

Why It Works

Contains flavonoids and volatile oils with mild mood-lifting and energy-enhancing properties. Used for centuries in Mexico for sexual vitality. May increase blood flow to genitals and enhance sensitivity. Also mild nervine (calms anxiety that inhibits libido).

How to Make It

Ingredients:

- 1-2 teaspoons dried damiana leaf
- 1 cup hot water

Instructions:

1. Place damiana in teapot.
2. Pour hot water, cover.
3. Steep 10-15 minutes.
4. Strain, drink.

   Or tincture: 1 part dried leaf to 5 parts vodka (40%), 4 weeks.

How to Use It

For libido/mood: 1 cup tea or 2-3 mL tincture, 1-2 times daily. Effects build over weeks of consistent use.

Can take before intimacy: Some people notice enhanced sensation with acute dose.

Safety Notes

Very safe. Mild effects—not a dramatic aphrodisiac but gentle support. Generally well-tolerated. Pleasant, slightly bitter taste. Can be used long-term.

REMEDY 20: Pine Pollen - Natural Testosterone Support

What It Heals

One of few herbs with actual testosterone: low androgen symptoms (low energy, low libido, depression) in women, supports male hormonal health, builds strength and vitality.

Why It Works

Contains phytoandrogens—plant testosterone. Provides actual testosterone-like compounds. Can be beneficial for women with **very low androgens** but must be used cautiously (many women have excess androgens, not deficiency).

How to Make It

Note: Pine pollen is harvested as powder. Tincture (alcohol) extracts testosterone; powder does not.

Pine Pollen Tincture (for testosterone):

- 1 part pine pollen powder
- 2 parts high-proof alcohol (80-90%)
- Let sit 4 weeks, shaking daily
- Strain

Or use as powder (doesn't extract testosterone but provides other nutrients).

How to Use It

For low androgen symptoms: 1-2 mL tincture, 1-2 times daily. Start low.

Or powder: ½-1 teaspoon in smoothies (doesn't provide testosterone, but provides nutrients).

Safety Notes

Not for everyone. Use cautiously if you have PCOS or excess androgens (will worsen symptoms). Start very low—powerful. Can cause acne, irritability if dose too high. Consult practitioner before use.

REMEDY 21: Sage - Hot Flash Eliminator

What It Heals

Rapid hot flash and night sweat relief: reduces perspiration dramatically, stops hot flashes within 30 minutes for many women, improves sleep quality (less night sweats).

Why It Works

Sage has **antiperspirant properties**—reduces perspiration throughout body. Contains thujaone and tannins that dry secretions. Traditionally used to "dry up" excessive sweating, breast milk when weaning, and stop night sweats.

How to Make It

Ingredients:

- 1-2 teaspoons dried sage leaf
- 1 cup hot water

Instructions:

1. Place sage in mug.
2. Pour hot water, cover.
3. Steep 10-15 minutes.
4. Strain, drink.

How to Use It

For night sweats: Drink 1 cup before bed.

For hot flashes: 1 cup, 2-3 times daily. Or take 2 mL tincture, 2-3 times daily.

Works rapidly—many women notice effects within 30 minutes to a few hours.

Safety Notes

Very safe for short-term use. **Not for long-term daily use** (high thujone content—use for 2-3 weeks, then take break). Not during nursing (will reduce milk supply—this is intentional if weaning). Generally well-tolerated.

REMEDY 22: Licorice Root - Mild Estrogen and Adrenal Support

What It Heals

Mild estrogenic support: perimenopausal transition, adrenal fatigue, low cortisol, supports hormone balance, eases transition off hormone therapy.

Why It Works

Contains phytoestrogens (mild estrogenic effects) and supports cortisol regulation (adrenals and ovaries work together—adrenal support aids hormonal transition). Also anti-inflammatory and soothing.

How to Make It

Ingredients:

- 1 teaspoon dried licorice root
- 2 cups water

Instructions:

1. Place root in pot with water.
2. Bring to boil.
3. Simmer 10-15 minutes.
4. Strain, drink.

Sweet, pleasant taste—natural sweetener.

How to Use It

For hormone support: 1-2 cups tea daily. Or tincture: 2 mL, twice daily.

Not for long-term continuous use—cycle 6 weeks on, 2 weeks off.

Safety Notes

Can raise blood pressure in some people (monitor BP if using long-term). Avoid if you have high blood pressure, heart disease, or kidney disease. Safe in normal doses for most people. Very sweet, pleasant taste.

REMEDY 23: Schisandra Berry - Adaptogen for Hormonal Stress

What It Heals

Five-flavor adaptogen: stress-related hormonal imbalance, fatigue, skin aging, liver support (metabolizes hormones), enhances resilience, improves mood.

Why It Works

Adaptogen supporting entire endocrine system plus liver detox (critical for hormone metabolism). Contains lignans (schisandrin) that support liver's ability to process and eliminate hormones. Reduces cortisol, improves stress response.

How to Make It

Ingredients:

- 1 tablespoon dried schisandra berries
- 3 cups water

Instructions:

1. Place berries in pot with water.
2. Bring to boil.
3. Simmer 20-30 minutes.
4. Strain (or leave berries in—edible).

How to Use It

For hormonal support: 2-3 cups tea daily. Or tincture: 2-3 mL, twice daily.

For liver/hormone metabolism: Take consistently for 2-3 months.

Safety Notes

Very safe for long-term use. Mild stimulant effect (some feel energized). Generally well-tolerated. Unique sour-sweet-salty-bitter-pungent flavor (hence "five-flavor").

REMEDY 24: Tribulus Terrestris - Libido and Fertility

What It Heals

Traditional aphrodisiac and fertility herb: low libido (both genders), PCOS support, fertility issues, enhances ovulation, improves egg quality.

Why It Works

Supports LH (luteinizing hormone) production—LH triggers ovulation. Also increases free testosterone (beneficial for low libido). Used in Ayurvedic and Chinese medicine for centuries for reproductive health.

How to Make It

Note: Typically purchased as extract or powder.

Look for: Standardized extract (40% saponins), 500-1,000 mg capsules.

How to Use It

For fertility: 500-1,000 mg daily, first half of cycle (day 1-14) to support ovulation.

For libido: 500-1,000 mg daily, long-term.

Safety Notes

Generally safe. May cause stomach upset (take with food). Not during pregnancy. Can increase androgens—use cautiously if you have PCOS with high androgens.

REMEDY 25: Pomegranate - Phytoestrogen and Antioxidant

What It Heals

Fruit for: menopausal symptoms, cardiovascular health, antioxidant support, skin aging, breast health, cognitive function.

Why It Works

Rich in phytoestrogens (especially in seeds) and powerful antioxidants (ellagic acid, punicalagins). Supports estrogen balance, reduces oxidative stress, protects cardiovascular system (heart disease risk increases after menopause).

How to Make It

Note: Eat fresh pomegranate or drink pure juice.

Fresh Pomegranate:

- Eat ½-1 pomegranate daily (including seeds for maximum phytoestrogens).

Pure Pomegranate Juice:

- Drink 4-8 oz daily (look for 100% pure, no added sugar).

How to Use It

For menopause: Drink 8 oz juice daily or eat fresh fruit regularly.

For cardiovascular health: 4-8 oz juice daily, long-term.

Safety Notes

Very safe. High in natural sugars—diabetics monitor blood sugar. May interact with certain medications (metabolized by liver enzymes—consult pharmacist). Generally well-tolerated.

REMEDY 26: Flax Seeds - Lignans and Omega-3s

What It Heals

Seed for: estrogen balance, breast health, cardiovascular health, menopausal symptoms, supports healthy estrogen metabolism, reduces hot flashes.

Why It Works

Rich in lignans—phytoestrogens that support healthy estrogen metabolism (convert "bad" estrogens to "good" estrogens). Also high in omega-3 ALA (anti-inflammatory). Fiber binds excess estrogen for elimination.

How to Make It

Ground Flax Seeds (must be ground):

1. Purchase whole flax seeds.
2. Store in refrigerator or freezer.
3. Grind fresh daily (coffee grinder or blender).
4. Use immediately—oxidizes rapidly once ground.

Add to: smoothies, oatmeal, yogurt, salads, baked goods.

How to Use It

For hormone balance: 1-2 tablespoons ground flax daily.

For menopause: 2 tablespoons daily (studies show reduces hot flashes).

Must be ground—whole seeds pass through undigested.

Safety Notes

Very safe. High fiber—ensure adequate water intake. May cause digestive changes initially (start with 1 tablespoon). Mild blood-thinning effect. Safe for most people long-term.

REMEDY 27: Saw Palmetto - Blocks Excess Testosterone

What It Heals

Herb for: PCOS (polycystic ovarian syndrome), excess androgens, hormonal acne, unwanted facial hair (hirsutism), male-pattern hair loss in women.

Why It Works

Blocks 5-alpha-reductase enzyme that converts testosterone to DHT (dihydrotestosterone). DHT causes acne, facial hair, and hair loss. By blocking this conversion, reduces androgenic symptoms.

How to Make It

Note: Purchased as extract (from berries).

Look for: Standardized extract (85-95% fatty acids and sterols), 160 mg capsules.

How to Use It

For PCOS/androgens: 160 mg extract, twice daily (320 mg total).

For acne/hirsutism: 160 mg, twice daily for 3-6 months minimum.

Safety Notes

Generally safe. May cause mild digestive upset (take with food). Can affect hormone levels—consult practitioner if on hormonal medications. Takes 3-6 months for full effects on hair/acne.

REMEDY 28: Peony & Licorice Formula - TCM for PCOS

What It Heals

Classic Chinese medicine formula for: PCOS, regulates cycles, reduces androgens, supports ovulation, balances estrogen-to-testosterone ratio.

Why It Works

White peony lowers testosterone. **Licorice** raises estrogen. Together, they balance the estrogen-to-testosterone ratio that's disrupted in PCOS. Used in China for centuries for "blood deficiency and liver Qi stagnation" (PCOS symptoms in TCM terms).

How to Make It

Ingredients:

- 2 tablespoons dried white peony root
- 1 teaspoon dried licorice root
- 4 cups water

Instructions:

1. Place both roots in pot with water.
2. Bring to boil.
3. Simmer 20-30 minutes.
4. Strain.

Traditional ratio: 20:1 (peony:licorice).

How to Use It

For PCOS: 2 cups tea daily for 3-6 months.

Or purchase as prepared formula (Shakuyaku-kanzo-to in Japanese, Shao Yao Gan Cao Tang in Chinese).

Safety Notes

Generally safe. Contains licorice—monitor blood pressure. Works best under TCM practitioner guidance for individualized dosing. Takes 3-6 months for full effects.

REMEDY 29: Kelp/Bladderwrack - Thyroid Support (Iodine)

What It Heals

Seaweed for: hypothyroidism (if iodine-deficient), supports thyroid hormone production, provides essential minerals, supports metabolism.

Why It Works

Provides iodine—essential for thyroid hormone synthesis (T3, T4). Many people are iodine-deficient (depleted soils, less iodized salt consumption). **Critical:** Only effective if hypothyroidism is due to iodine deficiency.

How to Make It

Note: Kelp is purchased as powder or dried seaweed.

Kelp Powder:

- Add ½ teaspoon to food daily (sprinkle on salads, soups, smoothies).

Or take as capsules: 150-300 mcg iodine daily.

How to Use It

For hypothyroidism: ½ teaspoon kelp powder daily (provides approximately 150-300 mcg iodine).

Important: Get thyroid tested first—determine if iodine deficiency is issue.

Safety Notes

Not for hyperthyroidism. Not for Hashimoto's (autoimmune thyroid—iodine can worsen). Can interact with thyroid medications. Get thyroid function tested before and during use. Too much iodine can suppress thyroid function.

REMEDY 30: Rhodiola Rosea - Energy, Mood, Resilience

What It Heals

Adaptogen for: fatigue, depression, stress-related hormonal imbalance, low energy affecting libido, mental fog, physical endurance.

Why It Works

Adaptogen supporting HPA (hypothalamic-pituitary-adrenal) axis—reduces cortisol, increases energy and mood without overstimulation. Contains rosavins and salidroside (active compounds). Improves stress resilience, which supports hormone balance (chronic stress disrupts reproductive hormones).

How to Make It

Note: Purchased as extract.

Look for: Standardized extract (3% rosavins, 1% salidroside), 200-400 mg capsules.

How to Use It

For energy/mood: 200-400 mg extract daily, morning or early afternoon (can be stimulating).

For stress/hormones: 200 mg twice daily.

Take on empty stomach for best absorption.

Safety Notes

Very safe. Can be stimulating—avoid evening doses. Start with lower dose. Generally well-tolerated. Not during pregnancy. Works within days to weeks.

REMEDY 31: Seed Cycling Protocol - Food as Hormone Medicine

What It Heals

Nutritional protocol for: irregular cycles, PMS symptoms, hormonal acne, low progesterone, estrogen dominance, supports fertility, teaches body natural rhythm.

Why It Works

Different seeds contain specific lignans and nutrients supporting either estrogen or progesterone:

Flax and pumpkin (follicular phase): Support healthy estrogen production while binding excess. Rich in omega-3s and zinc.

Sesame and sunflower (luteal phase): High in selenium and vitamin E—essential for progesterone production. Sesame lignans block excess estrogen.

Provides targeted nutritional support for each hormone at the right time.

How to Make It

Phase 1: Follicular (Days 1-14) - Estrogen Support:

- 1 tablespoon ground flax seeds
- 1 tablespoon ground pumpkin seeds

Phase 2: Luteal (Days 15-28) - Progesterone Support:

- 1 tablespoon ground sesame seeds
- 1 tablespoon ground sunflower seeds

Instructions:

1. Purchase raw, organic seeds in bulk.
2. Store in refrigerator/freezer.
3. Grind fresh daily (coffee grinder).
4. Add to smoothies, oatmeal, yogurt, salads.

Must be ground fresh—whole seeds undigested, pre-ground oxidize.

How to Use It

For cycle regulation: Follow protocol 3-6 months minimum. Day 1 = first day of menstruation.

If no regular cycle: Follow moon phases (new moon = day 1).

For menopause: Follow moon phases.

Safety Notes

Extremely safe—this is food. Generally well-tolerated. Can cause mild digestive changes initially (high fiber). Flax seeds moderate amounts during pregnancy. Results take 3+ months. Very gentle approach.

REMEDY 32: Castor Oil Packs for Reproductive Health

What It Heals

External therapy for: uterine fibroids (reduces size and symptoms), ovarian cysts, endometriosis (reduces pain/inflammation), pelvic pain, fertility support (improves circulation), menstrual cramping.

Why It Works

Castor oil contains ricinoleic acid—penetrates deeply through skin, increases circulation to reproductive organs, supports lymphatic drainage, reduces inflammation. Creates therapeutic heating effect supporting healing.

How to Make It

Materials:

- Cold-pressed, hexane-free castor oil
- Flannel cloth (wool or cotton)

- Plastic wrap
- Heating pad
- Old sheets/towels (stains)

Instructions:

1. Saturate flannel with castor oil (wet but not dripping).
2. Lie down, place cloth over lower abdomen.
3. Cover with plastic wrap.
4. Place heating pad on top (medium heat).
5. Relax 45-60 minutes.
6. Remove, clean skin with baking soda water.
7. Store cloth in jar (reuse, add more oil as needed).

How to Use It

For fibroids/cysts/endometriosis: 3-4 times per week consistently.

For fertility: Daily for several months (except during menstruation and after ovulation if trying to conceive).

For cramping: Use as needed during menstruation.

Best time: Evening before bed.

Safety Notes

Very safe. Messy—use old linens. **Avoid during menstruation** (increases flow). **Not during pregnancy.** Not over open wounds. Generally well-tolerated.

REMEDY 33: Yoni Steam - Vaginal Steam Therapy

What It Heals

Traditional practice for: menstrual cramping, irregular cycles, fertility support, postpartum healing, pelvic tension, supports tissue health, spiritual/emotional release.

Why It Works

Warm herbal steam increases circulation to pelvic area, relaxes tissues, delivers herbal properties through vaginal mucosa (highly absorptive). Used in many cultures (Korea, Central America, Africa) for reproductive health.

How to Make It

Herbal Steam Blend:

Ingredients (choose 2-3):

- Lavender (relaxing, antiseptic)
- Rose (heart-opening, soothing)
- Calendula (healing, anti-inflammatory)
- Mugwort (traditional, regulating)
- Basil (warming, circulation)

Instructions:

1. Boil water with 2-3 tablespoons chosen herbs.
2. Simmer 5 minutes.
3. Pour into heat-safe bowl.
4. Sit comfortably over steam (safely—not too hot).
5. Steam for 20-30 minutes.

How to Use It

For cycle support: 1-2 times per week.

Avoid during: Menstruation, pregnancy, active infection, IUD.

After steam: Rest, stay warm.

Safety Notes

Generally safe when done correctly. **Test temperature carefully**—vaginal tissue sensitive. Don't steam during menstruation (increases flow), pregnancy, or with IUD. Not if active infection. Controversial practice—use personal judgment.

REMEDY 34: Progesterone-Supporting Foods - Nutritional Foundation

What It Heals

Dietary support for: progesterone production, supports healthy luteal phase, reduces PMS, supports fertility, provides cofactors for hormone synthesis.

Why It Works

Your body cannot make adequate progesterone without specific nutrients—they're cofactors for hormone synthesis enzymes:

Vitamin B6: Essential for progesterone production (chickpeas, salmon, chicken, potatoes, bananas).

Magnesium: Cofactor for hormone synthesis (dark leafy greens, nuts, seeds, dark chocolate, avocado).

Zinc: Critical for hormone production and receptor function (oysters, beef, pumpkin seeds, lentils, chickpeas).

Vitamin C: Supports progesterone synthesis (citrus, berries, bell peppers, broccoli, kiwi).

How to Make It

Progesterone-Supporting Meal Plan:

Daily focus: Include these foods daily, especially in luteal phase (day 14-28):

Breakfast:

- Oatmeal with ground flaxseeds, berries, almonds

Lunch:

- Salmon with quinoa and steamed broccoli
- Large leafy green salad

Dinner:

- Grass-fed beef or lentils
- Roasted sweet potato
- Sautéed spinach

Snacks:

- Pumpkin seeds
- Dark chocolate
- Chickpea hummus with veggies

How to Use It

For hormone balance: Incorporate these foods daily as foundation of diet.

During luteal phase: Emphasize these foods especially day 14-28.

Supplement if needed: B-complex, magnesium, zinc (see remedies 37-39).

Safety Notes

Extremely safe—whole foods. Generally beneficial for everyone. Focus on nutrient-dense whole foods over supplements when possible.

REMEDY 35: Liver Detox for Hormone Balance

What It Heals

Liver support for: estrogen dominance, hormonal acne, PMS, irregular cycles, clears used hormones, supports healthy metabolism, reduces toxic burden.

Why It Works

Liver metabolizes and eliminates used hormones. Congested liver = hormone imbalance. Liver converts estrogen into forms that can be eliminated. If liver function poor, estrogen recirculates causing estrogen dominance.

Phase 1: Liver breaks down hormones.

Phase 2: Liver conjugates hormones for elimination (requires specific nutrients).

How to Make It

Liver Support Protocol:

Daily practices:

1. **Milk thistle tincture:** 2-3 mL, 3 times daily (see Chapter 9, Remedy 1).

2. **Dandelion root tea:** 2 cups daily (see Chapter 9, Remedy 2).

3. **Cruciferous vegetables daily:** Broccoli, cauliflower, Brussels sprouts, kale, cabbage (contain DIM—see Remedy 36).

4. **Castor oil pack:** Over liver area (right upper abdomen), 3-4 times per week (see Chapter 9, Remedy 5).

5. **Lemon water:** Upon waking (see Chapter 9, Remedy 6).

How to Use It

For hormone balance: Follow liver support protocol consistently for 3-6 months.

Combine with: Other hormone-balancing herbs for comprehensive approach.

Safety Notes

Very safe. Supports overall health. See Chapter 9 for detailed safety notes on individual remedies.

REMEDY 36: DIM (Diindolylmethane) - Estrogen Metabolism

What It Heals

Compound from cruciferous vegetables for: estrogen dominance, hormonal acne, heavy periods, PMS, supports healthy estrogen metabolism, reduces "bad" estrogens.

Why It Works

DIM supports liver's conversion of estrogen into beneficial metabolites (2-hydroxyestrone—protective) rather than harmful metabolites (16-hydroxyestrone—proliferative, linked to breast cancer risk). Helps body eliminate excess estrogen.

How to Make It

Food sources (cruciferous vegetables):

- Broccoli
- Cauliflower
- Brussels sprouts
- Kale
- Cabbage
- Bok choy

Eat daily: 1-2 cups cruciferous vegetables (raw or lightly cooked).

Supplement: DIM extract, 100-200 mg daily (if not eating adequate cruciferous vegetables).

How to Use It

For estrogen dominance: Eat cruciferous vegetables daily. Or supplement: 100-200 mg DIM daily.

For hormonal acne: 100 mg daily for 3-6 months.

Best with fat: Take supplement with food containing fat (improves absorption).

Safety Notes

Generally safe. High doses can cause digestive upset, headache (start low). May alter estrogen metabolism—consult practitioner if on hormonal medications. Safe for most women.

REMEDY 37: Magnesium - The Relaxation Mineral

What It Heals

Essential mineral for: PMS, anxiety, cramping, insomnia, muscle tension, headaches (hormonal), supports progesterone production, blood sugar regulation.

Why It Works

Magnesium is cofactor for progesterone production. Relaxes muscles (reduces cramping), calms nervous system (reduces PMS anxiety), regulates blood sugar (prevents insulin spikes that disrupt hormones). Most people are deficient (depleted soils, stress depletes magnesium).

How to Make It

Food sources:

- Dark leafy greens (spinach, Swiss chard)
- Nuts and seeds (almonds, pumpkin seeds, cashews)
- Dark chocolate
- Avocado
- Legumes
- Whole grains

Supplement forms:

- **Magnesium glycinate:** Best for sleep, anxiety, muscle relaxation (doesn't cause diarrhea)
- **Magnesium citrate:** Good for constipation (mild laxative effect)
- **Magnesium threonate:** Best for brain/cognitive support

How to Use It

For PMS/cramping/anxiety: 300-400 mg magnesium glycinate daily, especially during luteal phase.

For sleep: 400 mg glycinate before bed.

For constipation: 300-400 mg citrate daily.

Or Epsom salt baths: 2 cups Epsom salts (magnesium sulfate) in bath, 2-3 times per week (absorbed through skin).

Safety Notes

Very safe. High doses can cause diarrhea (reduce dose). Take with food if causes stomach upset. Generally well-tolerated. Essential nutrient.

REMEDY 38: B-Complex Vitamins - Hormone Synthesis Support

What It Heals

Essential vitamins for: all hormone production, energy, mood, stress resilience, metabolism, supports liver detoxification (metabolizes hormones), nervous system health.

Why It Works

B vitamins are essential cofactors for hormone synthesis, liver detoxification (Phase 1 and 2), and neurotransmitter production (serotonin, dopamine—affect mood during cycle). Stress and birth control deplete B vitamins. Most people need supplementation.

How to Make It

Food sources:

- **B6:** Chickpeas, salmon, chicken, potatoes, bananas
- **B12:** Animal products (meat, fish, eggs, dairy)
- **Folate:** Leafy greens, legumes, asparagus

- **B1, B2, B3:** Whole grains, legumes, nuts

Supplement: High-quality B-complex with methylated forms (methylfolate, methylcobalamin) if possible—better absorbed.

How to Use It

For hormone balance: Take B-complex daily with breakfast (B vitamins can be energizing).

Look for: 50-100 mg of most B vitamins (B12 typically higher—500-1,000 mcg).

Safety Notes

Very safe—water-soluble (excess excreted). Can cause bright yellow urine (normal—riboflavin). Take with food. Generally well-tolerated. Essential nutrients.

REMEDY 39: Zinc - Hormone Production and Skin

What It Heals

Essential mineral for: PCOS, hormonal acne, progesterone production, fertility, immune function, wound healing, supports hormone receptor function.

Why It Works

Zinc is essential for hormone production and receptor function. Deficiency extremely common (depleted soils). Critical for progesterone synthesis, insulin function (PCOS), skin healing (acne), immune function.

How to Make It

Food sources:

- Oysters (highest source)
- Beef, lamb
- Pumpkin seeds
- Lentils, chickpeas
- Cashews

Supplement: 15-30 mg elemental zinc daily. Forms: zinc picolinate, zinc glycinate (well-absorbed).

How to Use It

For hormone balance: 15-30 mg daily with food (can cause nausea on empty stomach).

For PCOS/acne: 30 mg daily for 3-6 months.

For fertility: 15-30 mg daily.

Safety Notes

Safe in appropriate doses. Can cause nausea if taken without food. **Don't exceed 40 mg daily long-term** (can interfere with copper absorption). Generally well-tolerated. Essential nutrient.

REMEDY 40: Complete Hormone Balance Protocol - 3-Month Restoration

What It Heals

Comprehensive program for: complete hormonal restoration, addresses root causes, sustainable long-term balance, individualized approach based on symptoms.

Why It Works

True hormone balance requires multi-phase approach addressing: toxin elimination, liver support, nutrient repletion, stress management, cycle-specific herbal support, lifestyle optimization. Single remedies help—comprehensive protocol transforms.

How to Make It

3-Month Hormone Balance Protocol:

PHASE 1: FOUNDATION (Weeks 1-4)

Eliminate hormone disruptors:

- Plastics (store food in glass)
- Conventional personal care products (switch to natural)
- Non-organic produce (especially "dirty dozen")
- Processed foods, refined sugar
- Reduce alcohol, caffeine

Support liver detoxification:

- Milk thistle: 2-3 mL, 3 times daily
- Dandelion root tea: 2 cups daily
- Cruciferous vegetables: 1-2 cups daily
- Castor oil pack over liver: 3x/week
- Lemon water: Daily upon waking

Nutrient repletion:

- Magnesium: 300-400 mg daily
- B-complex: Daily with breakfast
- Zinc: 15-30 mg daily
- Omega-3s: 1,000-2,000 mg EPA+DHA daily

Stress management:

- Adaptogenic herbs: Ashwagandha 300-600 mg, or rhodiola 200-400 mg daily
- Daily movement (yoga, walking)
- Sleep optimization: 7-9 hours nightly

PHASE 2: REGULATION (Weeks 5-8)

Continue Phase 1, plus add:

Cycle-specific herbs:

Every morning: Vitex 2-3 mL (consistency critical)

Follicular phase (days 1-14):

- Seed cycling: 1 tablespoon each ground flax + pumpkin seeds daily
- Focus on building blood if anemic (nettle infusion, dong quai after period)

Luteal phase (days 15-28):

- Seed cycling: 1 tablespoon each ground sesame + sunflower seeds daily
- Evening primrose oil: 1,500 mg daily
- Wild yam cream: Apply twice daily
- Extra magnesium: 400 mg before bed

Daily uterine tonic:

- Red raspberry leaf infusion: 2-3 cups daily

Weekly support:

- Castor oil pack over lower abdomen: 3-4x/week

PHASE 3: OPTIMIZATION (Weeks 9-12)

Continue foundation and cycle-specific support, plus add targeted herbs based on specific symptoms:

For PMS:

- Continue: Vitex, evening primrose, magnesium
- Add: Motherwort 2-3 mL as needed for anxiety

For heavy bleeding:

- Lady's mantle: 3 cups tea during menstruation
- Shepherd's purse: 3-5 mL tincture if severe

- Nettle infusion: 3-4 cups daily (iron)

For menopause:

- Black cohosh: 2-3 mL, 2-3 times daily
- Sage: 1 cup tea before bed (night sweats)
- Red clover infusion: 2-4 cups daily
- Maca: 1-2 teaspoons daily

For PCOS:

- Saw palmetto: 160 mg, twice daily
- Peony & licorice formula: 2 cups tea daily
- DIM: 100-200 mg daily
- Focus on blood sugar regulation (cinnamon, chromium)

For low libido:

- Maca: 1-2 teaspoons daily
- Damiana: 2-3 mL tincture, twice daily
- Shatavari: 1-2 teaspoons in warm milk, twice daily

For thyroid issues:

- Ashwagandha: 600 mg daily (if hypothyroid)
- Kelp: ½ teaspoon daily (if iodine-deficient—test first)
- Avoid if hyperthyroid or Hashimoto's

How to Use It

Follow protocol for minimum 3 months.

Track progress:

- Keep detailed cycle journal (symptoms, flow, mood, energy)
- Note changes by month
- Most women see significant improvement by month 3

After 3 months:

- Continue core practices (nutrients, adaptogens, liver support)
- Maintain cycle-specific herbs (vitex, seed cycling)
- Add/adjust targeted herbs as needed
- Consider working with herbalist or functional medicine practitioner for fine-tuning

Maintenance long-term:

- Daily: Nutrients, adaptogens, liver support
- Cyclically: Seed cycling, vitex
- Weekly: Castor oil packs
- Monthly: Evaluate and adjust

Safety Notes

Comprehensive protocols ideally supervised by knowledgeable practitioner. Start gently—too many changes at once can be overwhelming. Listen to body—adjust intensity if needed. Allow time—hormones don't balance overnight. Not during pregnancy (most herbs). Consult practitioner if on hormonal medications.

CHAPTER 8: BRAIN, MEMORY & MOOD

Focus: Cognitive Function, Mental Clarity, Emotional Balance

Your brain is **everything**.

It's where you think, feel, remember, create, decide, dream, and experience the world. It's the command center of your entire existence.

When your brain is healthy, you feel **sharp, focused, emotionally balanced, and mentally resilient**. When it's not: brain fog, memory loss, depression, anxiety, lack of motivation, difficulty concentrating, mental fatigue, emotional instability.

Modern life is **waging war on your brain**:

- **Chronic stress** (elevates cortisol, shrinks hippocampus, impairs memory)
- **Poor sleep** (prevents memory consolidation, accelerates cognitive decline)
- **Inflammatory diet** (damages neurons, disrupts neurotransmitters)
- **Environmental toxins** (heavy metals, pesticides—neurotoxic)
- **Digital overload** (fragments attention, reduces focus capacity)
- **Sedentary lifestyle** (reduces brain-derived neurotrophic factor—BDNF)

The result: **epidemic of cognitive decline, depression, anxiety, and premature brain aging**.

If you experience:

- **Brain fog** (can't think clearly, feel mentally sluggish)
- **Memory problems** (forget names, lose track of conversations, can't recall information)
- **Difficulty concentrating** (can't focus, easily distracted)
- **Depression** (low mood, lack of joy, hopelessness)
- **Anxiety** (worry, racing thoughts, panic)
- **Mental fatigue** (exhausted from thinking, decision fatigue)
- **Age-related cognitive decline** (struggling more than you used to)

Then this chapter is your **cognitive restoration toolkit**.

Modern psychiatry offers **pharmaceutical Band-Aids** (antidepressants, anti-anxiety medications, stimulants) that alter brain chemistry without addressing root causes—often with significant side effects.

Herbal medicine offers **neuroprotection, neuroregeneration, and neurotransmitter support** that works with your brain's innate healing capacity.

This chapter provides remedies for:

- ☑ **Memory and cognitive enhancement**
- ☑ **Depression and mood support**
- ☑ **Anxiety and stress relief**
- ☑ **Focus and concentration**
- ☑ **Neuroprotection and brain aging**
- ☑ **Mental energy and clarity**

Each remedy includes:

- ☑ **What it heals**
- ☑ **Why it works**
- ☑ **How to make it**

- ☑ **How to use it**
- ☑ **Safety notes**

Let's restore your cognitive vitality.

REMEDY 1: Lion's Mane Mushroom - Neurogenesis Powerhouse

What It Heals

Lion's mane is the premier **brain-regenerating mushroom**: supports neurogenesis (growth of new neurons), improves memory and cognitive function, protects against Alzheimer's and dementia, reduces brain fog, supports nerve regeneration, treats mild cognitive impairment, enhances focus and clarity.

Why It Works

Lion's mane contains **hericenones and erinacines**—unique compounds that cross the blood-brain barrier and stimulate production of **NGF (nerve growth factor)**. NGF is essential for:

- Growth of new neurons (neurogenesis)
- Maintenance of existing neurons
- Formation of myelin (insulation around nerves)
- Synaptic plasticity (learning and memory)

Studies show lion's mane significantly improves cognitive function in people with mild cognitive impairment. Also promotes remyelination (critical for MS, nerve damage).

How to Make It

Lion's Mane Decoction:

Ingredients:

- 2 tablespoons dried lion's mane mushroom (chopped)
- 4 cups water

Instructions:

1. Place mushroom in pot with water.
2. Bring to boil.
3. Reduce to lowest simmer.
4. Cover, simmer 2-3 hours (mushrooms require long extraction).
5. Strain (save mushroom—can re-simmer once more).
6. Drink throughout day.

Or purchase: Lion's mane extract powder (dual-extracted—alcohol and water for complete compounds). 1-2 grams daily in coffee, tea, or smoothies.

How to Use It

For cognitive enhancement: 1-2 grams extract powder daily, or 2-3 cups decoction daily.

For memory/cognitive decline: 2-3 grams extract daily for minimum 3-6 months (neurogenesis takes time).

For nerve regeneration: 3 grams daily, long-term.

Effects build over weeks to months—be patient.

Safety Notes

Extremely safe. Very well-tolerated. Rare allergic reactions (mushroom family). Can be used daily indefinitely. Safe for most people. Mild, slightly sweet taste.

REMEDY 2: Ginkgo Biloba - Memory and Circulation

What It Heals

One of oldest living tree species and most studied brain herbs: improves memory and recall, enhances cognitive function, increases blood flow to brain, protects against Alzheimer's and dementia, treats tinnitus (ringing in ears), supports vision health, improves circulation to extremities.

Why It Works

Ginkgo contains **flavonoids and terpenoids (ginkgolides, bilobalide)** that:

- **Increase cerebral blood flow** (more oxygen and nutrients to brain)
- Act as powerful **antioxidants** (protect neurons from free radical damage)
- **Inhibit platelet aggregation** (improves microcirculation)
- **Protect mitochondria** (energy production in brain cells)
- **Modulate neurotransmitters** (acetylcholine, dopamine, serotonin)

Extensively studied—shown to improve memory, cognitive speed, and quality of life in people with dementia.

How to Make It

Ginkgo Tincture:

Ingredients:

- 1 part dried ginkgo leaves
- 5 parts vodka (40-50%)

Instructions:

1. Place leaves in jar.
2. Cover with alcohol.
3. Seal, label with date.
4. Let sit 4-6 weeks, shaking daily.
5. Strain, bottle in amber bottles.

Or purchase: Standardized ginkgo extract (24% flavone glycosides, 6% terpene lactones)—most research uses this standardization.

How to Use It

For memory/cognition: 2-3 mL tincture, 2-3 times daily. Or standardized extract: 120-240 mg daily (divided into 2-3 doses).

For dementia prevention: 240 mg standardized extract daily, long-term.

For tinnitus: 240 mg daily for 8-12 weeks (effective for some people).

Takes **4-6 weeks for full effects**—consistent daily use required.

Safety Notes

Generally safe. **Mild blood-thinning effect**—consult doctor if on anticoagulants or before surgery. Can cause mild headache initially (improves with continued use). Rare: digestive upset, dizziness. Don't use with MAO inhibitors. Generally well-tolerated.

REMEDY 3: Bacopa Monnieri - Memory Enhancer

What It Heals

Ayurvedic "herb of grace" for scholars and monks: significantly improves memory formation and recall, enhances learning ability, reduces anxiety (calming without sedation), improves processing speed, protects neurons from damage, supports ADHD symptoms.

Why It Works

Bacopa contains **bacosides**—compounds that:

- **Enhance synaptic transmission** (communication between neurons)

- **Increase dendritic branching** (more connections between neurons—critical for learning)
- **Act as antioxidants** (protect neurons from oxidative stress)
- **Modulate serotonin and dopamine** (improves mood while enhancing cognition)
- **Reduce cortisol** (protects hippocampus from stress damage)

Multiple studies show significant improvements in memory, learning, and information processing. Effects are cumulative—stronger with longer use.

How to Make It

Bacopa Infusion:

Ingredients:

- 2 teaspoons dried bacopa (whole plant)
- 2 cups hot water

Instructions:

1. Place bacopa in teapot.
2. Pour hot water, cover.
3. Steep 15-20 minutes.
4. Strain, drink.

Or purchase: Bacopa extract (standardized to 20-50% bacosides). 300-450 mg daily.

How to Use It

For memory/learning: 300-450 mg extract daily, or 2-3 cups tea daily.

For anxiety with cognitive symptoms: 300 mg, twice daily.

Requires consistent use for 8-12 weeks to see full benefits (don't expect instant results).

Safety Notes

Very safe. Can cause mild digestive upset initially (take with food). May cause drowsiness in sensitive individuals (adjust timing). Can increase thyroid hormones slightly (beneficial for most, cautious if hyperthyroid). Generally well-tolerated. Safe long-term.

REMEDY 4: Rhodiola Rosea - Mental Energy and Resilience

What It Heals

Adaptogen for mental performance: reduces mental fatigue, improves focus and concentration under stress, enhances mood (mild antidepressant effect), increases mental endurance, reduces brain fog, supports physical and mental stamina, improves stress resilience.

Why It Works

Rhodiola contains **rosavins and salidroside** that:

- **Increase serotonin, dopamine, norepinephrine** (without depleting them—unlike stimulants)
- **Protect neurons from stress damage** (adaptogenic effect on HPA axis)
- **Improve mitochondrial function** (more energy production in brain cells)
- **Enhance mental clarity without jitters** (non-stimulant energy)

Studies show significant improvements in mental fatigue, cognitive function, mood, and stress tolerance. Works within hours but effects strengthen with continued use.

How to Make It

Note: Rhodiola is typically purchased as standardized extract.

Look for: 3% rosavins, 1% salidroside—matches research studies.

Rhodiola Tea (less effective than extract but pleasant):

- Simmer 1 tablespoon dried root in 3 cups water, 20-30 minutes
- Strain, drink

How to Use It

For mental fatigue/focus: 200-400 mg standardized extract daily, morning or early afternoon (can be stimulating).

For depression: 200 mg, twice daily.

Acute mental performance: 200-400 mg before cognitively demanding tasks.

Take on empty stomach for best absorption.

Safety Notes

Very safe. Can be stimulating—avoid evening doses. Start with lower dose (some people very sensitive). Not during pregnancy. Generally well-tolerated. Works quickly (days to weeks).

REMEDY 5: Ashwagandha - Anxiety and Stress Resilience

What It Heals

Adaptogen for stress-related cognitive impairment: reduces anxiety (comparable to pharmaceutical anxiolytics in studies), lowers cortisol, protects hippocampus from stress damage, improves memory (especially stress-impaired memory), reduces brain fog from chronic stress, supports sleep quality.

Why It Works

Ashwagandha contains **withanolides** that:

- **Reduce cortisol** (high cortisol damages hippocampus—memory center)
- **Modulate GABA receptors** (calming neurotransmitter—reduces anxiety)
- **Protect neurons** from stress-induced damage
- **Support neurotransmitter balance** (serotonin, dopamine)

Studies show 30-40% reduction in cortisol and significant anxiety reduction within 8 weeks. Protects brain from chronic stress damage.

How to Make It

Ashwagandha Golden Milk:

- 1 teaspoon ashwagandha powder
- 1 teaspoon turmeric powder
- 1 cup warm milk (dairy or non-dairy)
- 1 teaspoon honey
- Pinch black pepper

Instructions:

1. Heat milk gently.
2. Whisk in powders and pepper.
3. Add honey.
4. Drink before bed (promotes sleep).

Or use standardized extract: 300-600 mg daily.

How to Use It

For anxiety/stress: 300-600 mg extract or 1-2 teaspoons powder, once or twice daily.

For sleep and stress: Take before bed.

Continue for 8-12 weeks for full adaptogenic effects.

Safety Notes

Very safe long-term. Avoid with hyperthyroidism (can increase thyroid hormones). May cause drowsiness—use this therapeutically. Not during pregnancy. Generally well-tolerated.

REMEDY 6: St. John's Wort - Depression Support

What It Heals

One of most studied herbs for depression: treats mild to moderate depression (as effective as SSRIs in studies), reduces anxiety, improves mood, supports seasonal affective disorder (SAD), relieves nerve pain, supports wound healing topically.

Why It Works

St. John's wort contains **hypericin and hyperforin** that:

- **Inhibit reuptake of serotonin, dopamine, and norepinephrine** (similar mechanism to pharmaceutical antidepressants but gentler)
- **Modulate GABA** (calming)
- **Reduce inflammation in brain** (neuroinflammation contributes to depression)

Over 30 clinical trials show effectiveness comparable to SSRIs for mild-moderate depression, with fewer side effects. Takes 4-6 weeks for full effects (like pharmaceutical antidepressants).

How to Make It

St. John's Wort Tincture:

Ingredients:

- 1 part fresh St. John's wort flowering tops (or dried)
- 2 parts vodka (fresh) or 5 parts vodka (dried, 50%)

Instructions:

1. Harvest flowering tops (peak potency when flowering—bright yellow flowers).
2. Chop, pack in jar.
3. Cover with alcohol (turns red—hypericin releasing).
4. Seal, let sit 4-6 weeks, shaking daily.
5. Strain, bottle.

Fresh plant preferred—significantly more effective.

How to Use It

For depression: 2-3 mL tincture, 3 times daily (900 mg herb equivalent daily in studies).

Or standardized extract: 300 mg (0.3% hypericin), 3 times daily.

Requires 4-6 weeks for full antidepressant effect—be patient and consistent.

Safety Notes

Major drug interactions—St. John's wort induces liver enzymes that metabolize many medications:

- Birth control pills (can reduce effectiveness—use backup)
- Antidepressants (risk of serotonin syndrome—don't combine)
- Blood thinners, immunosuppressants, HIV medications, many others
- **Consult doctor if on any medications**

Photosensitizing—increases sun sensitivity (protect skin). Can cause mild digestive upset. Not during pregnancy. Effective but requires medical supervision if on medications.

REMEDY 7: Lemon Balm - Anxiety and Cognitive Calm

What It Heals

Gentle nervine for: anxiety (rapid-acting), stress-related cognitive impairment, improves focus and attention (calms without sedation), insomnia, digestive upset from stress, herpes outbreaks (topical—antiviral).

Why It Works

Lemon balm contains **rosmarinic acid and volatile oils** that:

- **Modulate GABA receptors** (calming neurotransmitter)
- **Inhibit acetylcholinesterase** (increases acetylcholine—improves memory and attention)
- **Reduce cortisol response to stress** (protects brain from stress damage)
- **Antiviral** (topically for cold sores)

Studies show significant anxiety reduction within 1-3 hours. Also improves cognitive performance during stress (maintains focus while calming).

How to Make It

Lemon Balm Tea:

Ingredients:

- 2 teaspoons dried lemon balm (or 4-6 fresh leaves)
- 1 cup hot water

Instructions:

1. Place lemon balm in mug.
2. Pour hot water, cover immediately (volatile oils escape).
3. Steep 10-15 minutes, covered.
4. Strain, drink.

Pleasant lemon flavor.

How to Use It

For anxiety: Drink 1 cup as needed (works within 1 hour). Or 2-3 mL tincture, repeat as needed.

For sleep: Drink 1 cup 30-60 minutes before bed.

For cognitive support during stress: 2-3 cups daily.

Safety Notes

Extremely safe. Very gentle. Can be used as needed or daily. May reduce thyroid function in very high doses long-term (normal doses safe). Safe for children and elderly. Generally universally well-tolerated. Pleasant taste.

REMEDY 8: Holy Basil (Tulsi) - Stress-Related Brain Fog

What It Heals

Adaptogen for stress-induced cognitive impairment: clears brain fog from chronic stress, improves focus and mental clarity, reduces anxiety, balances cortisol, protects neurons from stress damage, supports mood.

Why It Works

Holy basil contains **eugenol, rosmarinic acid, and ursolic acid** that:

- **Normalize cortisol** (prevents stress-induced hippocampus damage)
- **Reduce oxidative stress** in brain
- **Modulate neurotransmitters** (serotonin, dopamine)
- **Protect against stress-induced cognitive decline**

Called "The Incomparable One" in Ayurveda—revered for bringing clarity and calm.

How to Make It

Holy Basil Tea:

Ingredients:

- 2 teaspoons dried holy basil (or 4-6 fresh leaves)

- 1 cup hot water

Instructions:

1. Place holy basil in mug.
2. Pour hot water, cover.
3. Steep 10-15 minutes.
4. Strain, drink.

How to Use It

For brain fog/stress: 2-3 cups tea daily, or 2-3 mL tincture, twice daily.

Long-term adaptogenic support: Daily for 2-3 months minimum.

Safety Notes

Very safe for daily use. May lower blood sugar (monitor if diabetic). Generally well-tolerated. Safe for children and pregnancy (in tea form). Pleasant, slightly spicy flavor.

REMEDY 9: Gotu Kola - Cognitive Clarity and Longevity

What It Heals

Ayurvedic "herb of enlightenment": enhances memory and learning, improves concentration, reduces anxiety, promotes longevity, supports wound healing, improves circulation, treats cognitive decline.

Why It Works

Gotu kola contains **triterpenoids (asiaticoside, asiatic acid, madecassoside)** that:

- **Increase BDNF** (brain-derived neurotrophic factor—supports neuron growth and survival)
- **Enhance dendritic arborization** (more neural connections—improves learning)
- **Improve circulation to brain** (more oxygen and nutrients)
- **Reduce anxiety** (modulates GABA)

Used by yogis and monks for thousands of years to enhance meditation and mental clarity.

How to Make It

Gotu Kola Infusion:

Ingredients:

- 1-2 teaspoons dried gotu kola
- 1 cup hot water

Instructions:

1. Place herb in mug.
2. Pour hot water, cover.
3. Steep 15-20 minutes.
4. Strain, drink.

How to Use It

For cognitive enhancement: 2-3 cups tea daily, or 2-3 mL tincture, twice daily.

For anxiety with cognitive symptoms: 2 cups daily.

Long-term use enhances effects (weeks to months).

Safety Notes

Very safe. Rare: mild sedation, digestive upset. Not during pregnancy. Can be used long-term. Generally well-tolerated.

REMEDY 10: Rosemary - Memory and Focus

What It Heals

Culinary herb with cognitive benefits: improves memory and recall, enhances concentration, supports alertness, protects against Alzheimer's and dementia, improves mood, increases circulation to brain.

Why It Works

Rosemary contains **rosmarinic acid and carnosic acid** that:

- **Inhibit acetylcholinesterase** (increases acetylcholine—memory neurotransmitter)
- **Powerful antioxidants** (protect neurons from oxidative damage)
- **Improve cerebral circulation** (more oxygen to brain)
- **Protect against beta-amyloid** (Alzheimer's protein)

Even **aromatherapy with rosemary** improves cognitive performance—volatile compounds absorbed through olfactory system.

How to Make It

Rosemary Tea:

Ingredients:

- 1 teaspoon dried rosemary (or 2-3 fresh sprigs)
- 1 cup hot water

Instructions:

1. Place rosemary in mug.
2. Pour hot water, cover.
3. Steep 10-15 minutes.
4. Strain, drink.

Rosemary Essential Oil (aromatherapy):

- Diffuse rosemary essential oil while working or studying
- Or inhale directly from bottle before cognitive tasks

How to Use It

For memory/focus: Drink 2-3 cups tea daily. Or use aromatherapy while working.

Add fresh rosemary to cooking regularly.

Acute cognitive boost: Inhale rosemary essential oil before exams, presentations, or mentally demanding tasks.

Safety Notes

Very safe as culinary herb and tea. Essential oil safe for aromatherapy (don't ingest undiluted). Can be stimulating. Not in very high therapeutic doses during pregnancy (culinary amounts safe). Generally well-tolerated.

REMEDY 11: Passionflower - Anxiety Without Drowsiness

What It Heals

Gentle anxiolytic: reduces anxiety (as effective as benzodiazepines in some studies), calms racing thoughts, improves sleep quality, reduces muscle tension, treats nervous exhaustion, safe for daytime use (less sedating than valerian).

Why It Works

Passionflower contains **flavonoids and alkaloids** that modulate GABA receptors (primary calming neurotransmitter). Reduces anxiety without significant sedation—can be used during day while maintaining function.

How to Make It

Passionflower Tea:

Ingredients:

- 1-2 teaspoons dried passionflower
- 1 cup hot water

Instructions:

1. Place herb in mug.
2. Pour hot water, cover.
3. Steep 10-15 minutes.
4. Strain, drink.

How to Use It

For anxiety: 1 cup tea or 2-3 mL tincture as needed, 1-3 times daily.

For sleep: 1 cup 30-60 minutes before bed.

Can be used as needed (doesn't require daily buildup).

Safety Notes

Very safe. Mild—less sedating than valerian. Generally well-tolerated. Safe for most people. Not during pregnancy.

REMEDY 12: Valerian Root - Deep Sleep and Anxiety

What It Heals

Powerful nervine for: insomnia (significantly improves sleep quality), anxiety, restlessness, muscle tension, nervous exhaustion, promotes deep, restorative sleep.

Why It Works

Valerian contains **valerenic acid and valepotriates** that:

- **Modulate GABA receptors** (similar mechanism to benzodiazepines but safer)
- **Increase GABA availability** (calming neurotransmitter)
- **Promote slow-wave sleep** (deep, restorative sleep stages)

Used for centuries as sleep aid and anxiolytic. Works better with consistent use (effects strengthen over 2-4 weeks).

How to Make It

Valerian Root Tincture:

Ingredients:

- 1 part dried valerian root
- 5 parts vodka (50-60%)

Instructions:

1. Place root in jar.
2. Cover with alcohol.
3. Seal, let sit 4-6 weeks, shaking daily.
4. Strain, bottle.

Or decoction: Simmer 2 teaspoons root in 2 cups water, 15-20 minutes.

How to Use It

For sleep: 3-5 mL tincture or 1 cup decoction 30-60 minutes before bed.

For anxiety: 2-3 mL tincture, 2-3 times daily.

Works better with consistent use (2-4 weeks).

Safety Notes

Very safe. Strong, unpleasant smell (some liken to dirty socks—but it works). Can cause morning drowsiness in some people (adjust dose/timing). Rare: paradoxical stimulation (10% of people feel energized instead of sedated—if this happens, valerian isn't for you). Not during pregnancy. Safe long-term.

REMEDY 13: Skullcap - Nervous System Restorative

What It Heals

Nervine tonic for: anxiety, nervous exhaustion, restlessness, insomnia, muscle tension and spasms, withdrawing from substances (alcohol, benzodiazepines), nervous system repair.

Why It Works

Skullcap contains **flavonoids (baicalin, wogonin)** that:

- **Modulate GABA receptors** (calming)
- **Reduce nervous system excitability** (calms overstimulated nerves)
- **Act as antispasmodic** (relaxes muscles)
- **Restore nervous system** (tonic effect with long-term use)

Traditional use: "restores integrity to the nervous system." Gentle but effective.

How to Make It

Skullcap Tincture:

Ingredients:

- 1 part dried skullcap (aerial parts)
- 5 parts vodka (40-50%)

Instructions:

1. Place skullcap in jar.
2. Cover with alcohol, seal.
3. Let sit 4 weeks, shaking daily.
4. Strain, bottle.

How to Use It

For anxiety: 2-3 mL tincture, 2-3 times daily.

For sleep: 3-5 mL before bed.

For nervous system restoration: 2 mL, 3 times daily for 2-3 months.

Safety Notes

Very safe. Very gentle. Generally well-tolerated. Rare: mild sedation. Safe long-term. **Note:** Use only **Scutellaria lateriflora** (American skullcap)—Chinese skullcap is different species.

REMEDY 14: Mucuna Pruriens - Dopamine Support

What It Heals

Natural L-DOPA source for: Parkinson's disease support, depression (especially anhedonia—inability to feel pleasure), low motivation and drive, cognitive decline, mood enhancement, supports focus and mental energy.

Why It Works

Mucuna contains **L-DOPA**—direct precursor to dopamine. Dopamine is critical for:

- Motivation and drive
- Pleasure and reward
- Focus and attention
- Movement and coordination
- Mood regulation

L-DOPA crosses blood-brain barrier and converts directly to dopamine. Used in Ayurveda for Parkinson's and mood disorders. Some studies show as effective as pharmaceutical L-DOPA for Parkinson's.

How to Make It

Note: Mucuna is purchased as powder or extract.

Mucuna Powder:

- Mix ½-1 teaspoon in smoothie, juice, or water

How to Use It

For Parkinson's support: Start low (½ teaspoon), increase gradually under medical supervision. Can need 5-15 grams daily (work with doctor).

For mood/motivation: ½-1 teaspoon daily.

For cognitive support: ½ teaspoon in morning.

Take on empty stomach for best absorption.

Safety Notes

Generally safe but potent. **Can interact with medications**—especially MAO inhibitors, antidepressants, blood pressure medications. **Work with doctor if using for Parkinson's** (can affect medication dosing). High doses can cause nausea. Start low. Not during pregnancy. Consult practitioner.

REMEDY 15: Saffron - Depression and Mood

What It Heals

Precious spice with powerful mood effects: treats depression (as effective as antidepressants in studies), reduces anxiety, improves memory, protects against cognitive decline, enhances mood, supports sexual function (especially SSRI-induced dysfunction).

Why It Works

Saffron contains **crocin and safranal** that:

- **Modulate serotonin, dopamine, norepinephrine** (antidepressant effect)
- **Inhibit serotonin reuptake** (similar to SSRIs but gentler)
- **Powerful antioxidants** (protect neurons)
- **Anti-inflammatory** (reduces neuroinflammation contributing to depression)

Multiple studies show 30 mg saffron daily as effective as pharmaceutical antidepressants for mild-moderate depression. Works within 4-6 weeks.

How to Make It

Saffron Tea:

Ingredients:

- 10-15 saffron threads
- 1 cup hot water
- Optional: honey, cardamom

Instructions:

1. Place saffron in mug.
2. Pour hot water, cover.
3. Steep 10-15 minutes (water turns golden).
4. Drink (can eat threads).

Saffron is expensive—but small amounts effective.

How to Use It

For depression: 30 mg saffron daily (approximately 10-15 threads, twice daily). Or standardized extract: 30 mg daily.

Continue for 6-8 weeks for full antidepressant effects.

Safety Notes

Very safe at therapeutic doses. **High doses toxic** (over 5 grams—don't exceed recommended amounts). May cause mild sedation. Can lower blood pressure slightly. Not during pregnancy. Generally well-tolerated at proper doses.

REMEDY 16: Omega-3 Fatty Acids (EPA/DHA) - Brain Structure and Function

What It Heals

Essential fats for: depression (EPA particularly effective), cognitive decline, Alzheimer's prevention, ADHD, mood stabilization, brain development, reduces neuroinflammation.

Why It Works

Omega-3s (especially **DHA**) are structural components of brain cell membranes—**60% of brain is fat**, much of it DHA. EPA has **anti-inflammatory effects** in brain. Together they:

- Support neuron membrane fluidity (communication between neurons)
- Reduce neuroinflammation (inflammation contributes to depression, cognitive decline)
- Support BDNF production (neuron growth and survival)
- Improve neurotransmitter function

Studies show EPA particularly effective for depression—1,000-2,000 mg EPA daily improves mood significantly.

How to Make It

Food sources:

- Wild-caught fatty fish (salmon, mackerel, sardines, herring) 3-4 times per week
- Algae (vegan source of EPA/DHA)

Supplement:

- Purchase high-quality fish oil or algae oil (molecularly distilled, third-party tested)

How to Use It

For depression: 1,000-2,000 mg EPA daily (look for EPA-predominant formulas).

For cognitive health: 1,000 mg combined EPA+DHA daily.

For Alzheimer's prevention: 1,000-2,000 mg DHA daily.

Take with food (improves absorption).

Safety Notes

Very safe. Mild blood-thinning effect (beneficial for most, consult if on anticoagulants). Choose quality brands (tested for heavy metals, PCBs). Store in refrigerator. Generally well-tolerated.

REMEDY 17: Curcumin (Turmeric) - Neuroinflammation and Depression

What It Heals

Anti-inflammatory compound for: depression (inflammation-driven), cognitive decline, Alzheimer's prevention, brain fog, neuroprotection, enhances mood, improves memory.

Why It Works

Curcumin is **powerful anti-inflammatory and antioxidant** that:

- **Reduces neuroinflammation** (chronic brain inflammation contributes to depression, cognitive decline)
- **Increases BDNF** (supports neuron growth)
- **Modulates neurotransmitters** (serotonin, dopamine)
- **Reduces beta-amyloid plaques** (Alzheimer's pathology)

Studies show curcumin as effective as Prozac for depression in some trials. India (high turmeric consumption) has much lower Alzheimer's rates.

How to Make It

Golden Paste (high absorption):

- ½ cup turmeric powder
- 1 cup water
- 1.5 teaspoons black pepper (increases absorption 2,000%)
- ¼ cup coconut oil

Instructions:

1. Cook turmeric and water to thick paste.
2. Add pepper and oil, stir.
3. Store in jar.

Use: 1 teaspoon, 2-3 times daily in warm milk, smoothies, or food.

Or: Curcumin supplement (standardized extract with piperine or liposomal for absorption).

How to Use It

For depression: 500-1,000 mg curcumin extract daily.

For cognitive health: 500 mg daily, long-term.

Must include black pepper or absorption enhancer.

Safety Notes

Very safe. May cause loose stools in high doses. Mild blood-thinning effect. Stains everything. Generally well-tolerated.

REMEDY 18: Phosphatidylserine - Memory and Cognitive Decline

What It Heals

Phospholipid for: age-related memory decline, improves cognitive function, supports attention and focus, reduces cortisol (stress hormone), supports exercise recovery (mental and physical).

Why It Works

Phosphatidylserine is **structural component of neuron membranes**—critical for:

- Neuron-to-neuron communication
- Neurotransmitter release
- Cognitive processing speed
- Memory formation and recall

Also **reduces cortisol** (protects hippocampus from stress damage). Levels decline with aging—supplementation can improve cognitive function in older adults.

How to Make It

Note: Phosphatidylserine is extracted from soy or sunflower lecithin. Purchased as supplement.

Look for: 100 mg capsules (sunflower-derived preferred—soy-free).

How to Use It

For memory/cognition: 100-300 mg daily.

For stress/cortisol: 200-400 mg daily.

Take with food (fat-soluble).

Safety Notes

Very safe. Well-tolerated. Rare: mild digestive upset. Can be used long-term. Generally safe for most people.

REMEDY 19: Acetyl-L-Carnitine - Energy and Neuroprotection

What It Heals

Amino acid for: mental fatigue, cognitive decline, depression (especially in elderly), improves memory and processing speed, neuroprotection, supports mitochondrial function, reduces brain fog.

Why It Works

Acetyl-L-carnitine:

- **Supports mitochondrial energy production** (more ATP in brain cells—more mental energy)
- **Acetyl group supports acetylcholine** (memory neurotransmitter)
- **Neuroprotective** (protects against age-related decline)
- **Mood enhancement** (particularly in elderly with depression)

Studies show improvements in memory, processing speed, and mood in people with cognitive decline.

How to Make It

Note: Amino acid supplement—purchased as capsules or powder.

How to Use It

For mental energy/fatigue: 500-1,000 mg, 1-2 times daily.

For cognitive decline: 1,500-3,000 mg daily (divided doses).

Take on empty stomach for best absorption. Can be taken with omega-3s for synergistic effect.

Safety Notes

Generally safe. Can be stimulating (avoid evening doses). May cause mild digestive upset, fishy body odor (rare). Reduce dose if jittery. Generally well-tolerated.

REMEDY 20: Magnesium L-Threonate - Brain-Specific Magnesium

What It Heals

Unique magnesium form for: cognitive function, memory improvement, anxiety, depression, sleep quality, neuroprotection, brain aging prevention.

Why It Works

Most magnesium forms don't cross blood-brain barrier well. **Magnesium L-threonate** specifically designed to:

- **Cross blood-brain barrier** (increases brain magnesium levels)
- **Support synaptic plasticity** (learning and memory)
- **Enhance NMDA receptor function** (critical for memory)
- **Calm nervous system** (modulates neurotransmitters)

Studies show improvements in cognitive function, especially memory, in people with cognitive decline. Also powerful for anxiety and sleep.

How to Make It

Note: Specific patented form—purchased as supplement (Magtein® brand).

How to Use It

For cognitive support: 1,000-2,000 mg magnesium L-threonate daily (typically 3-4 capsules based on product).

For anxiety/sleep: 1,000 mg before bed.

Can combine with other magnesium forms (glycinate for muscle relaxation, citrate for constipation).

Safety Notes

Very safe. More expensive than other magnesium forms (but uniquely effective for brain). Rare: loose stools (reduce dose). Generally well-tolerated.

REMEDY 21–40: Additional Brain, Memory & Mood Remedies

21. Green Tea (L-Theanine + Caffeine) - Calm Focus

What it heals: Improves focus and attention without jitters, calm alertness, anxiety reduction, neuroprotection.

Why it works: L-theanine (amino acid in green tea) increases alpha brain waves (calm, focused state) while modulating caffeine's stimulation. Synergistic effect.

How to use: 2-3 cups quality green tea daily. Or L-theanine supplement: 100-200 mg with caffeine.

Safety: Very safe. Contains caffeine (monitor if sensitive).

22. Huperzine A - Acetylcholine Enhancer

What it heals: Memory improvement, cognitive enhancement, Alzheimer's support, age-related memory decline.

Why it works: Potent acetylcholinesterase inhibitor (increases acetylcholine—memory neurotransmitter). From Chinese club moss.

How to use: 50-200 mcg daily. Start low.

Safety: Generally safe. Can cause nausea, digestive upset. Don't combine with cholinesterase inhibitor drugs.

23. Vinpocetine - Cerebral Blood Flow

What it heals: Improves memory, enhances cognitive function, tinnitus, stroke recovery, increases blood flow to brain.

Why it works: Derived from periwinkle plant. Increases cerebral blood flow and glucose utilization in brain.

How to use: 5-10 mg, 3 times daily with food.

Safety: Generally safe. May lower blood pressure. Not during pregnancy.

24. N-Acetyl Cysteine (NAC) - Glutathione and Mental Health

What it heals: OCD, addiction, depression, anxiety, compulsive behaviors, trichotillomania, neuroprotection.

Why it works: Precursor to glutathione (master antioxidant). Modulates glutamate (excitatory neurotransmitter often dysregulated in OCD, addiction).

How to use: 600-1,200 mg, 1-2 times daily.

Safety: Very safe. May cause mild nausea (take with food).

25. SAMe (S-Adenosyl Methionine) - Methylation and Mood

What it heals: Depression, joint pain, liver support, cognitive function.

Why it works: Methyl donor supporting neurotransmitter synthesis (serotonin, dopamine, norepinephrine). Fast-acting antidepressant effect in studies.

How to use: 400-800 mg daily on empty stomach.

Safety: Generally safe. Can be activating (avoid if bipolar—risk of mania). Expensive.

26. Inositol - OCD and Anxiety

What it heals: OCD, panic disorder, anxiety, depression, PCOS (bonus—improves insulin sensitivity).

Why it works: Structural basis of secondary messengers in brain. High doses modulate serotonin receptors.

How to use: High doses required: 12-18 grams daily (powder in water, divided doses).

Safety: Very safe. Mild laxative effect (adjust dose). Generally well-tolerated.

27. Lithium Orotate - Mood Stabilization and Neuroprotection

What it heals: Mood swings, irritability, depression, neuroprotection, cognitive decline prevention.

Why it works: Low-dose lithium (not prescription dose) supports brain health. Increases BDNF, protects neurons, mood stabilizing.

How to use: 5-20 mg elemental lithium daily (lithium orotate form).

Safety: Generally safe at low doses. Very different from prescription lithium (which requires monitoring). Consult practitioner.

28. Brahmi Oil (Scalp Massage) - Traditional Ayurvedic Brain Tonic

What it heals: Memory enhancement, stress relief, cognitive clarity (traditional use—topical scalp application).

Why it works: Traditional Ayurvedic practice—brahmi-infused oil massaged into scalp believed to "cool" brain and enhance cognition. Some absorption through scalp, also relaxation benefit.

How to make: Infuse bacopa (brahmi) in coconut or sesame oil, 3-4 weeks. Strain.

How to use: Massage into scalp 20-30 minutes before washing hair, 2-3 times per week.

Safety: Very safe, calming practice.

29. Yerba Mate - Clean Energy and Focus

What it heals: Mental fatigue, improves focus and alertness, mood enhancement, physical energy.

Why it works: Contains caffeine, theobromine, theophylline (stimulants), plus antioxidants and minerals. Cleaner, less jittery than coffee for many people.

How to use: Brew 1-2 teaspoons in hot water, 5-10 minutes. Drink 1-2 cups daily.

Safety: Safe. Contains caffeine (avoid late day). Generally well-tolerated.

30. Kava Kava - Anxiety Relief (Non-Cognitive Impairment)

What it heals: Anxiety, stress, promotes relaxation without mental fog (unlike some sedatives).

Why it works: Kavalactones modulate GABA receptors. Calms anxiety while maintaining mental clarity (doesn't impair cognition like benzodiazepines).

How to use: 250-500 mg kavalactones, 1-2 times daily as needed.

Safety: Short-term use only (concern about liver toxicity with excessive long-term use). Not with alcohol. Not if liver disease.

---

31. Blue Vervain - Nervous System Exhaustion

What it heals: Nervous exhaustion, stress-related tension, anxiety with physical tension, insomnia.

Why it works: Nervine tonic that restores depleted nervous system. Particularly for "Type A" personalities—driven, stressed, tense.

How to use: 2-3 mL tincture, 2-3 times daily. Or tea: 1-2 teaspoons steeped 10 minutes.

Safety: Very safe. Bitter taste. Not during pregnancy.

---

32. Wood Betony - Headaches and Mental Clarity

What it heals: Tension headaches, anxiety, mental fog, improves circulation to head.

Why it works: Traditional "head herb"—improves cerebral circulation, reduces tension, calms mind.

How to use: 2-3 mL tincture as needed. Or tea: 1-2 teaspoons steeped 10 minutes.

Safety: Very safe. Pleasant taste.

---

33. California Poppy - Gentle Sedative and Anxiety

What it heals: Anxiety, insomnia, restlessness, overactive mind, gentle nervine (especially for children).

Why it works: Contains alkaloids that gently calm nervous system without heavy sedation. Much milder than opium poppy (different species—non-narcotic).

How to use: 2-3 mL tincture before bed or as needed for anxiety.

Safety: Very safe. Non-addictive. Safe for children (proper dosing).

---

34. Catnip - Calming (Yes, for Humans Too)

What it heals: Anxiety, restlessness, insomnia, digestive upset from stress, safe for children.

Why it works: Contains nepetalactone (calming compound). Paradoxically stimulates cats but calms humans.

How to use: Tea: 1-2 teaspoons steeped 10 minutes. 1-3 cups daily or before bed.

Safety: Extremely safe. Very gentle. Safe for children and elderly.

---

35. Milky Oats - Nervous System Nourishment

What it heals: Nervous exhaustion, stress-related depletion, anxiety, supports recovery from addiction, burnout.

Why it works: Nourishes and restores depleted nervous system. Must be made from fresh oat tops in "milky" stage (immature seeds).

How to use: Tincture (fresh milky oats): 3-5 mL, 3 times daily for weeks to months (restorative—not acute).

Safety: Extremely safe. Nourishing tonic.

---

36. Chamomile - Gentle Nervine and Digestive

What it heals: Mild anxiety, insomnia, digestive upset from stress, safe for all ages.

Why it works: Contains apigenin (binds GABA receptors—calming). Gentle, safe, effective.

How to use: Tea: 2-3 teaspoons steeped 10 minutes. 1-3 cups daily or before bed.

Safety: Extremely safe. Very gentle. Safe for children, elderly, pregnancy.

37. Lavender - Calming and Sleep

What it heals: Anxiety, insomnia, restlessness, headaches, mood enhancement.

Why it works: Linalool and linalyl acetate (calming compounds). Aromatherapy and internal use both effective.

How to use: Tea: 1 teaspoon dried flowers steeped 10 minutes. Or aromatherapy: inhale or diffuse essential oil before bed.

Safety: Very safe. Pleasant. Generally well-tolerated.

38. Reishi Mushroom - Stress, Sleep, and Longevity

What it heals: Chronic stress, anxiety, insomnia, immune support, supports longevity, calms spirit.

Why it works: Adaptogenic mushroom supporting stress resilience. Triterpenes have calming, sleep-promoting effects. "Mushroom of immortality."

How to use: Decoction: simmer 2 tablespoons 2-3 hours. Or extract powder: 1-2 grams daily.

Safety: Extremely safe. Very gentle, cumulative effects.

39. B-Vitamin Complex - Neurotransmitter Support

What it heals: Depression, anxiety, cognitive function, energy, mood regulation, stress resilience.

Why it works: B vitamins (especially B6, B9, B12) are cofactors for neurotransmitter synthesis (serotonin, dopamine, GABA, norepinephrine). Deficiency common, causes mood and cognitive issues.

How to use: High-quality B-complex (methylated forms preferred—better absorbed). Daily with breakfast.

Safety: Very safe. Water-soluble (excess excreted). Can cause bright yellow urine (normal).

40. Comprehensive Brain Health Protocol - 3-Month Cognitive Optimization

What it heals: Complete cognitive restoration—memory, focus, mood, neuroprotection, mental energy, emotional balance.

Why it works: Brain health requires multi-system approach: neuroprotection, neurotransmitter support, inflammation reduction, circulation enhancement, stress management, sleep optimization, nutrition.

How to Make It

3-Month Brain Health Protocol:

PHASE 1: FOUNDATION (Weeks 1-4)

Neuroprotection and inflammation reduction:

- Omega-3s: 1,000-2,000 mg EPA+DHA daily
- Curcumin: 500-1,000 mg extract daily
- Antioxidant-rich diet: berries, dark leafy greens, colorful vegetables

Neurotransmitter support:

- B-complex: High-quality, methylated forms, daily
- Magnesium L-threonate: 1,000-2,000 mg daily
- Protein intake: 0.8-1g per kg body weight (amino acids for neurotransmitter synthesis)

Sleep optimization (critical for memory consolidation):

- Sleep hygiene: 7-9 hours, dark room, cool temperature
- Evening routine: No screens 1 hour before bed
- If needed: Magnesium glycinate 400 mg, valerian or passionflower before bed

Stress management:

- Daily: 10-20 minutes meditation, deep breathing, or gentle movement
- Adaptogen: Ashwagandha 300-600 mg or rhodiola 200-400 mg daily

Eliminate brain toxins:

- Reduce alcohol (neurotoxic)
- Eliminate processed foods, refined sugar
- Reduce exposure to environmental toxins

PHASE 2: ENHANCEMENT (Weeks 5-8)

Continue Phase 1, plus add:

Memory and cognitive enhancement:

- Lion's mane: 1-2 grams extract powder daily
- Bacopa: 300 mg extract daily (builds over time)
- Ginkgo: 120-240 mg standardized extract daily

Focus and mental energy:

- Rhodiola: 200-400 mg morning/early afternoon
- Green tea: 2-3 cups daily (L-theanine + caffeine synergy)
- Or: L-theanine 100-200 mg with morning coffee

Circulation support:

- Rosemary: Use in cooking, aromatherapy while working
- Ginkgo: Continue (also supports circulation)
- Exercise: 30 minutes daily (increases BDNF, cerebral blood flow)

Gut-brain axis support:

- Probiotic-rich foods: Fermented vegetables, kefir, yogurt daily
- Prebiotics: Fiber-rich vegetables, inulin
- Gut health directly impacts mood and cognition

PHASE 3: TARGETED SUPPORT (Weeks 9-12)

Continue Phases 1 & 2, plus add targeted support based on specific needs:

For depression:

- St. John's wort: 300 mg, 3 times daily (if not on medications—check interactions)
- Or saffron: 30 mg daily
- Omega-3s: Emphasize EPA (2,000 mg)
- Exercise: Essential for depression (as effective as medication in studies)

For anxiety:

- Lemon balm: 2-3 cups tea daily or 2-3 mL tincture, 2-3 times daily
- Holy basil: 2-3 cups tea daily
- Passionflower or skullcap: As needed
- Magnesium: Ensure adequate (400 mg minimum)

For cognitive decline/memory issues:

- Increase lion's mane: 2-3 grams daily
- Add gotu kola: 2-3 cups tea daily
- Phosphatidylserine: 100-300 mg daily
- Acetyl-L-carnitine: 500-1,000 mg, twice daily
- Mental exercises: Learn new skills, puzzles, reading

For ADHD/focus issues:

- Rhodiola: 400 mg daily
- Green tea + L-theanine: Throughout day
- Bacopa: 450 mg daily
- Omega-3s: High dose (2,000 mg minimum)
- Eliminate sugar, food dyes, processed foods

For chronic stress/burnout:

- Ashwagandha: 600 mg daily
- Holy basil: 3 cups tea daily
- Reishi: 2 grams extract daily
- Milky oats or skullcap: Nervous system restoration
- Prioritize rest, boundaries, stress reduction practices

How to Use It

Follow protocol for 3 months minimum.

Track progress:

- Keep journal: mood, energy, focus, memory, sleep quality
- Note improvements by week
- Most people see significant changes by 6-8 weeks

After 3 months:

- Continue foundation practices (omega-3s, B-vitamins, magnesium, sleep, stress management)
- Maintain cognitive enhancers (lion's mane, bacopa, ginkgo)
- Cycle adaptogens (6-8 weeks on, 1-2 weeks off)
- Adjust targeted herbs based on ongoing needs

Lifestyle essentials (critical—no herb replaces these):

- Exercise: 30-60 minutes daily (increases BDNF dramatically)
- Sleep: 7-9 hours nightly (non-negotiable for brain health)
- Social connection: Reduces dementia risk significantly
- Mental stimulation: Learn new things, read, engage cognitively
- Purpose and meaning: Critical for mental health

Safety Notes

Comprehensive protocols best supervised by practitioner. Start gradually—don't add everything at once. Allow herbs time to work (cognitive herbs take weeks to months). Not all herbs during pregnancy. Consult practitioner if on psychiatric medications (interactions possible, especially St. John's wort). Listen to your body—adjust as needed.

CHAPTER 10: HEART, BLOOD & CIRCULATION

> **Focus:** Cardiovascular Health, Blood Pressure, Circulation

Your cardiovascular system is your **lifeline**.

Your heart beats 100,000 times daily, pumping 2,000 gallons of blood through 60,000 miles of blood vessels, delivering oxygen and nutrients to every cell while removing waste.

When this system functions optimally, you feel **energetic, vital, and alive**. When it's compromised: chest pain, shortness of breath, fatigue, high blood pressure, poor circulation, arrhythmias, increased risk of heart attack and stroke.

Heart disease is the **#1 killer** in modern society—not because humans are designed to have weak hearts, but because modern life attacks the cardiovascular system relentlessly:

- **Inflammatory diet** (damages arterial walls, promotes plaque)
- **Chronic stress** (elevates blood pressure, increases clotting)
- **Sedentary lifestyle** (weakens heart muscle, reduces circulation)
- **Toxin exposure** (heavy metals damage cardiovascular tissue)
- **Nutrient deficiencies** (magnesium, CoQ10, omega-3s—all critical for heart health)

The result: epidemic of hypertension, atherosclerosis, heart failure, and premature cardiovascular death.

If you experience:

- **High blood pressure**
- **Chest pain or tightness**
- **Palpitations or arrhythmias**
- **Poor circulation** (cold hands/feet, numbness)
- **Fatigue** (weak heart can't deliver adequate oxygen)
- **Shortness of breath**
- **High cholesterol**
- **Family history of heart disease**

Then this chapter is your **cardiovascular protection toolkit**.

Modern cardiology offers pharmaceuticals: statins, blood pressure medications, blood thinners—often necessary but with side effects and without addressing root causes.

Herbal medicine offers **cardiovascular strengthening, circulation enhancement, blood pressure regulation, and arterial protection** that work with your body's healing capacity.

This chapter provides remedies for:

- ☑ **Heart strengthening and support**
- ☑ **Blood pressure regulation**
- ☑ **Circulation enhancement**
- ☑ **Cholesterol management**
- ☑ **Blood thinning and clot prevention**
- ☑ **Arrhythmia support**

REMEDY 1: Hawthorn Berry - Heart Strengthener

What It Heals

Supreme heart tonic: strengthens heart muscle (improves contractility), regulates blood pressure (high or low), treats heart failure, reduces chest pain (angina), improves circulation, treats arrhythmias, supports recovery from heart attack.

Why It Works

Hawthorn contains **flavonoids and oligomeric procyanidins** that increase coronary blood flow (more oxygen to heart), improve heart muscle efficiency, dilate blood vessels, act as antioxidants. Extensively studied in Europe—shown to improve heart failure symptoms as effectively as some medications.

How to Make It

Hawthorn Berry Tincture:

Ingredients:

- 1 part dried hawthorn berries
- 5 parts vodka (50%)

Instructions:

1. Place berries in jar.
2. Cover with alcohol, seal.
3. Let sit 6 weeks, shaking daily.
4. Strain, bottle.

Or decoction: Simmer 2 tablespoons berries in 4 cups water, 20 minutes.

How to Use It

For heart support: 2-3 mL tincture, 3 times daily. Or 2-3 cups decoction daily.

For heart failure: 3-5 mL tincture, 3 times daily (work with cardiologist—don't replace medications).

Requires consistent use for 6-8 weeks for full effects.

Safety Notes

Extremely safe. Can be used long-term. May enhance heart medications (beneficial—work with doctor to potentially reduce medication doses). Very gentle. Generally well-tolerated.

REMEDY 2: Garlic - Blood Pressure and Cholesterol

What It Heals

Cardiovascular powerhouse: lowers blood pressure, reduces cholesterol (especially LDL), prevents atherosclerosis, thins blood (prevents clots), antimicrobial, immune support, reduces arterial plaque.

Why It Works

Garlic contains **allicin** (released when crushed) that relaxes blood vessels (lowers BP), reduces cholesterol synthesis, prevents platelet aggregation, acts as antioxidant. Studies show significant reductions in both blood pressure and cholesterol with regular use.

How to Make It

Raw Garlic (most potent):

- Crush 1-2 cloves, let sit 10 minutes (activates allicin)
- Consume raw with food

Fermented Garlic Honey:

1. Peel cloves, place in jar.
2. Cover with raw honey.
3. Let ferment 1-2 weeks at room temperature.
4. Eat 1-2 cloves daily.

How to Use It

For blood pressure/cholesterol: 1-2 raw cloves daily, or aged garlic extract 600-1,200 mg daily.

For prevention: Use liberally in cooking.

Safety Notes

Very safe as food. Mild blood-thinning effect (beneficial, but consult if on anticoagulants). Can cause heartburn, body odor. Not before surgery. Generally well-tolerated.

REMEDY 3: Cayenne Pepper - Circulation and Emergency Heart

What It Heals

Powerful circulatory stimulant: improves circulation throughout body, stops bleeding (paradoxically—hemostatic), prevents blood clots, reduces cholesterol, emergency heart attack remedy (controversial but traditional), warms extremities.

Why It Works

Cayenne contains **capsaicin** that stimulates circulation, strengthens arterial walls, reduces platelet aggregation. Traditional emergency use: ¼-1 teaspoon cayenne in water during heart attack (stimulates heart, increases circulation). Also stops external bleeding rapidly.

How to Make It

Cayenne Tincture:

- 1 part cayenne powder to 5 parts vodka (50%), 4 weeks
- Or purchase: standardized to 40,000+ heat units

Daily use: Add cayenne to food, or capsules.

How to Use It

For circulation: ¼-½ teaspoon cayenne in warm water daily. Or capsules: 400-500 mg, 1-3 times daily.

Emergency (traditional—seek medical attention simultaneously): 1 teaspoon cayenne powder in glass of water, drink immediately.

Start small and increase gradually—very hot.

Safety Notes

Safe as food. Can irritate digestive tract (start small). Very hot—handle carefully. May interact with blood pressure medications. Generally safe in appropriate amounts.

REMEDY 4: Motherwort - Heart Palpitations

What It Heals

Cardiac nervine: treats heart palpitations (especially stress-related), anxiety affecting heart, rapid heartbeat, arrhythmias, high blood pressure from stress, emotional heart issues.

Why It Works

Motherwort contains **leonurine and alkaloids** that calm heart rate, reduce palpitations, relax nervous system. Traditional "mother's herb"—calms emotional and physical heart disturbances.

How to Make It

Motherwort Tincture:

- 1 part fresh flowering tops (or dried)
- 2 parts vodka (fresh) or 5 parts (dried, 50%)
- 3-4 weeks

How to Use It

For palpitations: 2-3 mL tincture as needed when palpitations occur. Can repeat every 2-3 hours.

For prevention: 2 mL, twice daily.

Safety Notes

Very safe. Not during pregnancy (stimulates uterus). May increase menstrual flow. Generally well-tolerated.

REMEDY 5: Ginger - Circulation and Anti-Clotting

What It Heals

Warming circulatory herb: improves circulation, reduces blood clots, lowers cholesterol, anti-inflammatory (reduces arterial inflammation), warms cold hands/feet, digestive support.

Why It Works

Ginger contains **gingerols and shogaols** that inhibit platelet aggregation (prevents clots), reduce inflammation, improve circulation. Also supports digestion (important—gut health affects cardiovascular health).

How to Make It

Fresh Ginger Tea:

- 1-2 inches fresh ginger, sliced
- 3 cups water
- Simmer 10-15 minutes

Daily: Add to cooking, smoothies, or take as tea.

How to Use It

For circulation: 2-3 cups tea daily. Or 1-2 grams dried powder daily.

For prevention: Use liberally in cooking.

Safety Notes

Very safe. Mild blood-thinning (beneficial). High doses may cause heartburn. Generally well-tolerated.

REMEDY 6: Dan Shen (Red Sage) - Chinese Heart Medicine

What It Heals

Traditional Chinese cardiovascular herb: improves circulation, reduces blood clots, treats angina, protects against heart attack, reduces atherosclerosis, improves heart failure symptoms.

Why It Works

Dan shen contains **tanshinones** that improve microcirculation, reduce blood viscosity, protect heart muscle from ischemic damage. Extensively used in China for cardiovascular disease.

How to Make It

Decoction:

- 2 tablespoons dried dan shen root
- 4 cups water
- Simmer 30 minutes

How to Use It

For heart disease: 2-3 cups decoction daily, or standardized extract per label directions.

Work with practitioner—potent herb.

Safety Notes

Generally safe but potent. Blood-thinning effect (consult if on anticoagulants). Work with knowledgeable practitioner. Not during pregnancy.

REMEDY 7: Arjuna - Ayurvedic Heart Tonic

What It Heals

Powerful Ayurvedic cardiotonic: strengthens heart muscle, reduces cholesterol, lowers blood pressure, treats heart failure, reduces angina, supports recovery from heart attack.

Why It Works

Arjuna bark contains **arjunolic acid and flavonoids** that strengthen heart muscle, improve ejection fraction (heart pumping efficiency), reduce cholesterol, act as antioxidants. Studies show significant improvements in heart failure.

How to Make It

Decoction:

- 2 tablespoons arjuna bark powder
- 4 cups water
- Simmer 20-30 minutes

How to Use It

For heart support: 2-3 cups decoction daily. Or powder: 1-2 teaspoons twice daily in warm milk or water.

Safety Notes

Very safe. Well-tolerated. Can be used long-term. Generally safe with heart medications (work with doctor).

REMEDY 8: Olive Leaf - Blood Pressure and Arterial Health

What It Heals

Mediterranean medicine: lowers blood pressure, improves arterial elasticity, reduces cholesterol, antimicrobial, antioxidant, supports immune system.

Why It Works

Olive leaf contains **oleuropein** that relaxes blood vessels (lowers BP), reduces oxidative stress, prevents LDL oxidation (critical step in atherosclerosis).

How to Make It

Olive Leaf Tea:

- 1-2 teaspoons dried olive leaf
- 1 cup hot water
- Steep 15 minutes

How to Use It

For blood pressure: 2-3 cups tea daily. Or extract: 500 mg, twice daily.

Requires several weeks for full BP-lowering effects.

Safety Notes

Very safe. May lower blood pressure significantly (monitor). Generally well-tolerated.

REMEDY 9: Linden Flower - Gentle Heart Calmer

What It Heals

Gentle cardiovascular nervine: reduces stress-related high blood pressure, calms heart palpitations, relaxes blood vessels, reduces anxiety, promotes restful sleep.

Why It Works

Linden contains **flavonoids and volatile oils** that relax nervous system, gently dilate blood vessels, calm heart. Traditional European heart herb for stress-related cardiovascular issues.

How to Make It

Linden Tea:

- 2 teaspoons dried linden flowers
- 1 cup hot water
- Steep 10-15 minutes

How to Use It

For stress-related heart issues: 2-3 cups tea daily.

For relaxation: 1 cup before bed.

Safety Notes

Extremely safe. Very gentle. Generally well-tolerated. Pleasant, sweet flavor.

REMEDY 10: CoQ10 - Heart Energy

What It Heals

Essential nutrient for: heart failure, statin side effects (muscle pain, fatigue), high blood pressure, angina, supports heart muscle energy production, antioxidant.

Why It Works

CoQ10 is critical for **mitochondrial energy production**—heart muscle requires enormous energy (constantly beating). Statins deplete CoQ10 (cause of muscle pain). Supplementation improves heart function in heart failure.

How to Make It

Note: CoQ10 is synthesized compound—purchased as supplement.

Look for: Ubiquinol form (more bioavailable), 100-200 mg softgels.

How to Use It

For heart failure: 100-300 mg daily.

If on statins: 100-200 mg daily (essential).

For general heart health: 100 mg daily.

Take with fat for absorption.

Safety Notes

Very safe. Well-tolerated. May interact with blood thinners (monitor). Generally safe.

REMEDY 11-40: Additional Heart, Blood & Circulation Remedies

11. Magnesium - Heart Rhythm and Blood Pressure

Regulates heart rhythm, lowers blood pressure, prevents arrhythmias, relaxes blood vessels. 400-600 mg daily (glycinate or taurate forms for heart). Very safe.

12. Omega-3 Fatty Acids - Inflammation and Triglycerides

Reduces triglycerides, prevents arrhythmias, reduces blood clots, anti-inflammatory. 1,000-2,000 mg EPA+DHA daily. Very safe, mild blood-thinning.

13. Turmeric/Curcumin - Arterial Protection

Reduces arterial inflammation, prevents atherosclerosis, improves endothelial function. 500-1,000 mg curcumin extract daily with black pepper. Safe.

14. Hibiscus Tea - Blood Pressure Reducer

Significant blood pressure reduction (comparable to some medications in studies). 2-3 cups tea daily. Very safe, pleasant tart flavor.

15. Celery Seed - Blood Pressure and Diuretic

Lowers blood pressure, mild diuretic, reduces uric acid. Tea or extract daily. Safe, may interact with diuretics.

16. Reishi Mushroom - Cholesterol and Blood Pressure

Lowers cholesterol, reduces blood pressure, supports longevity, immune support. 1-2 grams extract daily. Very safe.

17. Green Tea - Cholesterol and Arterial Health

Reduces LDL cholesterol, improves arterial function, antioxidant. 3-4 cups daily. Safe, contains caffeine.

18. Dark Chocolate (High Cacao) - Blood Pressure and Mood

Flavanols improve endothelial function, lower blood pressure, improve mood. 1-2 oz 70%+ cacao daily. High quality only.

19. Ginkgo Biloba - Peripheral Circulation

Improves circulation to extremities, supports cerebral circulation. 120-240 mg standardized extract daily. Mild blood-thinning.

20. Horse Chestnut - Varicose Veins and Venous Health

Strengthens vein walls, reduces varicose veins, improves venous return. Standardized extract only. Not the raw nuts (toxic).

21. Butcher's Broom - Venous Circulation

Supports venous circulation, reduces leg swelling, treats hemorrhoids. Extract or tea daily. Generally safe.

22. Gotu Kola - Venous Integrity

Strengthens blood vessel walls, improves circulation, wound healing. 2-3 cups tea daily. Very safe.

23. Yarrow - Blood Pressure and Circulation

Regulates blood pressure (high or low), improves circulation, hemostatic. Tea or tincture daily. Safe.

24. Bilberry - Capillary Strength

Strengthens capillaries, improves vision, supports circulation. Standardized extract daily. Very safe.

25. Grape Seed Extract - Arterial Protection

Powerful antioxidant, improves endothelial function, reduces oxidative stress. 100-300 mg daily. Very safe.

26. L-Arginine - Nitric Oxide Production

Precursor to nitric oxide (vasodilator), improves blood flow, lowers blood pressure. 3-6 grams daily. Generally safe.

27. L-Carnitine - Heart Muscle Support

Supports heart muscle energy, treats angina, improves exercise tolerance. 1,000-2,000 mg daily. Safe.

28. Taurine - Heart Rhythm and Blood Pressure

Regulates heart rhythm, lowers blood pressure, supports heart muscle. 500-2,000 mg daily. Very safe.

29. Potassium-Rich Foods - Blood Pressure Regulation

Critical for blood pressure regulation. Bananas, potatoes, leafy greens, avocados daily. Safe unless kidney disease.

30. Red Yeast Rice - Natural Statin

Contains naturally occurring statins, lowers cholesterol. Standardized extract. Similar side effects to statins—use with CoQ10.

31. Niacin (Vitamin B3) - Cholesterol Management

Raises HDL ("good") cholesterol, lowers triglycerides. 500-2,000 mg daily (flush form causes temporary skin flushing). Monitor with doctor.

32. Nattokinase - Fibrinolytic Enzyme

Breaks down blood clots, improves circulation, derived from fermented soybeans. 2,000 FU daily. Blood-thinning effect.

33. Salvia Miltiorrhiza (Dan Shen) - Covered in Remedy 6

Refer to Remedy 6 for full details.

34. Coleus Forskohlii - Blood Pressure

Relaxes blood vessels, lowers blood pressure, supports weight loss. Standardized extract. Generally safe.

35. Rauwolfia - Blood Pressure (Potent)

Powerful blood pressure reducer (contains reserpine—pharmaceutical isolated from this). Requires medical supervision. Not for self-treatment.

36. Guggul - Cholesterol Management

Lowers cholesterol, improves lipid profile. Standardized extract 500 mg, 2-3 times daily. May interact with medications.

37. Astragalus - Heart Failure Support

Supports heart muscle, immune support, adaptogen. Decoction or extract daily. Very safe long-term.

38. Cordyceps - Athletic Heart Performance

Improves oxygen utilization, enhances athletic performance, supports heart function. 1-3 grams extract daily. Safe.

39. Vitamin K2 - Arterial Calcium Regulation

Prevents arterial calcification, directs calcium to bones (not arteries). 100-200 mcg daily. Safe, but consult if on warfarin.

40. Comprehensive Heart Health Protocol

Foundation (Daily):

- Hawthorn: 2-3 mL tincture, 3 times daily
- Garlic: 1-2 cloves raw or aged extract
- Omega-3s: 1,000-2,000 mg EPA+DHA
- Magnesium: 400-600 mg
- CoQ10: 100-200 mg

For High Blood Pressure:

- Add: Hibiscus tea 2-3 cups, celery seed, olive leaf
- Reduce: Sodium, stress

For High Cholesterol:

- Add: Red yeast rice (with CoQ10), niacin, turmeric
- Increase: Fiber, omega-3s

For Poor Circulation:

- Add: Ginkgo, cayenne, ginger
- Exercise: Essential

Lifestyle (Critical):

- Exercise: 30-60 minutes daily (most important intervention)
- Mediterranean diet: Fish, olive oil, vegetables, fruits, whole grains
- Stress management: Meditation, deep breathing
- Sleep: 7-9 hours
- No smoking
- Moderate alcohol (or none)

Work with cardiologist—don't replace necessary medications. Herbs support and may allow medication reduction under medical supervision.

CHAPTER 11: SKIN, WOUNDS & FIRST AID

> Focus: Wound Healing, Burns, Infections, Emergency Medicine

Your skin is your **first line of defense**.

It's your largest organ—16-22 square feet protecting you from the outside world. It blocks pathogens, regulates temperature, synthesizes vitamin D, eliminates toxins, and constantly regenerates.

When your skin is damaged—cuts, burns, infections, rashes, wounds—your body has remarkable healing capacity. But modern life often impairs this:

- **Nutrient deficiencies** (vitamin C, zinc, protein—all essential for wound healing)
- **Chronic inflammation** (slows healing, increases scarring)
- **Poor circulation** (reduces oxygen and nutrients to wounds)
- **Stress** (elevates cortisol, impairs immune function and tissue repair)
- **Toxin exposure** (disrupts healing processes)

The result: slow-healing wounds, frequent infections, excessive scarring, chronic skin conditions.

If you need support for:

- **Cuts and lacerations** (clean, prevent infection, accelerate healing)
- **Burns** (first, second, third degree)
- **Bruises and contusions**
- **Skin infections** (bacterial, fungal, viral)
- **Rashes and dermatitis**
- **Chronic wounds** (diabetic ulcers, pressure sores)
- **Insect bites and stings**
- **Emergency first aid**

Then this chapter is your **natural medicine cabinet**.

Modern medicine offers antiseptics, antibiotics, and wound care—often necessary for serious injuries. But for everyday wounds and infections, herbal medicine provides **antimicrobial, vulnerary (wound-healing), and tissue-regenerating** remedies that work powerfully.

This chapter provides remedies for:

- ☑ **Wound healing and tissue repair**
- ☑ **Infection prevention and treatment**
- ☑ **Burns and scalds**
- ☑ **Bruises and trauma**
- ☑ **Skin infections (bacterial, fungal, viral)**
- ☑ **Emergency first aid protocols**

REMEDY 1: Calendula - Universal Wound Healer

What It Heals

Supreme vulnerary: accelerates wound healing, prevents infection, reduces inflammation, treats cuts/scrapes/lacerations, burns, surgical wounds, reduces scarring, treats skin infections, eczema, diaper rash.

Why It Works

Calendula contains **triterpenes, flavonoids, and resins** that stimulate tissue regeneration, increase collagen production, have antimicrobial properties, reduce inflammation. Promotes formation of healthy granulation tissue (wound closure). One of safest, most effective wound remedies.

How to Make It

Calendula Oil:

Ingredients:

- 1 cup dried calendula flowers
- 2 cups olive oil

Instructions:

1. Place flowers in jar.
2. Cover with oil completely.
3. Let sit in warm, sunny spot 3-4 weeks, shaking daily.
4. Strain through cheesecloth.
5. Store in amber bottle.

Calendula Salve:

1. Melt 1 cup calendula oil with 2-3 tablespoons beeswax in double boiler.
2. Test consistency (drop on cool plate).
3. Pour into tins, let cool.

How to Use It

For wounds: Clean wound, apply calendula oil or salve, cover with bandage. Reapply 2-3 times daily.

For burns: Apply generously after cooling burn. Reapply frequently.

For skin infections: Apply 3-4 times daily.

Can be used on open wounds (unlike comfrey—calendula doesn't trap infection).

Safety Notes

Extremely safe. Can be used on all ages including infants. Rare allergic reactions (Asteraceae family). Generally universally well-tolerated. Gentle, effective.

REMEDY 2: Plantain - Nature's Band-Aid

What It Heals

Common "weed" with powerful healing properties: draws out infections/splinters/stings, stops bleeding, heals wounds, treats insect bites/stings, reduces swelling and pain, soothes poison ivy/oak.

Why It Works

Plantain contains **allantoin** (tissue regeneration), **aucubin** (antimicrobial), and **mucilage** (soothing). Drawing properties pull toxins, venom, splinters to surface. Vulnerary properties accelerate healing.

How to Make It

Fresh Plantain Poultice (most effective):

Instructions:

1. Find fresh plantain leaves (common lawn weed).
2. Wash leaves.
3. Chew or crush to release juices (or use mortar and pestle).
4. Apply directly to wound, bite, or sting.
5. Secure with bandage.
6. Replace every few hours.

Plantain Salve:

- Infuse dried plantain in oil (3-4 weeks), make salve with beeswax

How to Use It

For wounds: Apply fresh poultice or salve 2-3 times daily.

For splinters/stings: Apply fresh crushed leaf, leave on several hours or overnight. Draws out foreign material.

For bites: Apply immediately and reapply frequently.

Emergency field medicine: Chew leaf, apply to wound—ancient but effective.

Safety Notes

Extremely safe. Can be used on all ages. No known contraindications. Free (grows everywhere). Generally well-tolerated.

REMEDY 3: Yarrow - Battlefield Wound Herb

What It Heals

Traditional battlefield medicine: stops bleeding rapidly (hemostatic), prevents infection, reduces pain, accelerates wound healing, treats internal bleeding (nosebleeds, heavy periods).

Why It Works

Yarrow contains **alkaloids and flavonoids** that constrict blood vessels (stops bleeding), have antimicrobial properties, reduce inflammation. Called "soldier's woundwort"—used for millennia for battlefield injuries.

How to Make It

Fresh Yarrow Poultice:

Instructions:

1. Harvest fresh yarrow (leaves and flowers).
2. Crush or chew to release juices.
3. Apply directly to bleeding wound.
4. Apply pressure with clean cloth.
5. Bleeding typically stops within minutes.

Yarrow Powder (for wounds):

- Dry yarrow completely, grind to fine powder
- Sprinkle directly on bleeding wounds

Yarrow Oil/Salve:

- Infuse dried yarrow in oil, make salve

How to Use It

For bleeding wounds: Apply fresh crushed yarrow or powder directly, apply pressure. Bleeding stops rapidly.

For bruises/sprains: Apply yarrow compress or salve 2-3 times daily.

Internal: Tea for nosebleeds, heavy periods (2-3 cups daily during bleeding).

Safety Notes

Very safe externally. Rare allergic reactions (Asteraceae family). Not for internal use during pregnancy. Can cause photosensitivity in some people. Generally well-tolerated.

REMEDY 4: Comfrey - Bone and Tissue Healer

What It Heals

Called "knitbone" for remarkable healing properties: accelerates bone healing, heals sprains/strains, repairs torn muscles/ligaments, treats bruises, reduces swelling, heals skin wounds rapidly.

Why It Works

Comfrey contains **allantoin**—stimulates cell proliferation and tissue regeneration at remarkable rate. Literally speeds up healing of bones, cartilage, tendons, ligaments, skin.

Critical: External use only—internal use can damage liver (pyrrolizidine alkaloids).

How to Make It

Comfrey Salve:

Ingredients:

- 1 cup comfrey-infused oil (dried comfrey leaf or root in olive oil, 3-4 weeks)
- 2-3 tablespoons beeswax

Instructions:

1. Melt oil and beeswax in double boiler.
2. Pour into tins, let cool.
3. Label: "EXTERNAL USE ONLY"

How to Use It

For injuries: Apply liberally to affected area 3-4 times daily. Massage gently into skin.

For broken bones: Apply over bone (after medical treatment) 2-3 times daily—accelerates healing.

For sprains/bruises: Apply immediately after injury and continue until healed.

Do not apply to open wounds (heals so rapidly it can trap infection inside).

Safety Notes

EXTERNAL USE ONLY—do not ingest. Do not apply to open wounds or broken skin (can trap infection). Not during pregnancy/nursing (topical absorption of PAs). Discontinue if skin irritation. Very effective but requires caution.

REMEDY 5: Honey (Raw) - Antimicrobial Wound Healer

What It Heals

Ancient wound medicine: prevents and treats infection, accelerates wound healing, treats burns, treats diabetic ulcers and chronic wounds, reduces scarring, antimicrobial.

Why It Works

Raw honey has **antimicrobial properties** (hydrogen peroxide production, low pH, high sugar content dehydrates bacteria), supports tissue regeneration, reduces inflammation. Medical-grade honey (Manuka) used in hospitals for wound care. Creates moist healing environment (reduces scarring).

How to Make It

Note: Use raw, unprocessed honey. Manuka honey (UMF 10+) for medical-grade wound care.

Honey Wound Dressing:

1. Clean wound thoroughly.
2. Apply generous layer of raw honey.
3. Cover with sterile bandage.
4. Change daily.

How to Use It

For wounds: Clean wound, apply thick layer of honey, bandage. Change daily until healed.

For burns: Apply immediately after cooling burn. Reapply 2-3 times daily.

For diabetic ulcers: Medical-grade Manuka honey under healthcare supervision.

Safety Notes

Very safe for external use. **Never give honey internally to infants under 1 year** (botulism risk). Generally well-tolerated. Can be messy. Effective and widely available.

REMEDY 6: Lavender - Burns and Pain Relief

What It Heals

Burn remedy and pain reliever: treats burns (first and second degree), prevents infection, reduces pain, promotes healing, treats insect bites, reduces anxiety during injury recovery.

Why It Works

Lavender contains **linalool and linalyl acetate**—antimicrobial, anti-inflammatory, analgesic (pain-relieving), promotes tissue regeneration. One of few essential oils safe to apply undiluted (though dilution preferred for large areas).

How to Make It

Lavender-Infused Oil:

Ingredients:

- 1 cup dried lavender flowers
- 2 cups olive or coconut oil

Instructions:

1. Place lavender in jar.
2. Cover with oil.
3. Let sit 3-4 weeks, shaking daily.
4. Strain, store in amber bottle.

Or use: Lavender essential oil (high quality, therapeutic grade).

How to Use It

For burns: Cool burn with cold water first, then apply lavender oil or 1-2 drops essential oil. Reapply every few hours.

For wounds: Apply diluted lavender essential oil (2-3 drops per tablespoon carrier oil) 2-3 times daily.

For pain: Apply topically or inhale aromatherapy.

Safety Notes

Very safe. Rare allergic reactions. Essential oil can be applied undiluted for burns in small amounts (René-Maurice Gattefossé famously treated his burn with pure lavender oil—led to modern aromatherapy). Generally well-tolerated.

REMEDY 7: Tea Tree Oil - Antimicrobial Powerhouse

What It Heals

Broad-spectrum antimicrobial: treats skin infections (bacterial, fungal, viral), prevents wound infection, treats acne, fungal infections (athlete's foot, ringworm), cuts/scrapes.

Why It Works

Tea tree oil contains **terpinen-4-ol**—powerful antimicrobial compound effective against bacteria (including MRSA), fungi, and viruses. Disrupts microbial cell membranes.

How to Make It

Note: Tea tree essential oil is steam-distilled—purchase high-quality, pure oil.

Diluted Tea Tree Spray:

- 10-15 drops tea tree oil
- 2 oz water in spray bottle
- Shake before each use

How to Use It

For infections: Dilute 2-3 drops in 1 tablespoon carrier oil, apply 2-3 times daily.

For fungal infections: Apply diluted oil 2-3 times daily until cleared (can take weeks for nail fungus).

For wound care: Add 1-2 drops to wound cleaning solution.

Always dilute (can irritate skin undiluted).

Safety Notes

Generally safe topically when diluted. Can cause skin irritation undiluted. **Never ingest** (toxic internally). Not for pets (toxic to cats/dogs). Keep away from children. Effective but requires proper use.

REMEDY 8: Aloe Vera - Burn and Wound Soother

What It Heals

Supreme burn remedy: treats burns (first, second degree), sunburn, minor wounds, skin irritation, promotes healing, reduces scarring, anti-inflammatory.

Why It Works

Aloe gel contains **polysaccharides, glycoproteins, and enzymes** that reduce inflammation, promote tissue regeneration, provide moisture (prevents scarring), antimicrobial properties.

How to Make It

Fresh Aloe Gel:

Instructions:

1. Cut mature aloe leaf.
2. Stand upright 10-15 minutes to drain yellow latex.
3. Rinse thoroughly.
4. Peel away skin.
5. Scoop out clear inner gel.
6. Apply directly or blend with small amount of water.

Or purchase: 99-100% pure aloe vera gel (no added ingredients).

How to Use It

For burns: Apply generously immediately after cooling burn. Reapply every few hours.

For sunburn: Apply liberally, reapply frequently.

For wounds: Apply thin layer 2-3 times daily.

Store fresh gel in refrigerator up to 1 week.

Safety Notes

Very safe for external use. Ensure yellow latex removed (can irritate). Generally well-tolerated. Cooling, soothing. Widely available.

REMEDY 9: Goldenseal - Antimicrobial for Infections

What It Heals

Powerful antimicrobial: treats skin infections, prevents wound infection, antimicrobial for cuts/scrapes, treats conjunctivitis (pink eye), mouth infections.

Why It Works

Goldenseal contains **berberine**—potent antimicrobial alkaloid effective against bacteria, fungi, protozoa. One of strongest herbal antimicrobials available.

How to Make It

Goldenseal Powder (for wounds):

- Purchase dried goldenseal root powder
- Apply directly to wound (stings but very effective)

Goldenseal Wash:

- 1 teaspoon goldenseal powder in 1 cup warm water
- Use as wound wash

How to Use It

For infected wounds: Dust powder directly on wound, or wash with goldenseal water 2-3 times daily.

For pink eye: Goldenseal tea (cooled), apply with cotton ball to closed eye 3-4 times daily.

Overharvested—use sparingly and sustainably.

Safety Notes

Generally safe externally. Can sting on open wounds. Not for internal use during pregnancy. Overharvested—use Oregon grape (contains berberine) as sustainable alternative. Can temporarily stain skin yellow.

REMEDY 10: Echinacea - Immune-Boosting Wound Care

What It Heals

Immune stimulant for wound healing: prevents infection, accelerates healing, treats bites/stings (especially spider/snake), treats abscesses, supports immune response to wounds.

Why It Works

Echinacea contains **alkylamides and polysaccharides** that stimulate immune function, increase white blood cell activity, have antimicrobial properties. Native Americans used topically for venomous bites/stings.

How to Make It

Echinacea Poultice:

Ingredients:

- Fresh echinacea root (or dried)
- Small amount of water

Instructions:

1. Grind root to paste (add water if needed).
2. Apply directly to wound, bite, or sting.
3. Cover with bandage.
4. Reapply every few hours.

Or use: Echinacea tincture—apply directly to wound.

How to Use It

For bites/stings: Apply poultice or tincture immediately and every 2-3 hours.

For wounds: Apply tincture or poultice 2-3 times daily.

Internal support: Take echinacea tincture internally (3-5 mL, 3-4 times daily) for immune support during infection.

Safety Notes

Very safe. Rare allergic reactions (Asteraceae family). Not for long-term daily use (use during acute infections only). Generally well-tolerated.

REMEDY 11-40: Additional Skin, Wounds & First Aid Remedies

11. Witch Hazel - Astringent and Anti-Inflammatory

Reduces inflammation, stops minor bleeding, treats bruises, hemorrhoids, insect bites, skin irritation. Apply topically as needed. Very safe.

12. Arnica - Bruise and Trauma Healer

External use only—treats bruises, reduces swelling, accelerates healing of trauma. Oil or cream 3-4 times daily. Never on broken skin. Toxic if ingested.

13. St. John's Wort Oil - Nerve Pain and Burns

Heals burns, treats nerve pain/damage, accelerates wound healing. Infused oil applied topically. Photosensitizing—protect from sun.

14. Myrrh - Antimicrobial and Astringent

Treats infected wounds, mouth sores, prevents infection. Tincture applied topically. Strong antimicrobial.

15. Thyme - Antiseptic Wash

Powerful antimicrobial for wound washing. Strong thyme tea used as wash. Essential oil diluted for topical use.

16. Rosemary - Circulation and Healing

Improves circulation to wounds, antimicrobial, promotes healing. Infused oil or essential oil (diluted) topically.

17. Sage - Antiseptic and Drying

Antimicrobial, dries excessive secretions, treats infections. Tea as wash or powder on wounds.

18. Usnea (Old Man's Beard Lichen) - Natural Antibiotic

Powerful antimicrobial especially against gram-positive bacteria (staph, strep). Tincture applied topically. Sustainably harvested only.

19. Propolis - Bee Antimicrobial

Potent antimicrobial, accelerates healing, reduces inflammation. Propolis tincture or salve topically. Rare allergic reactions.

20. Turmeric Paste - Anti-Inflammatory Wound Care

Reduces inflammation, antimicrobial, promotes healing. Paste (turmeric powder + water) applied to wounds. Stains yellow.

21. Activated Charcoal - Toxin and Venom Draw

Draws out toxins, venom, infection. Poultice (charcoal powder + water) on bites, stings, infected wounds. Replace every few hours.

22. Clay Poultice (Bentonite) - Drawing and Healing

Draws infection, toxins, reduces inflammation. Mix clay with water to paste, apply to wounds/infections. Very safe.

23. Slippery Elm - Wound Poultice

Soothes inflammation, promotes healing. Powder mixed with water to paste, applied to wounds. Very gentle.

24. Marshmallow Root - Soothing Poultice

Soothes irritated skin, draws out splinters/infections. Root ground to paste, applied as poultice. Very safe.

25. Baking Soda Paste - Burns and Stings

Neutralizes acids (ant bites), soothes burns, reduces pain. Paste (baking soda + water) applied topically. Very safe.

26. Apple Cider Vinegar - Antimicrobial Wash

Antimicrobial, restores skin pH, treats fungal infections. Diluted (1:1 with water) as wash. Can sting on open wounds.

27. Coconut Oil - Moisturizing Antimicrobial

Antimicrobial (lauric acid), moisturizes, promotes healing. Apply directly to wounds, burns, dry skin. Very safe.

28. Vitamin E Oil - Scar Reduction

Reduces scarring, promotes healing, antioxidant. Apply to healing wounds (after closure) daily. Generally safe.

29. Castor Oil - Deep Wound Healing

Promotes deep tissue healing, reduces scarring, antimicrobial. Apply topically, can cover with bandage. Very safe, messy.

30. Chickweed - Soothing Skin Irritation

Soothes itching, rashes, eczema, minor wounds. Fresh poultice or infused oil. Very gentle, safe.

31. Jewelweed - Poison Ivy/Oak Relief

Neutralizes urushiol (poison ivy/oak oil), reduces itching/inflammation. Fresh plant rubbed on affected area immediately. Very safe.

32. Oak Bark - Astringent for Weeping Wounds

Powerful astringent, dries weeping wounds, antimicrobial. Strong decoction as wash. Very drying.

33. Black Walnut Hull - Antifungal

Treats fungal skin infections (ringworm, athlete's foot). Tincture applied topically. Stains brown.

34. Neem Oil - Antifungal and Antibacterial

Broad-spectrum antimicrobial, treats skin infections, insect repellent. Diluted oil topically. Strong smell.

35. Gotu Kola - Scar Reduction and Wound Healing

Promotes collagen production, reduces scarring, improves wound healing. Infused oil or extract topically. Very safe.

36. Vitamin C (Topical and Internal) - Collagen Support

Essential for collagen synthesis, wound healing. Increase dietary vitamin C (citrus, berries, peppers) and consider topical vitamin C serum. Very safe.

37. Zinc (Topical and Internal) - Wound Healing Mineral

Critical for wound healing, immune function. Zinc oxide cream topically (diaper rash, minor wounds). Internal: 15-30 mg daily during healing. Safe in appropriate doses.

38. Colloidal Silver - Antimicrobial (Controversial)

Antimicrobial properties, used topically for wound care. Commercially prepared colloidal silver spray. Controversial—use sparingly, can cause argyria (skin discoloration) with excessive use.

39. Manuka Honey - Medical-Grade Wound Care

Superior antimicrobial honey, treats chronic wounds, burns, diabetic ulcers. UMF 15+ for medical use. Apply generously, bandage. Very safe, expensive.

40. Comprehensive First Aid Protocol

Immediate Wound Care:

1. **Stop bleeding:**
   - Apply direct pressure with clean cloth
   - Elevate if possible
   - If severe bleeding, apply yarrow powder/crushed plantain while maintaining pressure
   - Seek medical attention if bleeding doesn't stop
2. **Clean wound:**
   - Rinse with clean water
   - Remove debris gently

- Optional: wash with diluted tea tree oil, thyme tea, or goldenseal water

3. **Apply antimicrobial:**
   - Raw honey, calendula oil, or tea tree (diluted)
   - Or: goldenseal powder, propolis

4. **Bandage:**
   - Cover with sterile bandage
   - Change daily or when wet

5. **Support healing:**
   - Keep clean and moist (prevents scarring)
   - Apply calendula salve, honey, or aloe 2-3 times daily
   - Increase protein, vitamin C, zinc intake

For Burns:

1. **Cool immediately:**
   - Run under cool water 10-20 minutes
   - Never ice (damages tissue further)

2. **Assess severity:**
   - **First degree** (red, painful—like sunburn): Self-treat
   - **Second degree** (blistering): Can self-treat if small
   - **Third degree** (white/charred, painless): MEDICAL EMERGENCY

3. **Apply:**
   - Aloe vera gel generously
   - Raw honey
   - Lavender oil
   - Reapply frequently

4. **Bandage loosely** (don't pop blisters)

5. **Support healing:**
   - Stay hydrated
   - Increase protein and vitamin C

For Bites/Stings:

1. **Remove stinger** if present (scrape, don't pinch)

2. **Apply:**
   - Fresh plantain poultice (chew leaf, apply)
   - Or: baking soda paste
   - Or: activated charcoal poultice
   - Or: echinacea tincture

3. **Watch for allergic reaction** (severe swelling, difficulty breathing—seek emergency care)

4. **Reapply** poultice every 2-3 hours

For Infections:

1. **Signs of infection:**
   - Increased redness, warmth, swelling
   - Red streaks extending from wound
   - Pus or foul odor
   - Fever

2. **Herbal treatment:**
   - Clean with antimicrobial wash (tea tree, thyme, goldenseal)
   - Apply antimicrobial directly (goldenseal powder, propolis, honey)
   - Take echinacea internally (immune support)
   - Change bandage 2-3 times daily

3. **If worsening or not improving in 24-48 hours:** Seek medical attention (may need antibiotics)

Natural First Aid Kit:

Essential items:

- Calendula salve
- Raw honey (Manuka if possible)
- Lavender essential oil
- Tea tree essential oil
- Plantain salve or dried leaves
- Yarrow powder or dried herb
- Echinacea tincture
- Goldenseal powder or tincture
- Activated charcoal powder
- Aloe vera gel
- Bandages, gauze, tape
- Witch hazel
- Arnica cream
- Cayenne powder (stops bleeding)
- Baking soda
- Clean cloth/towels

Storage:

- Keep in waterproof container
- Store in cool, dry place
- Replace items as needed
- Label clearly
- Include basic first aid instructions

When to seek medical attention:

- Severe bleeding that won't stop
- Deep wounds (may need stitches)
- Puncture wounds (especially rusty metal—tetanus risk)
- Animal/human bites (infection risk)
- Signs of serious infection
- Third-degree burns
- Wounds on face (cosmetic concerns)
- Foreign objects embedded deeply
- Loss of sensation or movement
- Wounds in people with diabetes or compromised immunity

Herbal first aid complements but doesn't replace medical care when needed.

CHAPTER 12: SLEEP, STRESS & NERVOUS SYSTEM

> Focus: Restorative Sleep, Stress Resilience, Nervous System Repair

Your nervous system is your **command center**.

It controls everything—every breath, heartbeat, thought, movement, sensation, and emotion. When balanced, you feel **calm, focused, energized, and resilient**. When depleted or overstimulated: anxiety, insomnia, burnout, panic, chronic tension, exhaustion.

Modern life is a **nervous system assault**:

- **Chronic stress** (keeps nervous system in fight-or-flight constantly)
- **Sleep deprivation** (prevents nervous system repair and restoration)
- **Digital overstimulation** (blue light, constant notifications, information overload)
- **Caffeine and stimulants** (exhaust adrenal and nervous systems)
- **Nutrient depletion** (magnesium, B vitamins—critical for nervous system function)
- **Lack of downtime** (no space for parasympathetic restoration)

The result: epidemic of anxiety, insomnia, burnout, and nervous system exhaustion.

If you experience:

- **Insomnia** (difficulty falling asleep, staying asleep, or unrefreshing sleep)
- **Anxiety** (worry, racing thoughts, tension, panic attacks)
- **Chronic stress** (overwhelm, inability to relax)
- **Burnout** (exhaustion, lack of motivation, emotional flatness)
- **Nervous tension** (tight muscles, clenched jaw, headaches)
- **Nervous exhaustion** (wired and tired, depleted but can't rest)
- **Poor stress resilience** (easily overwhelmed, reactive)

Then this chapter is your **nervous system restoration guide**.

Modern medicine offers sedatives, anti-anxiety medications, sleeping pills—often effective short-term but dependency-forming, with side effects, and without addressing root causes.

Herbal medicine offers **nervines (nervous system tonics), adaptogens (stress resilience), and sedatives (sleep support)** that restore nervous system function rather than suppressing symptoms.

This chapter provides remedies for:

- ☑ **Deep, restorative sleep**
- ☑ **Anxiety and panic relief**
- ☑ **Stress resilience and adaptation**
- ☑ **Nervous system repair and restoration**
- ☑ **Tension and muscle relaxation**
- ☑ **Burnout recovery**

REMEDY 1: Valerian Root - Deep Sleep

What It Heals

Powerful sleep herb: treats insomnia (difficulty falling asleep, staying asleep), improves sleep quality (deeper, more restorative), reduces anxiety, relaxes muscles, treats restlessness and nervous tension.

Why It Works

Valerian contains **valerenic acid and valepotriates** that modulate GABA receptors (primary calming neurotransmitter), increase GABA availability, promote slow-wave sleep (deep, restorative sleep stages). Similar mechanism to benzodiazepines but safer. Effects strengthen with consistent use (2-4 weeks).

How to Make It

Valerian Root Tincture:

Ingredients:

- 1 part dried valerian root (chopped)
- 5 parts vodka (50-60%)

Instructions:

1. Place root in jar.
2. Cover with alcohol, seal.
3. Let sit 4-6 weeks, shaking daily.
4. Strain, bottle in amber bottles.

Or decoction: Simmer 2 teaspoons root in 2 cups water, 15 minutes.

How to Use It

For sleep: 3-5 mL tincture or 1 cup decoction 30-60 minutes before bed.

For anxiety: 2-3 mL tincture, 2-3 times daily.

Works better with consistent use—give it 2-4 weeks for full sleep-improving effects.

Safety Notes

Very safe. Strong, unpleasant smell (some say "dirty socks"—but effective). Can cause morning drowsiness (adjust dose/timing). **Paradoxical reaction in ~10% of people** (feel energized instead of sedated—if this happens, valerian isn't for you). Safe long-term. Not during pregnancy.

REMEDY 2: Passionflower - Anxiety Without Sedation

What It Heals

Gentle anxiolytic: reduces anxiety (racing thoughts, worry, tension), calms mind without heavy sedation, improves sleep quality, treats restlessness, safe for daytime use (less sedating than valerian).

Why It Works

Passionflower contains **flavonoids and alkaloids** that modulate GABA receptors, reduce anxiety without significant sedation. Studies show comparable effectiveness to benzodiazepines for anxiety with fewer side effects. Can be used during day while maintaining function.

How to Make It

Passionflower Tea:

Ingredients:

- 1-2 teaspoons dried passionflower (aerial parts)
- 1 cup hot water

Instructions:

1. Place herb in mug.
2. Pour hot water, cover.
3. Steep 10-15 minutes.
4. Strain, drink.

Or tincture: 1:5, 40% alcohol, 4 weeks.

How to Use It

For anxiety: 1 cup tea or 2-3 mL tincture as needed, 1-3 times daily.

For sleep: 1 cup tea or 3-5 mL tincture 30-60 minutes before bed.

Can combine with valerian for stronger sleep support.

Safety Notes

Very safe. Mild—less sedating than valerian. Can be used as needed or daily. Safe for most people. Not during pregnancy. Generally well-tolerated.

REMEDY 3: Ashwagandha - Stress Resilience and Cortisol

What It Heals

Premier adaptogen for stress: reduces anxiety (30-40% reduction in studies), lowers cortisol significantly, improves stress resilience, reduces stress-related insomnia, protects brain from stress damage, improves energy (paradoxically both calming and energizing).

Why It Works

Ashwagandha contains **withanolides** that normalize cortisol (high cortisol damages nervous system, disrupts sleep), modulate GABA receptors (anxiety reduction), protect neurons from stress-induced damage. Adaptogenic—helps body adapt to stress rather than suppressing stress response.

How to Make It

Ashwagandha Moon Milk:

Ingredients:

- 1 teaspoon ashwagandha powder
- 1 cup warm milk (dairy or non-dairy)
- 1 teaspoon honey
- Pinch cinnamon or cardamom

Instructions:

1. Heat milk gently.
2. Whisk in ashwagandha.
3. Add honey and spice.
4. Drink before bed.

Or: Standardized extract capsules, 300-600 mg daily.

How to Use It

For anxiety/stress: 300-600 mg extract or 1-2 teaspoons powder, once or twice daily.

For sleep: Take before bed (promotes sleep quality).

Requires 8-12 weeks for full adaptogenic effects—be patient.

Safety Notes

Very safe long-term. May cause drowsiness (use therapeutically). Avoid with hyperthyroidism. Not during pregnancy. Generally well-tolerated.

REMEDY 4: Lemon Balm - Nervous Tension and Anxiety

What It Heals

Gentle nervine: reduces anxiety rapidly (works within 1-3 hours), calms nervous tension, improves cognitive function during stress, treats insomnia (mild sedative), soothes stress-related digestive upset.

Why It Works

Lemon balm contains **rosmarinic acid and volatile oils** that modulate GABA receptors (calming), inhibit acetylcholinesterase (improves memory/attention), reduce cortisol response to stress. Calms without impairing function—maintains mental clarity while reducing anxiety.

How to Make It

Lemon Balm Tea:

Ingredients:

- 2 teaspoons dried lemon balm (or 4-6 fresh leaves)
- 1 cup hot water

Instructions:

1. Place lemon balm in mug.
2. Pour hot water, **cover immediately** (volatile oils escape).
3. Steep 10-15 minutes, covered.
4. Strain, drink.

How to Use It

For anxiety: 1 cup tea as needed (works within 1 hour). Or 2-3 mL tincture, repeat as needed.

For sleep: 1 cup 30-60 minutes before bed.

For stress: 2-3 cups daily.

Safety Notes

Extremely safe. Very gentle. Can be used as needed or daily. May reduce thyroid function in very high doses long-term (normal doses safe). Safe for children and elderly. Pleasant lemon flavor.

REMEDY 5: Chamomile - Gentle Sleep and Anxiety

What It Heals

Universal gentle nervine: mild anxiety, insomnia (promotes sleep onset), stress-related digestive upset, restlessness, safe for all ages (infants to elderly).

Why It Works

Chamomile contains **apigenin** (flavonoid that binds GABA receptors—calming effect), also anti-inflammatory, antispasmodic. One of safest, gentlest nervines—effective but mild. Perfect for children, sensitive individuals, or when stronger herbs too sedating.

How to Make It

Chamomile Tea:

Ingredients:

- 2-3 teaspoons dried chamomile flowers
- 1 cup hot water

Instructions:

1. Place flowers in mug.
2. Pour hot water, cover.
3. Steep 10-15 minutes.
4. Strain, drink.

How to Use It

For anxiety/stress: 1-3 cups daily as needed.

For sleep: 1 cup 30-60 minutes before bed.

For children: ½-1 cup before bed (safe from infancy).

Safety Notes

Extremely safe. Very gentle. Rare allergic reactions (Asteraceae family). Safe during pregnancy and nursing. Can be used daily indefinitely. Pleasant, apple-like flavor.

REMEDY 6: Skullcap - Nervous Exhaustion and Restoration

What It Heals

Nervine tonic for depleted nervous system: nervous exhaustion, anxiety with physical tension, restlessness, insomnia, muscle tension/spasms, recovery from addiction (alcohol, benzodiazepines), nervous system repair.

Why It Works

Skullcap contains **flavonoids (baicalin, wogonin)** that modulate GABA receptors (calming), reduce nervous system excitability, act as antispasmodic. Traditional use: "restores integrity to the nervous system"—tonic effect with long-term use rebuilds depleted nerves.

How to Make It

Skullcap Tincture:

Ingredients:

- 1 part dried skullcap (aerial parts)
- 5 parts vodka (40-50%)

Instructions:

1. Place skullcap in jar.
2. Cover with alcohol, seal.
3. Let sit 4 weeks, shaking daily.
4. Strain, bottle.

How to Use It

For anxiety: 2-3 mL tincture, 2-3 times daily.

For sleep: 3-5 mL before bed.

For nervous system restoration: 2 mL, 3 times daily for 2-3 months (restorative—builds over time).

Safety Notes

Very safe. Very gentle. Rare: mild sedation. Safe long-term. **Use Scutellaria lateriflora** (American skullcap)—Chinese skullcap different species. Generally well-tolerated.

REMEDY 7: Lavender - Calming and Sleep

What It Heals

Multi-use nervine: anxiety, insomnia, restlessness, nervous tension, headaches, mood enhancement. Effective both as tea and aromatherapy.

Why It Works

Lavender contains **linalool and linalyl acetate** (calming volatile compounds). Aromatherapy studies show significant anxiety reduction, improved sleep quality. Oral use also effective. One of most pleasant, safe nervines.

How to Make It

Lavender Tea:

Ingredients:

- 1 teaspoon dried lavender flowers
- 1 cup hot water

Instructions:

1. Place lavender in mug.
2. Pour hot water, cover.
3. Steep 10 minutes.
4. Strain, drink.

Aromatherapy: Diffuse lavender essential oil before bed, or place 2-3 drops on pillow.

How to Use It

For anxiety: 1 cup tea or inhale lavender essential oil as needed.

For sleep: 1 cup tea before bed, or diffuse oil in bedroom 30 minutes before sleep.

Safety Notes

Very safe. Pleasant. Rare allergic reactions. Can be used daily. Safe for most ages. Generally well-tolerated.

REMEDY 8: Holy Basil (Tulsi) - Stress Adaptation

What It Heals

Adaptogen for chronic stress: normalizes cortisol (prevents stress-induced damage), reduces anxiety, improves stress resilience, clears stress-related brain fog, balances mood.

Why It Works

Holy basil contains **eugenol, rosmarinic acid, ursolic acid** that normalize cortisol (prevents hippocampus damage from chronic stress), reduce oxidative stress in brain, modulate neurotransmitters. Revered in Ayurveda as "The Incomparable One"—brings clarity and calm.

How to Make It

Holy Basil Tea:

Ingredients:

- 2 teaspoons dried holy basil (or 4-6 fresh leaves)
- 1 cup hot water

Instructions:

1. Place holy basil in mug.
2. Pour hot water, cover.
3. Steep 10-15 minutes.
4. Strain, drink.

How to Use It

For chronic stress: 2-3 cups tea daily. Or 2-3 mL tincture, twice daily.

Long-term adaptogenic support: Daily for 2-3 months minimum.

Safety Notes

Very safe for daily use. May lower blood sugar (monitor if diabetic). Safe for children and pregnancy (in tea form). Pleasant, slightly spicy flavor.

REMEDY 9: Rhodiola - Mental Energy and Resilience

What It Heals

Adaptogen for mental fatigue: reduces mental fatigue and burnout, improves focus under stress, enhances mood (mild antidepressant), increases mental endurance, improves stress resilience without overstimulation.

Why It Works

Rhodiola contains **rosavins and salidroside** that increase serotonin, dopamine, norepinephrine (without depleting them), protect neurons from stress damage, improve mitochondrial function (mental energy). Works within hours but strengthens with continued use.

How to Make It

Note: Rhodiola typically purchased as standardized extract.

Look for: 3% rosavins, 1% salidroside—matches research.

How to Use It

For mental fatigue: 200-400 mg standardized extract, morning or early afternoon (can be stimulating).

For depression/mood: 200 mg, twice daily.

Take on empty stomach for best absorption.

Safety Notes

Very safe. Can be stimulating—avoid evening doses. Start low (some very sensitive). Not during pregnancy. Works quickly (days to weeks).

REMEDY 10: Reishi Mushroom - Sleep and Immune Support

What It Heals

"Mushroom of immortality": improves sleep quality (deeper sleep), reduces anxiety, supports stress resilience, immune support, promotes longevity, calms spirit.

Why It Works

Reishi contains **triterpenes** (ganoderic acids) that have calming, sleep-promoting effects, reduce anxiety, modulate immune system. Traditional use: "calms the spirit and nourishes the heart"—promotes peaceful, deep sleep.

How to Make It

Reishi Decoction:

Ingredients:

- 2 tablespoons dried reishi mushroom (sliced)
- 4 cups water

Instructions:

1. Place reishi in pot with water.
2. Bring to boil.
3. Simmer on lowest heat 2-3 hours (mushrooms require long extraction).
4. Strain (save mushroom—can re-simmer once).

Or: Extract powder, 1-2 grams daily in tea.

How to Use It

For sleep: 1-2 cups decoction in evening. Or 1-2 grams extract powder before bed.

For stress/immune: 2-3 cups decoction daily.

Long-term tonic—safe for years of daily use.

Safety Notes

Extremely safe. Very gentle. Can cause mild digestive upset initially. Safe long-term. Generally well-tolerated.

REMEDY 11-40: Additional Sleep, Stress & Nervous System Remedies

11. Magnesium - Relaxation Mineral

Essential for nervous system: relaxes muscles, reduces anxiety, improves sleep, regulates stress response. 400-600 mg glycinate or threonate before bed. Very safe.

12. L-Theanine - Calm Focus

Amino acid from green tea: promotes calm alertness (alpha brain waves), reduces anxiety without sedation. 100-200 mg as needed. Very safe.

13. GABA Supplement - Direct Calming

Calming neurotransmitter: reduces anxiety, promotes sleep. 500-1,000 mg before bed or as needed. Generally safe.

14. 5-HTP - Serotonin Precursor

Converts to serotonin: improves mood, reduces anxiety, promotes sleep. 50-100 mg before bed. Don't combine with antidepressants.

15. Hops - Sleep Aid

Sedative herb: improves sleep (often combined with valerian), reduces anxiety, bitter digestive. Tea or tincture before bed. Safe.

16. California Poppy - Gentle Sedative

Mild nervine: anxiety, insomnia, restlessness, safe for children. 2-3 mL tincture before bed. Non-narcotic (different from opium poppy). Very safe.

17. Catnip - Calming (For Humans)

Paradoxically calms humans (stimulates cats): anxiety, restlessness, insomnia, safe for children. 1-3 cups tea daily. Extremely safe.

18. Milky Oats - Nervous System Nourishment

Restorative nervine: nervous exhaustion, stress-related depletion, recovery from addiction, burnout. Fresh milky oat tincture: 3-5 mL, 3 times daily for weeks/months. Very safe.

19. Blue Vervain - Type-A Tension

Nervine for driven personalities: nervous tension with physical rigidity, stress-related muscle tension, anxiety. 2-3 mL tincture, 2-3 times daily. Not during pregnancy.

20. Wood Betony - Headaches and Clarity

Traditional "head herb": tension headaches, anxiety, mental fog, improves circulation to head. Tea or tincture as needed. Very safe.

21. Bacopa - Anxiety with Cognitive Support

Adaptogen: reduces anxiety while improving memory, supports learning, calms without sedation. 300-450 mg extract daily for 8-12 weeks. Very safe.

22. Kava Kava - Strong Anxiety Relief

Powerful anxiolytic: significant anxiety reduction, muscle relaxation, maintains mental clarity. 250-500 mg kavalactones as needed. **Short-term only** (liver concerns with excessive long-term use).

23. Mucuna Pruriens - Dopamine Support

L-DOPA source: improves mood, motivation, supports stress resilience. ½-1 teaspoon powder daily. Potent—consult practitioner.

24. Cordyceps - Energy Without Overstimulation

Adaptogenic mushroom: improves energy, stress resilience, supports adrenals without jitters. 1-3 grams extract daily. Safe.

25. Schisandra - Adaptogen for Stress

Five-flavor berry: supports stress resilience, liver function (metabolizes stress hormones), improves mood. 2-3 mL tincture, twice daily. Very safe.

26. Eleuthero (Siberian Ginseng) - Endurance and Resilience

Adaptogen: improves physical and mental endurance, stress resilience, immune support. Extract or tea daily. Safe long-term.

27. Gotu Kola - Anxiety and Clarity

Ayurvedic nervine: reduces anxiety, improves mental clarity, promotes meditation. 2-3 cups tea daily. Very safe.

28. Oatstraw - Nervous System Nourishment

Restorative tonic: nourishes depleted nervous system, reduces stress, improves resilience. Long infusion daily. Extremely safe, nourishing.

29. Motherwort - Heart Palpitations from Anxiety

Cardiac nervine: anxiety-related heart palpitations, emotional stress affecting heart. 2-3 mL tincture as needed. Not during pregnancy.

30. Hawthorn - Heart and Emotional Support

Heart tonic with emotional benefits: reduces anxiety, supports heart (emotional and physical), calms spirit. 2-3 mL tincture, 3 times daily. Very safe.

31. Rose - Emotional Heart Opening

Gentle nervine: emotional stress, grief, heartbreak, anxiety with sadness, calms and uplifts. Rose tea or glycerite daily. Very safe, beautiful.

32. Linden - Gentle Relaxation

Mild nervine: stress-related tension, anxiety, insomnia, safe for children. 2-3 cups tea daily. Very safe, pleasant.

33. Damiana - Mood Lifter

Mild nervine and aphrodisiac: mild depression, anxiety, low mood, supports libido. Tea or tincture daily. Safe.

34. St. John's Wort - Depression and Anxiety

Covered in Chapter 11—effective for mild-moderate depression and anxiety. 300 mg, 3 times daily. Major drug interactions.

35. Saffron - Mood Enhancement

Powerful mood elevator: depression, anxiety, improves sleep. 30 mg daily. Very safe at therapeutic doses.

36. CBD Hemp Oil - Anxiety and Sleep

Cannabidiol: reduces anxiety, improves sleep, supports stress resilience. 20-50 mg daily. Generally safe, legal (hemp-derived).

37. Essential Oil Aromatherapy - Multi-Sensory Calming

Lavender, chamomile, bergamot, ylang ylang: diffuse before bed, apply to pulse points (diluted), inhale. Very safe, pleasant.

38. Epsom Salt Bath - Magnesium Absorption and Relaxation

Magnesium sulfate absorbed through skin: relaxes muscles, calms nervous system, promotes sleep. 2 cups in warm bath 20-30 minutes before bed, 2-3 times weekly. Very safe.

39. Meditation and Breathwork - Direct Nervous System Regulation

Not herbal but essential: 4-7-8 breathing (inhale 4, hold 7, exhale 8), box breathing, body scan meditation. Practice daily. Activates parasympathetic nervous system directly. Free, powerful.

40. Comprehensive Sleep and Stress Protocol

Sleep Optimization (4-Week Protocol):

Week 1: Sleep Hygiene Foundation

- Consistent sleep/wake times (even weekends)
- Dark, cool room (65-68°F)
- No screens 1 hour before bed
- Limit caffeine (none after 2 PM)
- Exercise daily (but not within 3 hours of bedtime)
- Evening routine: dim lights, warm bath, reading

Week 2: Add Herbal Support

- **Evening ritual:**
  - 6 PM: Holy basil or lemon balm tea (start winding down)
  - 8 PM: Magnesium 400-600 mg
  - 8:30 PM: Ashwagandha moon milk or chamomile tea
  - 9 PM: Valerian or passionflower tincture (3-5 mL)
  - 9:15 PM: Lavender aromatherapy (diffuse in bedroom)
  - 9:30 PM: Bed

Week 3: Optimize

- Continue Week 1-2
- Add: Reishi decoction with dinner
- Consider: L-theanine 200 mg evening
- Practice: 10 minutes meditation or breathwork before bed

- Reduce: Alcohol (disrupts sleep architecture)

Week 4: Refine and Maintain

- Continue what works
- Adjust herbs based on response
- Track: Sleep journal (quality, duration, dreams, how you feel)
- Most people see significant improvement by Week 4

Stress Resilience Protocol:

Daily Foundation:

- Adaptogen AM: Ashwagandha, rhodiola, or holy basil (choose based on needs)
- Nervine PM: Lemon balm, skullcap, or passionflower
- Magnesium: 400-600 mg daily
- B-complex: Daily with breakfast
- Omega-3s: 1,000-2,000 mg EPA+DHA

Acute Stress Response:

- Lemon balm or passionflower tincture: 2-3 mL as needed
- 4-7-8 breathing: 4 rounds
- Walk outside: 10-15 minutes
- Lavender aromatherapy: Inhale deeply

Nervous System Restoration (For Burnout):

- Milky oats tincture: 3-5 mL, 3 times daily for 2-3 months
- Ashwagandha: 600 mg daily
- Reishi: 2 grams extract daily
- Skullcap: 2-3 mL, 3 times daily
- Magnesium: 600 mg daily
- Rest: Non-negotiable—reduce commitments, say no
- Therapy/support: Address underlying stress sources

Lifestyle Essentials (No Herb Replaces These):

- Sleep: 7-9 hours nightly (most important)
- Exercise: 30-60 minutes daily (reduces stress hormones, improves sleep)
- Nature: Daily time outdoors (grounding, calming)
- Connection: Social support reduces stress significantly
- Purpose: Meaningful activity protects against burnout
- Boundaries: Learn to say no, protect your energy
- Downtime: Schedule unstructured rest (nervous system needs recovery)

When to Seek Professional Help:

- Severe insomnia (>3 weeks despite interventions)
- Panic attacks
- Suicidal thoughts
- Severe anxiety interfering with daily function
- Depression lasting >2 weeks

CHAPTER 13: SURVIVAL & EMERGENCY MEDICINE

Focus: Wilderness First Aid, Emergency Remedies, Self-Reliance

[IMAGE SUGGESTION: Rugged outdoor medicine arrangement featuring wild-harvested yarrow, plantain, pine needles, birch bark, willow bark, charcoal, and survival first-aid items displayed on weathered wood with natural backcountry lighting.]

When modern medicine isn't available, **plant knowledge saves lives**.

For 99.9% of human history, there were no hospitals, pharmacies, or ambulances. Our ancestors survived—and thrived—using plant medicine, traditional knowledge, and wilderness first aid skills.

Today, we've become dependent on modern medical systems. But situations arise where you're on your own:

- **Wilderness emergencies** (hiking, camping, remote locations)
- **Natural disasters** (hurricanes, earthquakes, floods—infrastructure collapse)
- **Supply chain disruptions** (can't access pharmacy or hospital)
- **Travel to remote areas** (developing countries, rural settings)
- **Emergency preparedness** (pandemic, civil unrest, grid failure)

In these moments, **herbal medicine and wilderness first aid skills are critical**.

This chapter is different. This is **survival medicine**—immediate, practical remedies for emergencies when professional medical care isn't accessible. This is about:

- Stopping bleeding
- Preventing infection
- Managing pain
- Treating shock
- Addressing dehydration
- Handling trauma
- Supporting the body through crisis

Critical disclaimer: These remedies do **not replace professional medical care**. Always seek emergency medical attention when available. This knowledge is for situations where you have no other option.

This chapter provides remedies for:

- **Bleeding control and wound care**
- **Infection prevention and treatment**
- **Pain management**
- **Fever reduction**
- **Poisoning and toxic exposure**
- **Emergency trauma support**

REMEDY 1: Yarrow - Emergency Bleeding Control

What It Heals

Battlefield medicine for severe bleeding: stops hemorrhaging rapidly (arterial and venous), prevents infection, reduces pain, accelerates wound healing. Used by soldiers for millennia—called "soldier's woundwort."

Why It Works

Yarrow contains **achilleine and flavonoids** that constrict blood vessels (hemostatic), promote clotting, have antimicrobial properties. Works within minutes for most bleeding. One of most important survival herbs—can save life from hemorrhage.

How to Make It

Fresh Yarrow Poultice (Emergency):

Instructions:

1. Find fresh yarrow (common roadside/field plant—feathery leaves, white/pink flower clusters).
2. Harvest leaves and flowers.
3. **Chew thoroughly** to release juices (if no other way to crush).
4. Apply directly to bleeding wound.
5. Pack tightly into wound.
6. Apply direct pressure with clean cloth.
7. Bleeding typically stops within 5-15 minutes.

Dried Yarrow Powder:

- Carry dried yarrow powder in emergency kit
- Sprinkle directly on bleeding wounds
- Apply pressure

How to Use It

For severe bleeding:

1. Apply direct pressure immediately
2. Pack wound with yarrow (fresh or powder)
3. Continue pressure 10-15 minutes
4. Don't remove yarrow (will restart bleeding)
5. Bandage over yarrow
6. Seek medical attention as soon as possible

For nosebleeds: Pack nostrils with yarrow, pinch nose 10 minutes.

Safety Notes

Very safe for emergency use. Rare allergic reactions. Can be used on all wounds. Extremely effective hemostatic. **Learn to identify yarrow before emergency**—practice now.

REMEDY 2: Plantain - Universal Wound Poultice

What It Heals

Common "weed" with lifesaving properties: draws out infections/toxins, stops bleeding, treats wounds, neutralizes venomous bites/stings, reduces pain and swelling, prevents tetanus (traditional use).

Why It Works

Plantain contains **allantoin** (tissue regeneration), **aucubin** (antimicrobial), **tannins** (astringent—stops bleeding). Drawing properties pull venom, bacteria, foreign material to surface. Available almost everywhere—grows in lawns, roadsides, fields worldwide.

How to Make It

Fresh Plantain Poultice (Field Medicine):

Instructions:

1. Find fresh plantain (broad or narrow leaf—both work).
2. Wash if possible (or wipe clean).
3. **Chew leaves thoroughly** (releases medicinal compounds).
4. Apply chewed leaf directly to wound/bite/sting.
5. Secure with bandage or cloth.

6. Replace every 2-4 hours until emergency passes.

"Spit poultice" is ancient but remarkably effective emergency medicine.

How to Use It

For wounds: Apply fresh poultice 2-4 times daily.

For venomous bites/stings: Apply immediately, reapply every 2 hours (draws venom).

For infected wounds: Apply fresh poultice, leave several hours or overnight (draws infection).

For splinters/embedded objects: Apply poultice overnight (draws to surface).

Safety Notes

Extremely safe. Can be used on all ages. No contraindications in emergency use. **Learn to identify before emergency**—extremely common plant. Free, available almost everywhere.

REMEDY 3: Activated Charcoal - Poisoning and Toxin Removal

What It Heals

Universal antidote for oral poisoning: binds toxins in digestive tract (prevents absorption), treats drug overdose, food poisoning, toxic plant ingestion, chemical exposure, treats gas/bloating.

Why It Works

Activated charcoal has **enormous surface area with negative electrical charge**—binds positively-charged toxins, drugs, chemicals, preventing absorption into bloodstream. Used in emergency rooms worldwide for poisoning. Most effective within 1 hour of ingestion.

How to Make It

Emergency Field Charcoal:

Instructions (if no commercial charcoal available):

1. Make hot fire with hardwood (oak, maple, birch).
2. Let burn completely to white-hot coals.
3. Extinguish, let cool.
4. Grind to fine powder.
5. Mix with water to create slurry.

Better: Keep commercial activated charcoal in emergency kit (much more effective—higher surface area).

How to Use It

For poisoning:

- Adult: 50-100 grams activated charcoal mixed with water (drink immediately)
- Child: 1 gram per kg body weight
- **Give within 1 hour of ingestion** for maximum effectiveness
- Can repeat dose every 4 hours if needed
- **Do not induce vomiting** unless instructed by poison control

Seek emergency medical care (charcoal buys time but doesn't replace treatment).

Does NOT work for: Alcohol, heavy metals, strong acids/alkalis, petroleum products.

Safety Notes

Very safe for acute use. Makes stool black (normal). Can cause constipation. **Give 2 hours away from any medications/supplements** (binds everything—including beneficial substances). **Not for daily use** (depletes nutrients).

REMEDY 4: Willow Bark - Natural Pain Relief and Fever

What It Heals

Original aspirin source: reduces pain (headaches, muscle pain, injuries), reduces fever, anti-inflammatory (sprains, arthritis), thins blood (prevents clots in emergency situations).

Why It Works

Willow bark contains **salicin**—converted by body to salicylic acid (same active compound as aspirin). Reduces pain, fever, inflammation through COX enzyme inhibition. Indigenous peoples used for thousands of years before pharmaceutical aspirin synthesized from willow.

How to Make It

Willow Bark Decoction:

Ingredients:

- 2 tablespoons fresh willow bark (inner bark—scrape from branches)
- 4 cups water

Instructions:

1. Harvest young willow branches (any willow species—white willow highest salicin).
2. Scrape inner bark (layer just under outer bark).
3. Chop bark, place in pot with water.
4. Bring to boil.
5. Simmer 15-20 minutes.
6. Strain, drink.

Or: Chew fresh inner bark directly (bitter but effective).

How to Use It

For pain/fever: Drink 1 cup decoction every 4-6 hours as needed.

For inflammation: 2-3 cups daily.

Emergency field use: Chew fresh inner bark (swallow juice, spit out fiber).

Takes 30-60 minutes to work (slower than pharmaceutical aspirin but effective).

Safety Notes

Generally safe. Same contraindications as aspirin: **avoid if allergic to aspirin**, bleeding disorders, before surgery, with blood thinners. Can cause stomach upset (take with food). Not for children with viral infections (Reye's syndrome risk—same as aspirin). Pregnancy: consult before use.

REMEDY 5: Pine Needle Tea - Vitamin C and Survival Nutrition

What It Heals

Wilderness vitamin C source: prevents scurvy (vitamin C deficiency), supports immune function, treats respiratory infections, provides hydration and minerals, general survival nutrition.

Why It Works

Pine needles contain **5x more vitamin C than oranges** (weight for weight), plus vitamin A, antioxidants, antimicrobial compounds. Prevents scurvy during extended wilderness survival. Available year-round in most climates. Also warming, improves circulation.

How to Make It

Pine Needle Tea:

Instructions:

1. Harvest fresh pine needles (Eastern white pine, Scotch pine—avoid Norfolk Island pine, yew, ponderosa during pregnancy).
2. Use young, green needles (highest vitamin C).

3. Chop ¼-½ cup needles.

4. Pour 2 cups hot water over needles.

5. Steep 10-15 minutes.

6. Strain, drink.

Tastes citrusy, slightly resinous.

How to Use It

For vitamin C: Drink 2-3 cups daily (prevents scurvy in survival situations).

For respiratory infections: 3-4 cups daily (antimicrobial, expectorant).

For hydration: Drink throughout day (provides minerals, slight energy).

Safety Notes

Generally very safe. **Avoid ponderosa pine during pregnancy** (can cause miscarriage). Avoid Norfolk Island pine and yew (toxic). Most common pine species safe. High in vitamin K (consult if on blood thinners). Free, available year-round.

REMEDY 6: Cayenne Pepper - Shock, Bleeding, Heart Emergency

What It Heals

Emergency circulatory stimulant: stops bleeding (internal and external—paradoxically), treats shock, heart attack emergency (controversial but traditional), improves circulation, warms in hypothermia.

Why It Works

Cayenne contains **capsaicin**—powerful circulatory stimulant. Increases blood flow to core organs, stimulates heart, raises blood pressure (beneficial in shock/hemorrhage). Also hemostatic (stops bleeding by equalizing blood pressure). Traditional emergency use for heart attacks—stimulates heart, prevents shock.

How to Make It

Emergency Cayenne Powder:

Keep in survival kit: Cayenne powder in waterproof container.

Emergency Heart Tincture:

- 1 part cayenne powder
- 5 parts vodka
- 2 weeks minimum (shake daily)
- Keep in emergency kit

How to Use It

For shock/hemorrhage:

- Mix 1 teaspoon cayenne in glass of warm water
- Drink immediately
- Stimulates circulation, prevents shock
- Repeat every 15 minutes if needed

For heart attack (traditional—seek medical care simultaneously):

- 1 teaspoon cayenne powder in water, drink
- Or 1 teaspoon cayenne tincture in water
- Stimulates heart, increases circulation
- **Not a replacement for emergency medical care**

For external bleeding:

- Sprinkle cayenne powder directly on wound
- Stings intensely but stops bleeding

For hypothermia:

- Cayenne tea warms core body temperature

Safety Notes

Generally safe in emergency use. Very hot—can cause intense burning sensation. Not for internal use if stomach ulcers. May interact with blood pressure medications. **Emergency use only—not daily supplement at these doses**.

REMEDY 7: Birch Bark - Pain Relief and Antiseptic

What It Heals

Wilderness analgesic and wound care: pain relief (contains methyl salicylate—similar to aspirin), reduces fever, antiseptic for wounds, emergency bandage material, treats burns.

Why It Works

Birch bark contains **methyl salicylate** (wintergreen-like compound—pain reliever), **betulin** (antimicrobial, wound healing). Outer bark is waterproof (emergency bandage), inner bark medicinal. Indigenous emergency medicine for millennia.

How to Make It

Birch Bark Tea (Pain/Fever):

Instructions:

1. Harvest birch bark sustainably (collect from dead/fallen trees—don't girdle living trees).
2. Use inner bark (scrape from inside of outer bark).
3. Chop 2 tablespoons inner bark.
4. Simmer in 4 cups water, 15-20 minutes.
5. Strain, drink.

Birch Bark Bandage:

- Use outer bark as waterproof wound covering
- Place over clean wound
- Secure with cordage or cloth

How to Use It

For pain/fever: 1 cup tea every 4-6 hours.

For wounds: Apply inner bark (antimicrobial) or use outer bark as protective covering.

For burns: Apply inner bark paste (scrape/chew inner bark, apply to burn).

Safety Notes

Generally safe. Same contraindications as aspirin/willow bark. Birch allergies rare but possible. Sustainable harvesting critical—don't damage living trees. Available in northern climates year-round.

REMEDY 8: Honey - Antimicrobial Wound Care

What It Heals

Ancient emergency medicine: prevents infection in wounds, treats infected wounds, burn treatment, energy source in survival situations, treats dehydration (oral rehydration).

Why It Works

Raw honey has **antimicrobial properties** (hydrogen peroxide production, low pH, osmotic effect), supports tissue regeneration, provides instant energy. Never spoils—can be stored indefinitely. Hospitals use medical-grade honey (Manuka) for serious wound care.

How to Make It

Keep in survival kit: Small jar of raw honey (never spoils, lightweight, multi-use).

How to Use It

For wounds:

1. Clean wound if possible.
2. Apply thick layer of honey directly to wound.

3. Cover with clean bandage.
4. Change daily.
5. Prevents infection, accelerates healing.

   For burns: Apply immediately after cooling burn.

   For energy: 1 tablespoon provides quick glucose (survival situations, hypoglycemia).

   For dehydration: Add to water (makes more palatable, provides electrolytes and energy).

   For sore throat/cough: 1 tablespoon as needed (antimicrobial, soothing).

   Safety Notes

   Very safe for external use and adults internally. **Never give to infants under 1 year** (botulism spore risk). Can attract insects in wilderness (cover wound). Extremely versatile survival item.

REMEDY 9: Garlic - Antibiotic Alternative

What It Heals

Natural antibiotic: treats bacterial infections (respiratory, skin, gut), prevents infection in wounds, treats food poisoning, supports immune function, cardiovascular support.

Why It Works

Garlic contains **allicin** (released when crushed)—broad-spectrum antimicrobial effective against bacteria, fungi, viruses, parasites. Used successfully before antibiotics existed. Can be lifesaving when pharmaceutical antibiotics unavailable.

How to Make It

Raw Garlic (Most Potent):

Instructions:

1. Crush 2-4 cloves garlic.
2. Let sit 10 minutes (activates allicin).
3. Consume raw (swallow whole or chop finely, swallow with water).
4. Or mix with honey (makes more palatable).

Garlic Poultice (External Infection):

- Crush garlic to paste
- Mix with small amount of olive oil (prevents skin burn)
- Apply to infected area
- Leave 20-30 minutes maximum (can burn skin)
- Wash off

How to Use It

For infection: 2-4 cloves raw garlic, 3-4 times daily until infection clears.

For food poisoning: 4-6 cloves immediately, then 2-3 cloves every 2-3 hours.

For wound infection: Garlic poultice (diluted) 2-3 times daily.

More effective raw—cooking destroys allicin.

Safety Notes

Generally safe. Can cause heartburn, digestive upset (take with food). **Can burn skin undiluted** (always dilute for topical use). Thins blood (beneficial but note if bleeding disorder). Strong odor. Extremely effective natural antibiotic.

REMEDY 10: Colloidal Silver - Antimicrobial Water Purification

What It Heals

Controversial but traditional antimicrobial: water purification (kills bacteria, viruses), wound infection prevention, treats infections when antibiotics unavailable.

Why It Works

Silver ions have **antimicrobial properties**—disrupt bacterial cell membranes, prevent replication. Used historically before antibiotics. NASA uses silver for water purification in space. **Controversial in medical community**—use only in emergency when no alternatives.

How to Make It

Note: Colloidal silver is commercially produced (silver particles suspended in water). Quality varies widely.

Keep in emergency kit: Commercial colloidal silver (10-20 PPM).

Emergency water purification: Add to questionable water source (consult label for amount).

How to Use It

For water purification: Follow product instructions (typically several drops per liter).

For wound care: Spray on wounds to prevent infection.

For infection: Gargle or apply topically (internal use controversial—use only in emergency without alternatives).

Safety Notes

Controversial—FDA doesn't recognize as safe/effective. **Argyria risk** (permanent blue-gray skin discoloration) with excessive internal use. **Use only in emergency** when antibiotics unavailable. Prefer garlic, honey, other proven antimicrobials for internal use. May be useful for water purification and external wound care.

REMEDY 11-40: Additional Survival & Emergency Remedies

11. Sage - Antiseptic and Drying Agent

Powerful antimicrobial, dries wounds/secretions, treats infections. Strong sage tea as wound wash. Chew fresh leaves for sore throat/infection. Very safe.

12. Usnea (Old Man's Beard Lichen) - Natural Antibiotic

Powerful against gram-positive bacteria (staph, strep). Tincture on infected wounds or taken internally. **Ensure correct identification**—toxic look-alikes exist. Sustainably harvest only.

13. Echinacea - Immune Support for Infections

Stimulates immune response to infections. Tincture or fresh root poultice on bites/wounds. 3-5 mL tincture, 3-4 times daily. Safe short-term.

14. Goldenseal/Oregon Grape - Berberine Antibiotic

Potent antimicrobial (berberine). Powder on infected wounds or tea as wash. Oregon grape more sustainable than goldenseal. Short-term use.

15. Thyme - Respiratory and Wound Antiseptic

Powerful antimicrobial (thymol). Strong tea for respiratory infections or wound wash. Essential oil diluted for topical use. Safe.

16. Elderberry - Immune Support and Antiviral

Reduces viral infections (flu, colds). Syrup or tea, 3-4 times daily at first symptoms. Very safe, effective.

17. Ginger - Nausea, Warming, Circulation

Treats nausea (motion sickness, food poisoning), improves circulation, warms in hypothermia. Fresh or dried tea. Very safe.

18. Peppermint - Digestive Emergency and Cooling

Treats nausea, digestive upset, IBS, cools in heat emergency. Tea or chew fresh leaves. Very safe.

19. Rehydration Solution - Dehydration Emergency

Lifesaving in diarrhea/vomiting: 1 liter clean water + 6 teaspoons sugar + ½ teaspoon salt. Sip slowly. WHO oral rehydration formula.

20. Comfrey - Bone/Tissue Healing (External)

Accelerates bone/tissue healing. **External only** (liver toxicity if ingested). Poultice on fractures, sprains after medical treatment. Very effective.

21. Arnica - Bruise and Trauma (External)

Reduces bruising, swelling, trauma. **External only** (toxic internally). Never on broken skin. Oil or cream on injuries. Effective.

22. Calendula - Universal Wound Healer

Safe, effective wound healing. Oil or salve on all wounds. Prevents infection, accelerates healing. Extremely safe.

23. Lavender - Burns and Anxiety

Treats burns, reduces pain, calms anxiety during crisis. Essential oil on burns. Aromatherapy for psychological trauma. Very safe.

24. Tea Tree Oil - Antimicrobial (External)

Broad-spectrum antimicrobial. Diluted on infected wounds, fungal infections. **Never ingest.** Effective topically.

25. Aloe Vera - Burns and Wounds

Soothes burns, promotes healing. Fresh gel directly on burns/wounds. Extremely safe, effective.

26. Slippery Elm - Soothing Poultice and Nutrition

Soothes irritated tissues, emergency nutrition. Powder as poultice or gruel (survival food). Very safe, nourishing.

27. Dandelion - Diuretic and Nutrition

Treats edema, provides nutrition (leaves edible—vitamin-rich). Entire plant edible. Very safe, free.

28. Nettle - Nutrition and Hemostatic

Mineral-rich nutrition, stops bleeding. Young leaves cooked (vitamin/mineral source). Also hemostatic. Very safe when cooked.

29. Chickweed - Edible and Soothing

Nutritious wild edible, soothes skin irritation. Eat raw in salads or poultice on rashes. Very safe, common.

30. Purslane - Omega-3 Survival Food

Highest plant source of omega-3s, nutritious wild edible. Eat raw or cooked. Very safe, common weed.

31. Acorns - Emergency Carbohydrate Source

Carbohydrate-rich survival food. **Must leach tannins** (soak in multiple water changes) before eating. Grind to flour. Time-intensive but nutritious.

32. Cattail - Complete Survival Food

Entire plant edible at different seasons. Roots (starch), pollen (protein), shoots (vegetable). Abundant in wetlands. Very safe.

33. Sphagnum Moss - Absorbent Wound Dressing

Highly absorbent, antimicrobial. Historical wound dressing (WWI/WWII). Pack wounds, change frequently. Sustainably harvest.

34. Spider Web - Emergency Suture/Hemostatic

Traditional but risky: Spider silk for wound closure, hemostatic properties. **Risk of infection**—use only in dire emergency without alternatives. Clean thoroughly first.

35. Maggot Therapy - Wound Debridement (Extreme Emergency)

Medical maggots (specific species) debride necrotic tissue, prevent infection. **Only in life-threatening gangrene** without medical care. Extremely dangerous if wrong species. **Last resort only**.

36. Urine - Emergency Antiseptic (Controversial)

Controversial and risky: Fresh urine is sterile. Historical use for wound cleaning in absolute emergency. **Only if literally no water**—urine preferable to leaving wound dirty. Many risks. True emergency only.

37. Tobacco Poultice - Venomous Bites (Traditional)

Traditional but not recommended: Wet tobacco applied to venomous bites/stings. **Better options exist** (plantain, charcoal). Included for historical knowledge only.

38. Tourniquets - Life-Threatening Hemorrhage

Extreme emergency only: Severe arterial bleeding from limbs when direct pressure fails. Apply above wound, tighten until bleeding stops. **Can cause limb loss**—use only when death from bleeding otherwise certain. Seek immediate emergency care.

39. Improvised Antibiotics - Expired Medications

Controversial survival situation: Expired antibiotics lose potency but don't become toxic. **If life-threatening infection and literally no other option**, expired antibiotics may be better than nothing. **Highly risky**—proper dosing unknown, resistance risk. True emergency only.

40. Comprehensive Survival Medicine Protocol

Emergency Response Priorities (Survival Medicine):

1. Safety First

- Remove from danger
- Assess scene safety
- Don't become second victim

2. ABCs (Primary Survey)

- **Airway:** Clear, open
- **Breathing:** Check, support if needed
- **Circulation:** Control bleeding, treat shock

3. Stop Severe Bleeding

- Direct pressure (most important)
- Elevation if possible
- Pressure points if trained
- Yarrow, cayenne, plantain if available
- Tourniquet only if life-threatening and other methods fail

4. Treat Shock

- Lay flat, elevate legs
- Keep warm

- Cayenne tea (stimulates circulation)
- Monitor consciousness
- Reassure

5. Clean and Dress Wounds

- Clean water if available (boiled/filtered)
- Remove debris
- Honey, calendula, plantain, or garlic
- Cover with clean bandage
- Change daily
- Watch for infection

6. Manage Pain

- Willow bark or birch bark tea
- Immobilize injuries
- Elevation reduces swelling
- Cool compress for acute injuries

7. Prevent Infection

- Clean wounds thoroughly
- Antimicrobial herbs (garlic, honey, goldenseal)
- Keep covered
- Change dressings
- Watch for infection signs

8. Support Hydration and Nutrition

- Clean water (boil, filter, or purify)
- Oral rehydration solution if diarrhea/vomiting
- Wild edibles if extended survival
- Pine needle tea (vitamin C)
- Conserve energy

9. Monitor and Reassess

- Check vitals regularly
- Watch for complications
- Infection signs: increased redness, warmth, swelling, red streaks, pus, fever
- Seek medical care as soon as accessible

Survival Medicine Kit (Minimal):

Herbal Medicines:

- Cayenne tincture or powder
- Yarrow powder
- Activated charcoal
- Raw honey
- Garlic (fresh or powder)
- Goldenseal or Oregon grape powder
- Calendula salve
- Lavender essential oil
- Tea tree essential oil
- Echinacea tincture

Supplies:

- Bandages, gauze, tape
- Tourniquets (commercial)
- Emergency blanket
- Water purification tablets
- Oral rehydration salts
- Tweezers, scissors
- Disposable gloves
- Waterproof matches/lighter
- Cordage
- Knife
- Emergency whistle
- First aid manual

Knowledge (Most Important):

- Plant identification
- Wound care
- CPR
- Basic first aid
- Water purification
- Fire starting
- Shelter building
- Wild edibles

Practice before emergency:

- Take wilderness first aid course
- Learn plant identification
- Practice making remedies
- Test kit in field conditions
- Know your limits

When to Evacuate:

- Severe bleeding uncontrolled
- Suspected internal injuries
- Head/spine/chest trauma
- Difficulty breathing
- Loss of consciousness
- Severe burns
- Broken bones (except simple fractures if you're trained)
- Signs of serious infection
- Snakebite (venomous)
- Allergic reactions
- Any life-threatening condition

Herbal medicine supports but doesn't replace:

- Professional medical training
- Emergency evacuation when needed
- Common sense and good judgment
- Prevention (avoiding injuries in first place)

The best emergency medicine is prevention.

CHAPTER 14: A LIFETIME OF SELF-HEALING

Focus: Long-Term Vitality, Self-Reliance, Legacy

This is where everything comes together.

You've learned to make **250+ remedies**. You've studied the plants that heal inflammation, balance hormones, strengthen your heart, calm your mind, protect your brain, and save lives in emergencies.

But knowledge without practice fades. Skills unused atrophy. Remedies unmade don't heal anyone.

This final chapter is about **integration**—making herbal medicine a permanent part of your life, not just a book you read once. It's about:

- **Aging powerfully** instead of declining
- **True self-reliance** that can't be taken away
- **Teaching the next generation** so this knowledge doesn't die with you
- **Creating systems** that sustain health for decades

You're not just learning remedies. You're **reclaiming an ancestral birthright**—the ability to heal yourself and those you love.

Let's build your lifetime practice.

Section 1: Aging With Strength - The Longevity Protocol

Modern culture treats aging as inevitable decline—weakness, disease, dependence, deterioration.

This is a lie.

True aging is:

- Accumulated wisdom
- Deep resilience
- Stable energy
- Mental clarity
- Physical capability
- Freedom from chronic disease

The difference between these two paths? **How you live every single day.**

The Fundamental Truth About Aging

You don't suddenly become old at 65. You become old through **decades of accumulated damage**:

- Chronic inflammation (destroys tissues)
- Oxidative stress (ages cells)
- Mitochondrial dysfunction (depletes energy)
- Hormonal decline (accelerates aging)
- Toxin accumulation (damages systems)
- Nutrient depletion (prevents repair)
- Sedentary lifestyle (weakens everything)

Herbal medicine addresses every single one of these.

The Daily Longevity Protocol

Morning (Within 30 Minutes of Waking):

1. **Lemon water** (liver flush, hydration)
2. **Adaptogen of choice:**
   - Ashwagandha (stress resilience, thyroid)
   - Rhodiola (mental energy, mood)
   - Holy basil (stress, clarity)
   - Or rotate monthly
3. **Movement:** 10-20 minutes (walk, yoga, tai chi)

Breakfast:

4. **Nutrient-dense meal:**
   - Protein (eggs, fish, beans)
   - Healthy fats (avocado, nuts, olive oil)
   - Vegetables
5. **Longevity smoothie** (2-3 times weekly):
   - Berries (antioxidants)
   - Greens (minerals, chlorophyll)
   - Maca powder (hormones, energy)
   - Ground flax seeds (lignans, omega-3s)
   - Turmeric + black pepper (anti-inflammatory)
   - Reishi or lion's mane powder (brain, immune)

6. **Supplements:**
   - Omega-3s: 1,000-2,000 mg EPA+DHA
   - Vitamin D3: 2,000-5,000 IU (test levels)
   - Magnesium: 400-600 mg
   - B-complex (methylated forms)

Midday:

7. **Herbal tea rotation:**
   - Monday: Green tea (EGCG, antioxidants)
   - Tuesday: Nettle (minerals, blood building)
   - Wednesday: Red clover (phytoestrogens, cardiovascular)
   - Thursday: Tulsi (adaptogen, stress)
   - Friday: Gotu kola (brain, longevity)
   - Saturday/Sunday: Personal choice

Afternoon:

8. **Movement:** 30-60 minutes
   - Strength training (2-3x/week—critical for aging)
   - Walking (daily)
   - Flexibility work (yoga, stretching)
9. **Second adaptogen dose** (if taking twice daily)

Evening:

10. **Dinner:** Anti-inflammatory, nutrient-dense
11. **Liver support** (3-4x weekly):
    - Milk thistle tincture
    - Dandelion root tea
    - Cruciferous vegetables
12. **Calming ritual:**
    - Chamomile or lemon balm tea
    - Magnesium (before bed)
    - Ashwagandha moon milk (2-3x weekly)

Weekly:

13. **Castor oil pack** (liver, 1-2x)
14. **Epsom salt bath** (magnesium, relaxation, 2-3x)
15. **Deep rest day** (recovery essential)

Monthly:

16. **Assess and adjust:**
    - Energy levels
    - Sleep quality
    - Mood
    - Digestion
    - Pain/inflammation
    - Cognitive function
17. **Rotate herbs** (prevent tolerance, ensure variety)

Specific Longevity Herbs (Long-Term Daily Use)

Brain Protection:

- Lion's mane: 1-2 grams extract daily (neurogenesis)
- Ginkgo: 120-240 mg daily (circulation, memory)
- Bacopa: 300-450 mg daily (memory, neuroprotection)

Cardiovascular:

- Hawthorn: 2-3 mL tincture, 3x daily (heart strengthening)
- Garlic: 1-2 cloves raw daily or aged extract (BP, cholesterol)
- Omega-3s: 1,000-2,000 mg daily (inflammation, heart)

Immune and Cancer Prevention:

- Reishi: 1-2 grams extract daily (longevity, immune)
- Turmeric: 500-1,000 mg curcumin daily (anti-inflammatory, anti-cancer)
- Green tea: 3-4 cups daily (EGCG, polyphenols)

Hormones:

- Women: Vitex, red clover, or maca (based on needs)
- Men: Saw palmetto, nettle root (prostate), maca

- Both: Adaptogens (support entire endocrine system)

Cellular Protection:

- Antioxidant rotation: berries, green tea, turmeric, reishi, schisandra
- Detox support: milk thistle, dandelion, cruciferous vegetables
- Mitochondrial support: CoQ10, PQQ, alpha-lipoic acid

The Non-Negotiables (No Herb Replaces These)

1. **Sleep:** 7-9 hours nightly (when body repairs)
2. **Movement:** Daily (prevents all-cause mortality dramatically)
3. **Strength training:** 2-3x weekly (prevents sarcopenia—muscle loss with aging)
4. **Social connection:** Regular (reduces dementia risk 50%+)
5. **Purpose:** Meaningful activity (longevity factor in Blue Zones)
6. **Stress management:** Daily practice (chronic stress accelerates aging)
7. **Fasting/time-restricted eating:** 12-16 hour overnight fast (autophagy, cellular repair)
8. **Nature exposure:** Daily sunlight, outdoor time (vitamin D, circadian rhythm, mental health)

What to Expect

Months 1-3:

- More stable energy
- Better sleep
- Improved digestion
- Reduced inflammation/pain
- Mental clarity improves

Months 6-12:

- Significant reduction in chronic symptoms
- Weight normalization
- Hormones balancing
- Stronger immunity (fewer colds/infections)
- Noticeable physical improvements

Years 2-5:

- Reversal of "age-related" conditions

- Sustained energy and vitality
- Sharp cognitive function
- Strong physical capability
- Independence maintained

Decades:

- Aging like those in Blue Zones (Okinawa, Sardinia, Ikaria)
- Healthy until very end of life (compression of morbidity)
- Active, engaged, contributing into 80s, 90s, 100s+
- Death from old age, not chronic disease

This is not fantasy. This is how humans are designed to age when we support our biology.

Section 2: Travel Kits - Medicine Wherever You Go

Whether traveling across the country or around the world, **don't leave your health to chance**.

The Essential Travel Apothecary

Small Kit (Weekend/Short Trips):

1. **Digestive:**
   - Digestive bitters tincture (digestion, bloating)
   - Ginger chews or capsules (nausea, motion sickness)
   - Activated charcoal (food poisoning, toxins)
   - Peppermint essential oil (nausea, headaches)

2. **Immune:**
   - Echinacea tincture (immune boost at first symptoms)
   - Elderberry syrup or lozenges (antiviral)
   - Garlic capsules (natural antibiotic)
   - Vitamin C (1,000 mg, take at first sign of illness)

3. **Sleep/Stress:**
   - Valerian or passionflower tincture (sleep, time zones)
   - Magnesium glycinate (sleep, muscle tension)
   - Lavender essential oil (anxiety, sleep, aromatherapy)

4. **First Aid:**
   - Calendula salve (wounds, burns, skin irritation)
   - Tea tree oil (antiseptic, fungal infections)
   - Arnica cream (bruises, muscle soreness)
   - Cayenne powder (bleeding, circulation)

5. **Pain/Inflammation:**
   - Willow bark or turmeric capsules (pain, inflammation)
   - Topical pain relief (St. John's wort oil or CBD)

   Large Kit (Extended Travel/International):

   Add to small kit:

6. **Antimicrobials:**
   - Goldenseal or Oregon grape (infections)
   - Usnea tincture (natural antibiotic)
   - Colloidal silver spray (wound care, water purification)
   - Propolis tincture (throat, infections)

7. **Digestive Support:**
   - Probiotics (gut health, prevent traveler's diarrhea)
   - Slippery elm lozenges (sore throat, digestive soothing)
   - Anti-parasitic formula (wormwood, black walnut, cloves)

8. **Respiratory:**
   - Mullein tincture (lungs, cough)
   - Thyme essential oil (respiratory infections)
   - Eucalyptus essential oil (congestion)

9. **Liver Support:**
   - Milk thistle capsules (alcohol, toxin exposure)
   - Dandelion root tea bags (liver, digestion)

10. **Adaptogenic Support:**
    - Ashwagandha or rhodiola capsules (stress, jet lag)
    - Eleuthero (energy, immune)

11. **Emergency:**
    - Yarrow powder (bleeding)
    - Activated charcoal capsules (poisoning)
    - Rescue Remedy (trauma, shock—flower essences)
    - Basic bandages, tweezers, safety pins

Travel-Specific Protocols

Jet Lag Recovery:

- Day of travel: Rhodiola morning, magnesium + melatonin evening
- First 3 days: Expose to sunlight morning in new timezone
- Ashwagandha: Helps reset cortisol rhythm
- Stay hydrated: Add electrolytes

Traveler's Diarrhea Prevention:

- Probiotics: Start 1 week before travel, continue throughout
- Activated charcoal: At first sign of digestive upset
- Goldenseal: If bacterial infection suspected
- Rehydration solution: Critical if diarrhea occurs

Altitude Sickness:

- Ginkgo biloba: 120-240 mg daily starting 2 days before ascent
- Rhodiola: Improves oxygen utilization
- Coca tea: Traditional Andean remedy (where legal)
- Hydration: Critical

Immune Protection (Flying, Crowded Places):

- Elderberry: Before and during travel
- Echinacea: At first symptoms
- Vitamin C: 1,000 mg 2-3x daily during travel
- Hand sanitizer: Use frequently (or essential oil spray)

Packing Tips

- **Tinctures in dropper bottles:** Leak-proof, concentrated, TSA-compliant (under 3.4 oz)
- **Powders in capsules:** Pre-fill capsules, label clearly

- **Salves in small tins:** Won't spill
- **Essential oils:** Small bottles, rubber-banded together
- **Label everything:** Include ingredients, dosage, date made
- **Waterproof bag:** Protect from spills
- **Carry-on:** Keep essentials with you (checked bags get lost)
- **Documentation:** For international travel, carry herbal medicine documentation if questioned at customs

International Considerations

- **Research regulations:** Some herbs illegal in certain countries
- **Generally safe to carry:** Common tinctures, capsules, salves
- **Potentially problematic:** Kava (some countries ban), ephedra (banned most places), coca (illegal except Peru/Bolivia)
- **When in doubt:** Capsules less likely to raise questions than loose herbs
- **Be prepared to explain:** "Natural health supplements" usually sufficient

Section 3: Growing Your Own Herbs - True Self-Reliance

The ultimate self-reliance is **growing your own medicine**.

Benefits:

- **Free** (after initial investment)
- **Highest quality** (you control growing conditions)
- **Always available** (no supply chain dependence)
- **Fresh** (maximum potency)
- **Connection** (relationship with plants deepens healing)
- **Resilience** (independent of pharmacy, economy, infrastructure)

Easiest Herbs to Grow (Beginner-Friendly)

1. Calendula

- **Growing:** Direct seed after frost, full sun, poor soil tolerated
- **Harvest:** Flowers continuously—pick every few days
- **Uses:** Salves, oils, wound healing
- **Why start here:** Foolproof, beautiful, incredibly useful

2. Chamomile

- **Growing:** Direct seed spring, full sun, self-sows
- **Harvest:** Flowers when fully open
- **Uses:** Tea (anxiety, sleep, digestion)
- **Why:** Easy, productive, gentle medicine

3. Peppermint

- **Growing:** Plant starts, part shade tolerates, **very invasive** (grow in containers)
- **Harvest:** Leaves anytime, best before flowering
- **Uses:** Tea (digestion, headaches, cooling)
- **Why:** Nearly impossible to kill, spreads aggressively

4. Lemon Balm

- **Growing:** Plant starts or seed, part shade tolerates, self-sows vigorously
- **Harvest:** Leaves anytime
- **Uses:** Tea (anxiety, stress, sleep)
- **Why:** Extremely easy, prolific, pleasant

5. Lavender

- **Growing:** Plant starts, full sun, well-drained soil, drought-tolerant
- **Harvest:** Flowers just opening
- **Uses:** Tea, aromatherapy, salves
- **Why:** Beautiful, fragrant, multi-use

6. Holy Basil (Tulsi)

- **Growing:** Seed or starts, full sun, warm weather
- **Harvest:** Leaves and flowers
- **Uses:** Tea (adaptogen, stress)
- **Why:** Easy as regular basil, powerful medicine

7. Echinacea

- **Growing:** Seed or starts, full sun, drought-tolerant once established
- **Harvest:** Flowers and roots (roots after 3 years)
- **Uses:** Tincture (immune support)
- **Why:** Beautiful perennial, powerful medicine

8. Yarrow

- **Growing:** Seed or division, full sun, neglect-tolerant
- **Harvest:** Flowers and leaves
- **Uses:** Tincture, powder (bleeding, fever)
- **Why:** Drought-tolerant, spreads, critical first aid herb

9. Plantain

- **Growing:** Doesn't need planting—already in your lawn
- **Harvest:** Leaves spring through fall
- **Uses:** Fresh poultice, salve (wounds, bites)
- **Why:** Free, everywhere, extremely useful

10. Nettle

- **Growing:** Spreads aggressively, shade tolerant, **use gloves**
- **Harvest:** Young leaves spring (wear gloves)
- **Uses:** Infusion (minerals, nutrition)
- **Why:** Extremely nutritious, free once established

Garden Design for Medicine

Small Space (Container Garden):

- Calendula (large pot)
- Chamomile (medium pot)
- Lemon balm (container—too invasive for ground)
- Peppermint (container—too invasive for ground)
- Lavender (pot with drainage)
- Holy basil (pot)

Medium Space (4x8 Raised Bed):

- Section 1: Calendula
- Section 2: Echinacea (perennial—leave in place)
- Section 3: Chamomile
- Section 4: Lemon balm or holy basil
- Container nearby: Peppermint (don't plant in bed—invasive)

Large Space (Dedicated Herb Garden):

Perennial bed:

- Echinacea
- Yarrow
- Lavender
- Lemon balm (contained area)
- Nettle (far corner where it can spread)

Annual bed:

- Calendula
- Chamomile
- Holy basil

Containers (invasive species):

- Peppermint
- Spearmint

Basic Growing Principles

1. **Start small:** 3-5 herbs you'll actually use
2. **Grow what you need most:** Review your most-used remedies
3. **Full sun:** Most medicinal herbs need 6+ hours
4. **Good drainage:** Herbs hate wet feet
5. **Poor soil okay:** Most herbs don't need rich soil (intensifies medicinal compounds)
6. **Water when establishing:** Once established, most herbs drought-tolerant
7. **Harvest regularly:** Promotes new growth
8. **Don't over-fertilize:** Reduces medicinal potency

Harvesting and Drying

When to Harvest:

- **Leaves:** Morning after dew dries, before heat of day
- **Flowers:** Just opening (peak medicinal compounds)
- **Roots:** Fall (after aerial parts die back) or early spring
- **Seeds:** When mature but before they drop

How to Dry:

Hanging method (flowers, leafy stems):

1. Bundle 6-10 stems with rubber band
2. Hang upside down in dark, warm, dry area with good airflow
3. Dry until crispy (1-2 weeks)
4. Strip leaves/flowers from stems
5. Store in airtight jars

Screen drying (leaves, flowers):

1. Lay on screens in single layer
2. Place in dark, warm, dry area
3. Turn occasionally
4. Dry until crispy

Dehydrator (fastest):

- Set to 95-115°F (preserves volatile oils)
- Check every few hours
- Don't over-dry

Storage:

- Glass jars with tight lids
- Dark location (light degrades)
- Cool and dry
- Label with herb name and date
- Use within 1 year for best potency

Seed Saving

Build resilience by saving seeds:

Easy to save:

- Calendula (let flowers go to seed, collect when dry)
- Chamomile (self-sows readily—thin seedlings)
- Holy basil (let flower, collect seeds when brown)

Process:

1. Let best plants go to seed
2. Collect when fully dry on plant
3. Store in paper envelopes (labeled with variety and year)
4. Keep cool and dry
5. Viability: Most herb seeds 2-5 years

Buying vs. Growing

Grow yourself:

- Herbs you use fresh (peppermint, lemon balm, holy basil)
- Easy herbs (calendula, chamomile)
- Expensive to buy (echinacea, calendula)
- Local and abundant

Buy from reputable sources:

- Hard to grow in your climate (reishi mushrooms, ashwagandha roots)
- Require years to maturity (ginseng)
- Specific processing needed (fermented herbs)
- Endangered/overharvested (goldenseal—use Oregon grape instead)
- Require expertise (complex Chinese formulas)

Wildcrafting (Harvesting Wild Plants)

Benefits:

- Free
- Often more potent than cultivated
- Develops plant identification skills
- Deep connection to land

Critical Rules:

1. **100% positive identification:** Mistakes can be fatal. Use multiple field guides, apps, expert verification.
2. **Legal to harvest:** Check regulations—some areas prohibit, some plants protected.
3. **Sustainable harvesting:**
   - Take only 10-20% from any population
   - Never harvest rare or threatened species

- Leave enough for wildlife and regeneration
- Rotate harvesting areas

4. **Clean areas only:**
- Not near roads (heavy metal contamination)
- Not in sprayed areas (pesticides)
- Not in polluted areas

5. **Proper timing:** Harvest when medicinally optimal, not when convenient.

6. **Give thanks:** Traditional practice—respect for plants.

Easiest Wild Plants (Abundant, Easy to Identify):

- Dandelion (leaves, roots)
- Plantain (leaves)
- Yarrow (flowers, leaves)
- Nettle (young leaves—wear gloves)
- Violet (leaves, flowers)
- Red clover (flowers)
- Pine (needles)
- Mullein (leaves)

Never wildcraft without expert guidance:

- Mushrooms (many deadly look-alikes)
- Roots (harder to identify)
- Rare or endangered species
- In areas you're unfamiliar with

Section 4: Teaching Your Family - Legacy Of Healing

The greatest gift you can give is **the ability to heal**.

Why Teach Your Family

- **Self-reliance for them:** Skills they'll use for life
- **Protection:** Independence from failing systems
- **Connection:** Shared knowledge strengthens bonds

- **Legacy:** This wisdom outlives you
- **Empowerment:** Confidence in their own healing capacity

Teaching Children (Age-Appropriate)

Ages 3-7:

- **Garden together:** Let them water, harvest, smell herbs
- **Make it sensory:** Touch fuzzy lamb's ear, smell peppermint, taste chamomile tea
- **Simple remedies:** Calendula salve for scrapes, chamomile tea before bed
- **Stories:** Tell plant stories, folklore
- **No pressure:** Keep it playful, fun

Ages 8-12:

- **Identification:** Teach common herbs in garden and yard
- **Simple making:** Let them help make salves, teas
- **Uses:** Teach what each herb does
- **Responsibility:** Give them plants to care for
- **Empowerment:** Let them make their own chamomile tea for tummy ache

Teens:

- **Deeper knowledge:** Medicinal properties, body systems
- **Making remedies:** Supervise tincture-making, teach safety
- **First aid:** Wilderness medicine, emergency care
- **Independence:** Encourage their own experiments (safely)
- **Sharing:** Help them make gifts (salves, teas) for friends

Teaching Adults (Partner, Friends, Extended Family)

Start with need:

- "You mentioned trouble sleeping—want to try this valerian tincture I made?"
- "I made calendula salve—perfect for that burn"
- **Let results speak**

Invite participation:

- "Want to help me harvest calendula this weekend?"
- "I'm making tinctures—want to learn?"

- **Hands-on learning most effective**

    Share gradually:

- Don't overwhelm with information
- One remedy at a time
- Build on successes
- **Meet them where they are**

    Make it accessible:

- Start with gentle herbs (chamomile, peppermint)
- Simple preparations (tea before tinctures)
- Clear instructions written down
- **Remove barriers to entry**

    Creating Family Traditions

    Weekly:

- Sunday tea ritual (chamomile, lemon balm, family connection)
- Garden tending together (15-30 minutes)

    Seasonal:

- **Spring:** Plant garden together, identify wild greens
- **Summer:** Harvest and dry herbs, make sun tea
- **Fall:** Harvest roots, make elderberry syrup for winter
- **Winter:** Make salves and tinctures, plan next year's garden

    Ceremonial:

- First harvest celebration (gratitude for plants)
- Equinox/solstice tea gatherings
- **Create your own traditions**

    Building the Family Apothecary

    Involve everyone:

- Children: Label jars (practice writing, learn herb names)
- Teens: Make remedies under supervision
- Adults: Share research, try new herbs

- Elders: Share traditional knowledge

Create systems:

- Designated space (cabinet, shelf, room if possible)
- Clear organization (labels, categories)
- Inventory tracking (what needs restocking)
- Recipe book (family additions welcome)

Safety protocols:

- Lock cabinet if young children in house
- Clear labeling always
- Teach what's for adults only
- Emergency numbers posted

Documentation - The Family Herbal

Create a living document passed through generations:

Include:

- Favorite family remedies
- Success stories
- Photos of family making medicine together
- Garden plans and what grew well
- Notes on effectiveness
- Modifications made
- Children's drawings of plants
- **Each generation adds**

Format:

- Handwritten journal (most personal)
- Digital with photos (easy to backup, share)
- **Both** (belt and suspenders)

Sections:

- Growing herbs
- Making remedies

- First aid protocols
- Seasonal health support
- Family health history (what works for your genetics)
- Recipes refined over years

When They Resist

Common objections:

"That's not real medicine."

- **Don't argue.** Share research if they're interested.
- **Let results speak.** Use for yourself, they'll notice.
- **Respect their choice.** Plant seeds, don't push.

"I don't have time."

- **Start simple.** One cup of chamomile tea = 5 minutes.
- **Show efficiency.** Tinctures last years, taken in seconds.
- **Offer to make for them.** Lower barrier.

"What if it doesn't work?"

- **Acknowledge uncertainty.** Everything doesn't work for everyone.
- **Start low-risk.** Gentle herbs for minor issues first.
- **Encourage experimentation.** Track results, adjust.

"I'm scared I'll do it wrong."

- **Validate fear.** It's reasonable when new.
- **Start supervised.** Do it together first.
- **Teach safety.** Knowledge reduces fear.

Your response:

- **Live it.** Best teaching is modeling.
- **Share freely.** Give remedies as gifts.
- **Be patient.** Transformation takes time.
- **No pressure.** Coercion backfires.

When they see you **healthy, vibrant, capable, independent**—they'll become curious naturally.

Section 5: Integration - Making This Sustainable

Knowledge means nothing without **consistent practice**.

The Reality Check

You will not:

- Make all 250+ remedies
- Grow every herb
- Use every protocol
- Remember everything

You will:

- **Choose 10-20 core remedies** you use regularly
- **Grow 5-10 herbs** suited to your climate and needs
- **Master a few key skills** deeply
- **Reference this book** when needed

That's not only okay—it's optimal.

Your Personalized System

Step 1: Identify Your Top Needs

Review the book. Which chapters spoke to you?

- Chronic health issues
- Prevention priorities
- Family needs
- Personal interests

Example:

- *"I have anxiety and insomnia, my partner has high blood pressure, and my kid gets frequent colds."*

Step 2: Choose Core Remedies (10-20 Maximum)

Based on needs above:

- **For you:** Valerian tincture, ashwagandha, lemon balm tea, magnesium
- **For partner:** Hawthorn tincture, garlic, hibiscus tea
- **For kid:** Elderberry syrup, echinacea tincture, calendula salve

- **For everyone:** First aid kit (calendula, plantain, yarrow)

That's ~12 remedies. Totally manageable.

Step 3: Make/Buy on Schedule

Year 1 Schedule:

- **January:** Learn, read, plan
- **February:** Order supplies, seeds, dried herbs
- **March:** Start seeds indoors
- **April:** Plant garden
- **May:** Buy tincture supplies, make first batch
- **June:** Make elderberry syrup, harvest calendula
- **July:** Dry herbs, make infused oils
- **August:** Continue harvesting, make salves
- **September:** Harvest roots, make tinctures
- **October:** Finish drying, stock apothecary
- **November:** Assess what worked, plan year 2
- **December:** Gift remedies, teach family

Step 4: Create Rituals

Daily:

- Morning adaptogen (ashwagandha in coffee)
- Evening tea (chamomile or lemon balm)

Weekly:

- Garden tending (30 minutes)
- Make one batch of something (salve, tea blend, tincture)

Seasonal:

- Spring: Plant
- Summer: Harvest and dry
- Fall: Make tinctures and salves
- Winter: Rest, study, plan

Step 5: Track and Adjust

Keep simple journal:

- What you made
- What you used
- What worked
- What didn't
- What ran out
- What needs restocking

Adjust yearly: More of what worked, less of what didn't.

The 80/20 Principle

20% of remedies solve 80% of issues.

Your core 10-20 remedies will handle almost everything. The other 230+ are there **when you need them—** which is exactly right.

Mastery comes from depth, not breadth.

Better to know 10 remedies intimately than 250 superficially.

When Life Gets Overwhelming

Minimum viable practice:

If you can only do **three things**:

1. **Grow or buy chamomile/lemon balm.** Make tea when stressed.
2. **Keep first aid herbs.** Calendula salve, yarrow powder.
3. **Take adaptogen daily.** Ashwagandha or rhodiola.

These three maintain connection to plant medicine even during chaos.

When you have more capacity, expand again.

Life ebbs and flows. Your practice will too. **That's human.**

Measuring Success

Not by:

- Number of remedies made
- Size of apothecary
- Perfectly manicured herb garden

But by:

- **Reduction in suffering** (yours and family's)
- **Increase in vitality** (energy, mood, health)
- **Growth in confidence** ("I can handle this")
- **Deepening relationship with plants**
- **Independence from systems** (pharmacy, medical dependence)
- **Skills you can't lose** (knowledge in your hands

FINAL WORDS: THE PATH FORWARD

You've reached the end of this book.

But this is not an ending—it's a **beginning**.

You now have knowledge that **95% of humans have lost**. Knowledge that sustained our species for hundreds of thousands of years. Knowledge that **can't be taken from you**.

- The economy crashes? You have medicine.
- Pharmacies close? You have medicine.
- Supply chains fail? You have medicine.
- You can't afford care? You have medicine.

More importantly:

You have **agency**. The ability to act, to heal, to help. You're not helpless, dependent, or at the mercy of failing systems.

You have **resilience**. When crisis comes (and it will), you can respond. You have skills, knowledge, resources.

You have **connection**. To plants, to earth, to ancestors who lived this way, to your body's innate wisdom.

You have **legacy**. When you teach your children, this knowledge lives beyond you.

What Happens Next

Option 1: This Book Sits on Your Shelf

You feel inspired for a few days. Then life intervenes. The book gathers dust. Nothing changes.

You remain dependent on systems that don't serve you. You stay disconnected from your healing power.

Option 2: You Start Small Today

You choose **one remedy** to make this week.

You plant **one herb**.

You make **one cup of tea** before bed tonight.

Small actions compound. One remedy becomes five becomes twenty. One herb becomes a garden becomes wildcrafting. One cup of tea becomes daily ritual becomes lifestyle becomes transformation.

Six months from now, you look back amazed at how much has changed.

Five years from now, this is just who you are: The person who grows medicine, makes tinctures, treats family illnesses, teaches neighbors, passes knowledge to children.

The person who healed themselves.

Your First Action

Close this book.

Go to your kitchen.

Make one cup of chamomile tea.

Sit quietly. Sip slowly. Feel the warmth, taste the herbs, notice the calm spreading through your body.

This simple act—**making plant medicine and taking it**—is revolutionary.

You just became your own healer.

Everything else builds from here.

The Invitation

This knowledge is **yours** now.

Use it. Share it. Adapt it. Improve it. Pass it on.

Heal yourself. Heal your family. Heal your community.

Reclaim what was stolen.

Remember what was forgotten.

Become what you were always meant to be:

Self-reliant. Capable. Connected. Whole.

Your ancestors are watching. They're proud.

Now go. **Plant. Harvest. Make. Heal.**

The rest of your life begins today.